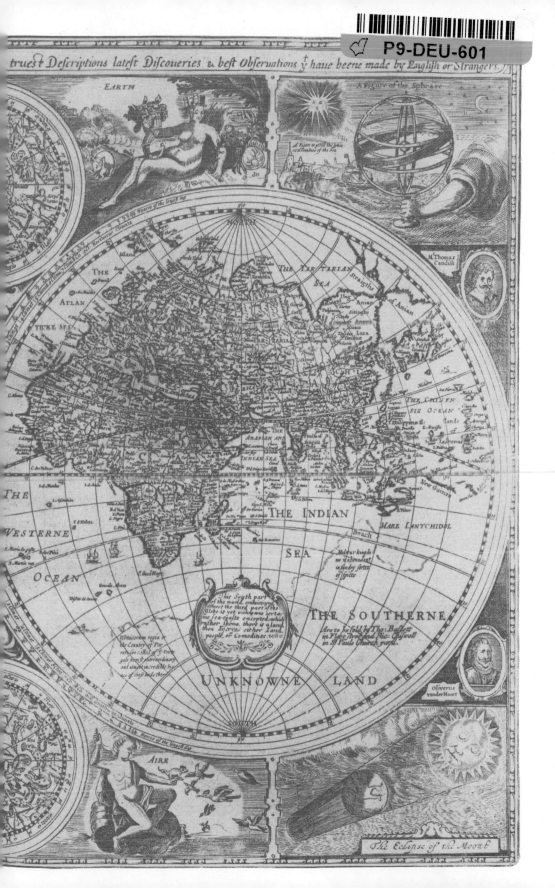

THE MIND OF THE TRAVELER

The Mind
of the Traveler

FROM GILGAMESH TO GLOBAL TOURISM

ERIC J. LEED

BasicBooks
A Division of HarperCollins*Publishers*

Map on endpapers courtesy of the Bettmann Archive.

Library of Congress Cataloging-in-Publication Data
Leed, Eric, 1942–
    The mind of the traveler: from Gilgamesh to global tourism/Eric
Leed.
      p.   cm.
Includes bibliographical references and index.
ISBN 0—465-04621-5
1. Travel.   I. Title.
G151.L44   1991
910–dc20   90–55590
                                                    CIP

Copyright © 1991 by Basic Books, Inc.
PRINTED IN THE UNITED STATES OF AMERICA
Designed by Ellen Levine
91   92   93   94   95   CG/HC   10   9   8   7   6   5   4   3   2   1

FOR MY FATHER:
BJARNE OLAF LEED

CONTENTS

PREFACE

T his study of travel began many journeys ago with the first one,
in August of 1942, as I was carried in my mother's womb from
Honolulu, Hawaii, to Missoula, Montana, where I arrived on December 11 of that year. The first journey I remember was made in late
November of 1945, in a moving van, from Missoula to Opheim, just
south of the Canadian border. I remember the driver, in a leather
jacket cracked and polished with wear, the way he smiled and how
my mother looked at him, how he put the chains on the big tires in
a driving snow, and myself wondering at this miracle and whether
this god could have any relation to myself. When my father came
back from the war, he took me on a train from Montana to San
Francisco, California, a sad journey—I was first separated from my
mother who had gone, with my older brother, on a bus. A long,
exhausting, sleepless trip, and my father tells me I was so angry that
I slapped the tickets from the hand of the kindly conductor who
offered them to me as a souvenir of the trip (my belated apologies,
sir). I had arrived in a battleship-gray postwar world, populated by
men who sat hunkered in rooms, in their underwear, drinking Four
Roses whiskey and water, talking in a low murmuring hum, barking
or laughing, while I listened to the radiators bang.

There were other journeys after that, remembered because a
good dog had to be left behind, or because I suddenly arrived in

unfamiliar territory, bearing a new, white face. These journeys blend into each other and are indistinguishable; my father became a fisherman following the fish; my mother followed him; my brother and I followed her to places where the curtains still went up and homes were made, but each time thinner and poorer in furnishings. But these were necessary journeys, not self-chosen or under one's own power, and in the company of familiar others.

The solitary educational journey began in 1960 on a bus from San Diego, California, to Eugene, Oregon. There I attended the University of Oregon for four years and found my first mentors and guides—Lloyd Sorenson and Stanley Pierson (history department), William Strange, who taught me Shakespeare, and Phin Capron, with whom I read modern literature. From that time Eugene became the object of repeated returns and still remains a destination of pilgrimage: it was there, on sabbatical in 1982, I began reading the literature of travel and thought about doing a general history of the subject.

But the general rule of travel—that the purposes and motives of the journey change and accrue in its course—is personally true. On the journey from the West to the East Coast and back to the Old World, to the past and origins, I learned that I was not alone, that others had gone before me and were embarked on parallel courses, and that I could depend on a few others to tell me what was there and what was not. I am forever thankful for the guidance and example of Hayden White, Sidney Monas, Michael Cherniavsky, and Norman O. Brown, who were at the University of Rochester, in Rochester, New York, from 1964 to 1968 when I was there as a graduate student. They showed me the paths of the inward journey from the peripheries back to the centers, what to expect in learning the way into the traditions, and how to use the books.

This is the matrix of this study, not its moment of conception— which occurred on a beach in Jacksonville, Florida, when talking about African labor migration with Dr. Thandekile Mvusi (history, Drake University) and the question of why men travel arose. At that moment, in 1982, I was looking for a topic to learn about; when I found the vastness of travel literature with its variegated nature and engrossing journeys, this conversation took root and deepened into further questions and answers. Between that conception and this moment, I have benefited from the thoughts, support, and recognitions of others.

Among my colleagues at Florida International University, I have been particularly reliant on Janet Chernela (sociology/anthropology) who lent me her brilliance, energy, and spark, and upon Darden Asbury Pyron (history) for his friendship and good advice. Howard Kaminsky and Andrea Leed gave me the title of this book. Many of the ideas herein have been poured into my ears, and their source is no longer easily identifiable, but conversations and correspondence with Eleanor Wilner, Nancy Munn (anthropology, University of Chicago), George Mosse (history, University of Wisconsin), Jean Bethke Elshtain (political science, Vanderbilt University), Jaime Melton (history, Emory University), and Kenneth Burke have opened channels of inquiry and thought pursued throughout this work. As Basho, the great seventeenth-century Japanese traveler and pioneer of haiku, observed, one of the pleasures of travel is "to find a genius among weeds and bushes, a treasure lost in broken tiles"[1]—and I would here like to thank the many strangers met on the road who became friends and shared with me their thoughts and lives, their motions and notions.

Among institutions, I am particularly beholden to Florida International University, in Miami, for two sabbatical years (1982 and 1989) during which I began the reading for this work and completed a first draft; and to Regenstein Library, University of Chicago, one of the biggest brains of all. I would particularly like to thank Gary Van Zante, who was bibliographer of the rare book room when I was there in 1989, and who enthusiastically let me in on his extensive holdings of travel and guide books. The first reading and critique of this work by my editor, Steve Fraser, and the masterful red-pencil work of my copy editor, Linda Carbone, at Basic Books, are largely responsible for transforming a draft into a book supplemental to those others and, I hope, useful to those who might wish to explore a rich and rewarding field.

Finally, and most important, I am grateful to my children—Drea, Inga, Zwe, Vusi, and Jason—for giving me the hope without which there would be no accomplishment.

A road form: the Appian Way *(Photo by Dora Jane Hamblin, from* The Appian Way, A Journey, *by Dora Jane Hamblin and Mary Jane Grunsfeld, © 1974. Used by permission.)*

FOR A HISTORY OF TRAVEL

What gives value to travel is fear. It is the fact that, at a certain moment, when we are so far from our own country ... we are seized by a vague fear, and the instinctive desire to go back to the protection of old habits. This is the most obvious benefit of travel. At that moment we are feverish but also porous, so that the slightest touch makes us quiver to the depths of our being.... This is why we should not say that we travel for pleasure. There is no pleasure in travelling, and I look upon it as an occasion for spiritual testing.... Pleasure takes us away from ourselves in the same way that distraction, as in Pascal's use of the word, takes us away from God. Travel, which is like a greater and graver science, brings us back to ourselves.

—Albert Camus, 1963

Travel is a common, frequent, everyday occurrence in our present. In fact, it is a source of our commonality, as in 1987 over forty million Americans traveled abroad, and many more at home. Comprising less than 5 percent of the world's population, U.S. citizens accounted for over 25 percent of the world spending for domestic and international travel—estimated at $2.3 trillion. If one counts all the California trips and journeys seasonally made, north and south, it is not merely a metaphor to say America is on the move and connected through mobilities. Travel, in the form of tourism, is becoming increasingly pervasive in our world. By the turn of the millennium, it will be the most important sector of world trade,

1

surpassing oil, and is currently the second largest retail industry in the United States. The impression of the commonality of travel is intensified when one includes in the ranks of travelers those who obviously belong but do not appear in the tourism statistics— business travelers, nomads, commuters, itinerant laborers, refugees, members of the armed services, diplomatic personnel, temporary and permanent immigrants. Indeed, in the first half of the twentieth century, military tourism was a common form of popular mobility and the only form of mass travel the masses could afford. A 1958 survey by the University of Michigan found that one adult American out of five had been overseas at some time in their lives, two out of three with the armed services.[1]

The term *mass tourism* conveys the scale of modern tourist business, the mass production of journeys, the infinite replication of trips to the point that even a formerly extraordinary voyage—to Machu Picchu, say, or to the Forbidden City or to Tashkent—has become something rather ordinary, a kind of norm rather than an escape from the norm. The sheer number of travelers crowding the terminals, roads, holy and sacred grounds, merchandising marts and markets alerts us to the fact that we are a society of travelers. In this society the journey is the ordinary way members link their lives and consume a world of meanings and places.

Though living in an era of mass tourism, the average American tourist is by no means representative of the masses of Americans. A survey of Americans traveling abroad in 1986 found that the average overseas tourist had an annual income of $55,519, was a member of the professional, managerial, or technical class (61 percent of overseas travelers), male (57 percent), forty-four years old, most likely to come from New York or California (46 percent), traveling for pleasure on a holiday (57 percent), was a repeat rather than a first-time traveler (91 percent), booked through a travel agency, traveled economy class (74 percent), and most likely going to one country (68 percent) in Western Europe or to the United Kingdom (60 percent).[2] Indeed, "travel for pleasure" remains as it was through the ages, a mark of success and status, while travel under compulsion of some necessity or in service of need is a mark of commonality and a common fate.

If one broadens the definition of travel to encompass all passage across significant boundaries that separate differing persona, kinds

of social relations, activities, then it becomes obvious that travel is
much more than common. It is an activity that weaves the fabric of
contemporary lives. Very few of us eat, sleep, work, and play in the
same place—this would be a definition of confinement and unfreedom. Normally our lives are segmented into places of work, play,
privacy, to be joined through territorial passage along the corridors
and passageways, road and rail networks of modern metropolitan
areas—those extended "cities" that differ so markedly from ancient
cities, like the city of Nejef in Iraq where the twentieth-century adventurer and travel writer Freya Stark once found herself:

> To sit there among the pressed houses, so crowded within the se-
> curity of their wall that there was scarcely room in front of the
> mosque for the little stone-flagged square, was to realize what for
> several thousand years of our history has constituted the feeling of
> safety, the close-packed enclosure of small cities crammed within
> walls. Outside are the wilderness, or the neighbouring unfriendly
> cities, or the raiding deserts; inside the intimacy where strangers or
> dissenters are watched with fear or anger.[3]

There, in the ancient city, citizens and insiders confront the outside
as a world of strangers held at bay with rampart and wall; here, in
modern metropolitan corridors, the vast majority of human relations are relations between strangers, who are served by a variety of
roads, markets, communicational networks, pathways that constitute
our cities. The contrast is sufficiently powerful to draw millions of
tourists out of our modernity back into those ancient cities of Mesopotamia, Egypt, ancient Europe, to experience the difference between contained lives and lives lived openly and in passage.

The commonality and familiarity of travel may also be seen in
the fact that travel is the most common source of metaphors used to
explicate transformations and transitions of all sorts. We draw upon
the experience of human mobility to define the meaning of death
(as a "passing") and the structure of life (as a "journey" or pilgrimage); to articulate changes of social and existential conditions in rites
of initiation (of "passage"). In their now-classic works, the anthropologists Arnold van Gennep, Victor Turner, and Mircea Eliade have
found rites and symbols of passage everywhere and in all periods of
human history.[4] If the essence of a metaphor or a symbol is the use

of the familiar to grasp the less familiar or ineffable,[5] then the universality of symbols and rites of passage testifies to the sheer normality of the experience of travel.

Travel is as familiar as the experience of the body, the wind, the earth, and this is why at all times and in all places it is a source of reference, a ground of symbols and metaphors, a resource of signification. The anthropologist and historian of religions Mircea Eliade laments the absence of genuine rituals of initiation in modern life and suggests that "modern man has lost all sense of traditional initiation."[6] But perhaps it is only that the reality of passage has replaced the ritual, and the most important transitions we experience are written into our journeys, which make of our lives a procession and spectacle more engrossing and transforming than any ritual could possibly be.

But the point is made: travel is, in contemporary civility, normal and a source of norms. Usually, contemporary lives are connected, segmented, sequenced through journeys—small ordinary journeys of a few miles or larger, extraordinary trips of hundreds and thousands of miles. Contemporary society, as many have noted, is a "mobile" society, but even more than that, it is a society of travelers. We may find in the history of travel the origins, the evolution, the manners, the forms of knowledge characteristic of our present, of this society of travelers. Contemporary life is perhaps unprecedented in the scale, quantity, and global organization of modern journeys, and yet it is clear that travel is not a new human experience. Mobility is the first, prehistorical human condition; sessility (attachment or fixation to one place), a later, historical condition. At the dawn of history, humans were migratory animals. Recorded history—the history of civilization—is a story of mobilities, migrations, settlements, of the adaptation of human groups to place and their integration into topography, the creation of "homes." In order to understand our present, we must understand how mobility has operated historically, in the past, as a force of change, transforming personalities, social landscapes, human topographies, creating a global civilization.

Travel has not yet been claimed as a field of history, nor is it clear that it need be, that an understanding of the way in which mobility transforms individuals, social relations, cultures would add significantly to our understanding of the past and the present. A case has to be made for the centrality of travel as an activity creative of a human condition, in the past as in the present—as I aim to do in this introduction.

TRAVEL AS EXPERIENCE

Often I feel I go to some distant region of the world to be reminded of who I really am. There is no mystery about why this should be so. Stripped of your ordinary surroundings, your friends, your daily routines ... you are forced into direct experience. Such direct experience inevitably makes you aware of who it is that is having the experience. That is not always comfortable, but it is always invigorating.

—Michael Crichton, 1988

The sheer familiarity and commonality of territorial passage in the past and the present makes it difficult to understand its effects upon individuals, societies, and cultures: these effects are so often assumed that we feel they require little or no demonstration. Travel is the paradigmatic "experience," the model of a direct and genuine experience, which transforms the person having it. We may see something of the nature of these transformations in the roots of Indo-European languages, where *travel* and *experience* are intimately wedded terms.

The Indo-European root of *experience* is **per* (the asterisk indicates a retroconstruction from languages living and dead). **Per* has been construed as "to try," "to test," "to risk"—connotations that persist in the English word *peril*. The earliest connotations of **per* appear in Latin words for "experience": *experior* and *experimentum*, whence the English *experiment*. This conception of "experience" as an ordeal, as a passage through a frame of action that gauges the true dimensions and nature of the person or object passing through it, also describes the most general and ancient conception of the effects of travel upon the traveler. Many of the secondary meanings of **per* refer explicitly to motion: "to cross space," "to reach a goal," "to go out." The connotations of risk and danger implicit in *peril* are also obvious in the Gothic cognates for **per* (in which *p* becomes an *f*): *fern* (far), *fare*, *fear*, *ferry*. One of the German words for experience, *Erfahrung*, is from the Old High German *irfaran*: "to travel," "to go out," "to traverse," or "to wander." The deeply rooted assumption that travel is an experience that tests and refines the character of the traveler is demonstrated by the German adjective *bewandert*, which currently means "astute," "skilled," or "clever" but originally (in fifteenth-century texts) meant merely "well traveled."[7]

These crossings of words and meanings reflect one of the first conceptualizations of travel as suffering, a test, an ordeal—meanings explicit in the original English word for travel: *travail*. Implicit is a notion of the transformations of travel as changes that strip, reduce, and waste the passenger. This ostensibly negative sense pervades ancient travel epics, including *The Epic of Gilgamesh*, the first work of Western travel literature (transcribed 1900 B.C.). At every stage of his passage, Gilgamesh is met with the same questions: "Why are your cheeks so starved and your face drawn? Why is despair in your heart and your face like the face of one who has made a long journey; yes, why is your face burned with heat and cold, and why do you come here wandering over the pasture in search of the wind?"[8]

Gilgamesh's journey is a prime example of heroic travel (which I will discuss in chapter 1): the fatigue, hardship, and danger it entails essentially reduce the character who undertakes it. The young Gilgamesh, who was a king too strong for his city, is sent on a journey as a way of decreasing his excessive appetite for labor, soldiers, and women so as to be compatible with the urban order in which he has originated. His journeys transform him from a predator upon his city into "the shepherd of the city." On his journey, Gilgamesh is, like Odysseus, stripped of his following, of his energies, of his chief companions, and of his ambitions. Ultimately he is brought to the extremity of the world, the Far West, the land of death and immortality. Because he falls asleep during a night in which he must stay awake, Gilgamesh fails to win immortality; and, on the way home, he loses his consolation prize, a rejuvenating plant. But his travels have the desired effect: he is reduced to a level coherent with the precincts of his city, and he is made wise: "This was the man to whom all things were known: this was the king who knew the countries of the world. He was wise, he saw mysteries and knew secret things, he brought us a tale of the days before the flood. He went on a long journey, was weary, worn-out with labour, returning he rested, he engraved on a stone the whole story."[9]

Here, in a compact and original form, are issues I consider at length in the following chapters: How do the transformations of travel produce the mind of the traveler, a certain mentality that has often been termed "modern," post-Renaissance, but that is as old as civilized travel? What features of the journey experience shape the identity of travelers, giving rise to the features of the stranger and the organization of traveling societies—nomadic peoples, military expeditions? These are the questions I address in part III of this study, on travel and identity. Here, too, in the introduction of Gilgamesh and his achievements, we find the basic premise of philosophical travel—the subject of part II: the concept that travel across space is travel into a past and a search for origins, for the story of the days before the last beginning, the "days before the flood."

THE ANCIENTS AND THE MODERNS: FROM SUFFERING TO FREEDOM

"Here we go, we're all together. . . . What did we do in New York? Let's forgive." We had all had our spats back there. "That's behind us, merely by miles and inclinations. . . ." We all jumped to the music and agreed. The purity of the road.
                                                                    Jack Kerouac, 1957

Ancient and modern conceptions of the "meaning" of travel are very different, as are their emphases on the transformations effected by a journey. The ancients valued travel as an explication of human fate and necessity; for moderns, it is an expression of freedom and an escape from necessity and purpose. Ancients saw travel as a suffering, even a penance; for moderns, it is a pleasure and a means to pleasure. Ancient epics of travel describe those motions through which individuals, in groups and often armed, confirmed an order of the world and demonstrated their status; travel today is marketed as a means of discovery, of acquiring access to something new, original, and even unexpected.

In general, the ancients most valued the journey as an explication of fate or necessity, as a revelation of those forces that sustain and shape, alter and govern human destinies. The travels narrated in the *Odyssey* and *The Epic of Gilgamesh* are god-decreed and thus not wholly voluntary nor pleasurable. Odysseus wanders on a long, frustrating journey toward home, personified by Penelope, the territorialized and virtuous woman whose exclusion of suitors preserves that home. When Odysseus finally arrives in Ithaca, disguised as a beggar, he thanks the swineherd Eumaeus for his hospitality in terms that adequately express the ancient conception of travel as a driven state of existence, a necessitated, even prophesied suffering: "You have given me rest from the pains and miseries of wandering. To be driven hither and then thither—nothing mortals endure can be worse than that, yet men will bear with such utter wretchedness, will accept such wandering and grief and sorrow for the sake of their accursed bellies."[10]

The sufferings of travel clearly frame and intensify the significance of the heroic traveler's actions. When Odysseus accepts the challenge of the nobles of Sphacteria to compete in their games, he cites the wastings and reductions of travel as factors that will make his victory even more significant: "As you see me now, I am ground down by distress and misery; I have had many trials to endure, fighting my way through hostile warriors and battering waves. Yet nevertheless, despite all sufferings, I will try my fortune in your contests. Your insult rankles and you have roused me."[11] The ability to rise to the new occasion despite the losses and frictions of the journey demonstrates, at the very least, that Odysseus, even though reduced, is still superior to the best efforts of the locals. The rhythm of this epic, the recurrent pattern of phallic self-assertion and exhaustion, of freedom and captivity, suggests that it is a narrative of male potencies deployed in the classical journey.

This emphasis upon travel as a test, as a loss that brings a gain of stature and certainty of self, suggests that the changes of character effected by travel are not so much the introduction of something new into the personality of the traveler as a revelation of something ineradicably present—perhaps courage, perdurance, the ability to endure pain, the persistence of skills and abilities even in a context of fatigue and danger. The transformations of passage are a species of "identification" through action, which adds to the being in motion only a consciousness of the irreducible form and individuality of that being. In the difficult and dangerous journey, the self of the traveler is impoverished and reduced to its essentials, allowing one to see what those essentials are.

In this sense, the heroic journey resembles what the critic and philosopher Kenneth Burke has spoken of as a "fictional death" *—

*Personal communication, 1978.

fictional rather than real because death is used as a context for the assertion of an essential and irreducible self; implicitly denied is the reality of death as a dissolution of form and a solvent of identity. The *topos* of the fictional death is prominent in funeral orations, in narrations of epic and heroic journeys as well as in war literature, in which it is frequently assumed that a "true" and genuine self is tried, proven, reduced to its essence by a journey through the valley of death. This *topos*, characteristic of ancient journeys, occurs in modern adventure travels and travels of discovery. Captain James Cook, upon reading the journals of his gentlemen companions, became indignant, believing that they had exaggerated the perils encountered on the around-the-world voyage of the *Endeavour* (1768–71); but he resigned himself to their hyperbole as inevitable:

> [S]uch are the dispositions of men in general in these voyages that they are seldom content with the hardships and dangers which will naturally occur, but they must add others which hardly ever had existence but in their imaginations, by magnifying the most trifling accidents and circumstances to the greatest hardships, and insurmountable dangers . . . as if the whole merit of the voyage consisted in the dangers and hardships they underwent, or that real ones did not happen often enough to give the mind sufficient anxiety; thus posterity are taught to look upon these voyages as hazardous to the highest degree.[12]

The dangers and fatigues of travel remain today, in some sense, a test of the heroism of the traveler. The great structural anthropologist Claude Lévi-Strauss, who ostensibly despises the mere tourist and the self-promoting adventurer ("adventure has no place in the anthropologist's profession"), nevertheless makes use of the traditional *topos* in gauging the value of what an ethnographer acquires on a voyage to the peripheries. The anthropologist "may endure months of travelling, hardships, and sickening boredom for the purpose of recording (in a few days, or even few hours) a hitherto unknown myth, a new marriage rule or a complete list of clan names."[13] In some sense, hardship, boredom, and physical effort contribute to the value of the rite or myth recorded, and to the stature of the anthropologist among equals.

Indeed, the fatigues and characteristic dangers of the journey may be precisely calibrated and itemized in one's hotel bill. A hotel in the Ecuadorean Amazon advertises, "The hosts try very hard to meet individual interests and provide levels of adventure according to what you feel you are up to—from easy guided walks on marked trails, to strenuous Outward Bound–style overnight hikes through the forest, which make you feel like the real Indiana Jones."[14]

The fatigues of travel, the sufferings of the journey, remain a cause and a measure of the extent to which a traveler is marked and tested by experience, becoming *bewandert*—"skilled" and "wise." It is this factor that distinguishes the mere tourist from the real and genuine traveler, for whom travel is a test rather than a pleasure. This traditional theme persists beneath the modern emphasis upon the pleasures of travel, which in any case do not exist, Albert Camus insists, for those traveling on cheap tickets or with no tickets at all.[15] For the poor contemporary traveler, travel retains its ancient significance and is given value by the fear that makes the individual "porous" and sensitive. However ancient the theme, Camus's emphasis is modern: the fear of the wayfarer, the loss of security implicit in unaccommodated travel is a gain of accessibility and sensitivity to the world. Travel, from the moment of departure, removes those furnishings and mediations that come with a familiar residence. It thus substantiates individuality in its sense of "autonomy," for the self is now separated from a confirming and confining matrix.

Today the very vicissitudes, strippings, and wastings that constituted the ancient sufferings of the traveler are prized as an ascetic, disciplined freedom, as the confirmation of an individuality that encounters directly a world held at bay by the walls and boundaries of one's home. " 'Being naked' always has associations of physical liberty, of harmony between the hand and the flower it touches, of a loving understanding between the earth and men who have become freed of human things."[16] The sufferings of travel constitute a simplification of life that enhances the objectivity of a world within which the traveler becomes aware of an irreducible subjectivity, a self. This contemporary conception of the strippings and wastings of travel as a freedom from mediations is only a present appearance of the ancient conception of travel as a penance and a purification which have a morally improving effect upon the traveler. The conception of travel as a penance is as old as the journey of the primal pair, evicted from the Garden for their sins and enjoined to travel and labor as an expiation for those sins. Departure breaks the bonds between the sinner and the site and occasions of the sin. It is a way of leaving trouble behind. This is perhaps the reason travel, as exile, was conceived to be at once punishment and cure, retribution and purification. The stripping away by the frictions of passage of all that is not of the essence of the passenger, the removal of defining associations, of bonds to the world of place—all effect changes in the character of the traveler that are strictly analogous to a cleansing, the reduction of the purified entity to its smallest, truest dimensions.

The penance of travel was also prescribed to the second biblical generation, as Cain was set upon his course of wanderings for his act of fratricide, the act that alienated him from the soil that had defined him and that he had watered with his brother's blood. Denying him any further attachment to the soil, God made wandering Cain's permanent condition: "When you till the ground, it will no longer yield you its wealth. You shall be a vagrant and a wanderer upon the earth." At the same moment, God decreed the sanctity of the wanderer whose travels and exile are his penance and make him sacrosanct, with the "mark of Cain": "So the Lord put a mark on Cain, in order that anyone meeting him should not kill him."[17]

Pilgrimage is the institutionalization of this transformation of travel, a formalization of the notion that travel purifies, cleanses, removes the wanderer from the site of transgressions. This notion is explicit in the charter of Buddhist pilgrimage, the *Aitareya Brahmana*: "There is no happiness for him who does not travel; living in the society of men, the best man often becomes a sinner; for Indra [Vedic deity of rain and thunder] is the friend of the traveler. Therefore wander."[18] Here the loss of travel may be a moral and psychological gain—as was understood by that modern Odysseus, Neil Cassady, fictionalized as Moriarity in Jack Kerouac's epic *On the Road*, who left behind any number of sins in a life spent in passage.[19] In chapter 2, on passage, I will examine the phenomenon noted by Kerouac and generations of travelers: the purity of the road.

Implicit in the conception of travel as a penance and a purge is the assumption that "self" and "place" are integrated realities, and that the self may be changed with change of place. The reductive effects of travel begin with the first term of a journey—departure, a separation requiring one to leave behind much that has previously defined the civil self. This event transforms the passenger into a species not unlike Rousseau's savage man, who has his own forces constantly at his disposal and carries himself "whole and entire" about with him. But such stripping away of defining relations and furnishings of the civil self is often painful, evoking protest, grief, and mourning. Departure is an occasion of human suffering. Though celebrated in modern travel, departure was traditionally undertaken only for the most urgent of motives. These may be explicit or implicit, and they change over time. In chapter 1, I discuss why a particular age places certain motives ahead of others, decreeing the propriety of traveling as a penance, a purification, a test, a liberation, a pleasure, a satisfaction of curiosity. In that chapter, too, I set out the rough but evident historical transition that is the backbone of this work: the transition from the ancient emphasis upon travel as a necessary suffering to the modern emphasis upon travel as an experience of freedom and the gaining of autonomy.

The ancients had no conception of travel as a voluntary and altruistic act. Even ancient tourism, which flourished under the *Pax Romana*, appears to Seneca as a driven state of existence, a distracted wandering:

> This is the reason why men undertake aimless wanderings, travel along distant shores and at one time by sea, at another by land, try to soothe the fickleness of disposition which is always dissatisfied with the present. "Now let us make for Campania: now I am sick of rich cultivation: let us see something of wild regions, let us thread the passes of Brulli and Lucania: yet amid this wilderness one wants something of beauty to relieve our pampered eyes after so long dwelling on savage wastes. Let us seek Tarentum with its famous harbor, its mild winter climate.... Let us now return to town; our ears have long missed its shouts and noise: it would be pleasant also to enjoy the sight of human bloodshed." Thus one journey succeeds another, and one sight is changed for another.[20]

The travels of Odysseus, Heracles, and many other ancient heroes were imposed upon them by an external "command"—from a god, a goddess, fate. The identity-defining travels of the medieval knight were, on the other hand, ostensibly voluntary and undertaken to no utilitarian purpose. The chivalric journey, which is the pattern and model for significant modern travel, is essentially self-referential, undertaken to reveal the essential character of the knight as "free," once the essence of nobility but since the seventeenth century considered an attribute of human nature. The voluntariness of departure and the solitude of the knight identified the new concept of adventure; travel became a demonstration of freedom from necessity, the mark of a status above the "commons." This transmutation

of the heroic journey into a freely chosen opportunity to demonstrate an identity—as freedom, self-display, and self-discovery—enters into the very definition of a new species of travel characteristic
of the postmedieval world: the voyage of discovery and, later, the
"scientific" expedition and the travels of curious and recording tourists. The celebration of travel as a demonstration of freedom and
means to autonomy becomes the modern *topos*, clearly evident in
William Wordsworth's evocation of the condition of the wanderer:

> *Whither shall I turn,*
> *By road or pathway, or through trackless field,*
> *Up hill or down, or shall some floating thing,*
> *Upon the river point me out my course?*[21]

The very indeterminacy of wandering, which Odysseus found hard
to bear, is the source of the freedom the Romantics prized in travel.
This association of travel and freedom may be traced to medieval
roots, where it was written into law. According to the laws of Henry
II, a lord who wished to free his serf had first to declare that intention in a church, a market, or a county court, to bestow a lance and
a sword upon his former bondsman, and then take him to a cross-
roads to show him that "all ways lie open to his feet."[22] These two
features—arms and the right of free departure—long remained the
distinguishing marks of the status of "free" man. Their opposites—
the forbidding of arms or of travel—were the marks of unfreedom.
The right to travel had entered into the Western definition of the
free autonomous individual whose associations to others are a result
of conscious acts of connection, of allegiance and contract.

In Wordsworth and the Romantics, and in modern travels generally, we find divorced those things with which travel had been
inextricably wedded in ancient conceptions. Travel became distin-
guishable from pain and began to be regarded as an intellectual
pleasure. Thus, Wordsworth's "Old Man Travelling" is a portrait of
"A man who does not move with pain, but moves / with thought."[23]

These factors—the voluntariness of departure, the freedom implicit in the indeterminacies of mobility, the pleasure of travel free
from necessity, the notion that travel signifies autonomy and is a
means for demonstrating what one "really" is independent of one
context or set of defining associations—remain the characteristics of

the modern conception of travel. Michael Crichton's explanation of why he travels draws upon these themes:

> And I felt a need for rejuvenation, for experiences that would take me away from things I usually did, the life I usually led. In my everyday life, I often felt a stifling awareness of the purpose behind everything I did. Every book I read, every movie I saw, every lunch and dinner I attended seemed to have a reason behind it. From time to time, I felt the urge to do something for no reason at all.

Done "for no reason at all" except to escape a world where all things are a means to an end, travel, in modern circumstances, is prized less as a means of revealing ungovernable forces beyond human control than for providing direct access to a new material and objective world. In the apprehension of that world, the passenger acquires a new awareness of self in the context of a direct experience that "inevitably makes you aware of who it is that is having the experience."[24]

If travel is, as the great African-American writer and folklorist Zora Neale Hurston observed, "the soul of civilization,"[25] then in the history of European travels we may find the soul of the West, its continuities, evolution, permutations. For the history of travel is in crucial ways a history of the West. It recounts the evolution from necessity to freedom, an evolution that gave rise to a new consciousness, the peculiar mentality of the modern traveler.

THE SOCIAL EFFECTS OF TRAVEL

To understand what was going on it is perhaps necessary to have participated in the freeway experience, which is the only secular form of communion Los Angeles has. Mere driving on the freeway is in no way the same as participating in it. Anyone can "drive" on the freeway, and many people with no vocation for it do, hesitating here and resisting there, losing the rhythm of the lane change, thinking about where they came from and where they are going. Actual participation requires a total surrender, a concentration so intense as to seem a narcosis, a rapture-of-the-freeway. The mind goes clean. The rhythm takes over. A distortion of time occurs.

—Joan Didion, 1979

Travel is a primary source of the "new" in history. The displacements of the journey create exotica ("matter out of place") and rarities, as well as generating that peculiar species of social being of unknown identity—the stranger. Travel also creates new social groups and bonds between strangers who meet in passing, and who are bound by a common motion, destination, or purpose. In Los Angeles mobility is a form of communion and a source of community. But this has always been so, and mobility has governed the shape and structure of nomadic societies, hunting and gathering societies, expeditions.

The communities formed by strangers and shaped in territorial passage have been primary agents of history—nomadic peoples and hordes, bands of warrior-citizens, military expeditions and brotherhoods, oath-bound associations of leaders and followers, crusaders and Vikings, those warring and trading companies that first consolidated Europe's world empire in the seventeenth centuries, modern scientific expeditions and tour groups. Such organizations have been primary historical actors, agents of empire, the medium for the extension of power and integration of cultural regions, civilizations. Such mobile societies, formed and shaped in passage, contain the seeds of historical transitions and are crucibles of historical change.

Those who bear the impress of many passages—professionals in the transport industries, sailors, teamsters, soldiers on expedition, missionaries and merchants, indefatigable tourists and anthropologists—are, in fact, the brokers of contacts among cultural domains, architects of a world that grows out of "external" relations, from the outside in. Indeed, the societies formed of such peoples, societies formed of common motion, substantiate our chronologies and establish the contiguity of the eras of Western history: the nomadic people who gave form to the ancient *polis*, the armed band of leaders and followers who were territorialized in medieval lordships, the armed company that was demilitarized and commercialized in the sixteenth and seventeenth centuries to give rise to the merchant company and ultimately the transnational corporation, distinctively "modern" forms of polity. The force mobility exercises in human affairs is evident in the features these societies share, and in the differences that distinguish them, features we should be able to observe in our present, in our own society of travelers.

Travel, clearly, provides a common idiom of human relations.

Companion, leader, follower, are all terms that originated in the experience of travel and are applied to other social relationships, just as metaphors of passage are applied to social and existential transitions. Among the Buid, a people native to the highlands of Mindanao, settlements are spoken of as "companion groups," a term originating in the company that goes, each year, to trade in lowland markets.[26] The Old Norse rites of marriage used the idiom of travel, in which the wife bound herself to her husband, "as the companion joined to her husband by the ties of a follower."[27]

The fact that travel actually *creates* relations, socialities, and communities can be observed in the present, in the communion of the freeway, as well as in the past, and is witnessed throughout travel literature. The community of strangers found by Samuel Dodsworth, Sinclair Lewis's character, aboard a transatlantic steamer in passage from the new back to the old world, differs neither in its components (strangers) nor in its structure from those groups that had made the journey west in the sixteenth century: "A racing view of all their companions of the voyage, their fellow-citizens in this brave village amid the desert of waters; strangers to be hated on sight, to be snubbed lest they snub first, yet presently to be known better and better loved and longer remembered than neighbors seen for a lifetime on the cautious land."[28]

Such communities born in the communion of motion often escape our explanatory models, which assume that societies are relatively stable, permanent, bounded, and centered entities. Our models and image of society are based on territorialized societies rooted in place. We have no model for those communities generated out of the "rapture-of-the-freeway" or the seductions of motion, for we have no real understanding of the passage experience or of the way in which motion alters the psychic state, the perceptions, the world of the traveler.

But traveling societies rooted in a moving present, and transitory by their very nature, have a certain persistence in the psychic state motion induces, a perdurance in the memory of passages. It is clear, for example, that travel affects the sense of time; in passage, as Didion says, "the mind goes clean.... A distortion of time occurs."[29] The transformations of the sense of time by motion through space has been a staple of travel literature from the beginning and a standard motive for journeying. In the first epic of travel, Gilgamesh sets out on his journey to escape the finality of his death, revealed to him by his god and reinforced every morning as he gazes over the city wall: "Here in the city man dies oppressed at heart, man perishes with despair in his heart. I have looked over the wall and seen bodies floating on the river, and that will be my lot also. . . . Therefore . . . I will go to the country where the cedar is cut."[30] The use of the journey to avoid the implications of temporality—finality and death—assumes the sessile condition, a continuous sameness of locale that intensifies a sense of temporal repetitions and may be escaped through departure. Thus, the abeyance of time in passage across space is a feature of travel particularly attractive to the civilized, the rooted, the territorialized. The same motives inspiring Gilgamesh may be found in the French anthropologist Michel Leiris's description of his reasons for leaving his home and undertaking a journey to Africa in the 1930s:

> Sick of his life in Paris, viewing travel as a private adventure, a method of concrete knowledge, an ordeal, a symbolic way to stop growing old, to deny time by crossing space, the author, interested in ethnography for the value he gives that science in the clarification of human relations, joins a scientific expedition crossing Africa.[31]

TERRITORIALIZATION AND PLACE

Nomadic cultures, or a cultural phenomenon like the seafaring life, do not inscribe themselves on any fixed place on earth. Yet a ship, constantly changing its location, is none the less a self-contained place, and so is a Gypsy camp, an Indian camp, or a circus camp, however often it shifts its geodetic bearings. Literally we say the camp is in a place; culturally it is a place.

—Susanne Langer, 1953

Civilized travel, at least travel within accomplished historical civilities, assumes the condition of sessility, settlement, and sedentarism—the territorialization of the human group and the localization of "place." The meanings traditionally invested in the journey, through a significant portion of human history, derive from the experienced contrasts mobility offers to a condition of sessility, which is presumed to be normal. It is only within the context of settlement that travel becomes a "liminal" experience, a moment betwixt and between established social orders and identities, no longer a way of life or a condition of existence as it is for nomadic and wandering peoples. Settlement fixes a mobile social order in space and thus often transforms the mobile social order—almost invariably a democratic organization of leaders and followers—into an order of hierarchy, aristocracy, and divine kingship. But it is this territorialization of place that ultimately makes travel conceivable as liberty rather than fate, as escape rather than performance of necessities. This transvaluation of the journey from a necessity into a liberty thus implies territorialization, those processes by which a once mobile ethnicity—a transportable structure of human relations and identities—is grounded in a site, which becomes a place of origin and an object of returns.

The always insightful German economist Karl Bücher correctly pinpointed the process of territorialization as a chief factor in the history of Western civilization: "In all probability, the whole course of further development down to our present day has been the gradual progress toward a settled condition and an ever closer attachment of man to the spot where he was born."[32]

Strictly speaking, all of those techniques by which groups root themselves in landscape—the mythicization and historicization of landscape, its peopling with gods and ancestors, their deeds and battles, the burial of the dead, the sessilization of certain portions of the population (traditionally, women, children, and servants), mapping, boundary making, the architecturalization of space in temples and gathering places, the peopling of cities with statues (which philosopher Susanne Langer terms "the first permanent inhabitants of cities"[33]), effigies and memorials—all belong to the history of travel.

Travel is, as I will argue throughout this book, a central rather than a peripheral force in historical transformations; and the creation of locale, the mapping of territory, the territorialization of humanity are achievements of mobility. Boundaries are made by those who cross them. Walls and gates assume a world of strangers and passengers. The stones are only materializations of associations and meetings, the flow and passage of humanity. The architecture of place—so often the object of the touristic gaze—is only a crystallization of repeated events of inclusion and exclusion, the performance of those methods that groups use to define members and nonmembers, defining themselves in the process. The great ancient centers—Delos, Memphis, Athens, Rome, Jerusalem, Mecca, Thebes are only monuments to generations of arrivals and returns, the skeletal remains of countless journeys. Here we may follow Susanne Langer's original suggestion that we view history from the perspective of mobility and motion, rather than from the position of the emplaced, because this promises a clarification and the removal of distortions caused by the premise of sessility.

The inability to regard place as anything but territorial, the eternal assumption that societies are boundaried, centered, contained, and enduring structures, is a distortion of retrospect, a view of history filtered through the results of history. The distortion of retrospect causes us to neglect the choices, events, and contingencies that create social structures and establish social bonds. The presumptions of the effects of travel, sessility and territorialization, enter deeply into our often unspoken assumption that societies are somehow pre-established rather than constantly in the process of formation and dissolution. It lends the eternality of locale to the transience of social relations and to analogies as convincing as they are spurious:

> A society is similar to a house divided into rooms and corridors. The more the society resembles ours in its form of civilization, the thinner are its internal partitions and the wider and more open are its doors of communication. In a semicivilized society, on the other hand, sections are carefully isolated, and passage from one to another must be made through formalities and ceremonies which show extensive parallels to the rites of territorial passage.[34]

Van Gennep's analogy here is persuasive to those who live in houses and dwell within established civilities. It assumes the stability and harmony between group and place that has been laboriously achieved in battles of entry, generations of arrivals and departures. In effect, the ritual model and most traditional history assume those structures whose origins we are trying to understand, and negate the climate of historical action—uncertainty and contingency—which breeds a human need for ritual and routine in the first place.

THE HISTORY OF TRAVEL AND THE HISTORY OF CULTURE

The community has been highly isolated and not confronted with members of contrastive ethnic groups. This absence of any systematic alternative to their own way of life has absolved them of the need to question features of their own customs and premises, and entails a very incomplete and unfocused self-image.
                                                        —Frederik Barth, 1975

One rationale for a history of travel lies in the value of the subject for our understanding of cultural change—historical alterations in established patterns of meaning. The invariably perceptive anthropologist Frederik Barth suggests that cross-cultural contacts in travel generate a new kind of cultural self-consciousness, a species of collective self-awareness.[35] The Baktaman, an isolated New Guinea hill tribe among whom Barth lived, could not explain to him—the curious stranger—the "meaning" of their rites, symbols, and initiations practiced from time immemorial. During his "contact year," Barth realized that with his questions and probings he was creating a body of "native explanation"; in his cultivation of informants, he was engendering a "native intelligentsia," who could explain themselves and their culture to others and demonstrate its logic. He, the curious and recording stranger, was an agent transforming the very culture he was observing.

The history of travel suggests that collective and individual identities arise from and are transformed by processes of mutual reflection, identification, and recognition in human relationships; that neither collective nor personal identities are implicit in the organism or the collective but arise from relations to others. The ancient Greek historian Thucydides makes the point that the Greeks were not conscious of themselves as a collectivity, as Hellenes, until their encounter with the Persians in the Persian wars (490–480 B.C.). Homer did not even use the word *Hellenic* in his story of the wars that joined Argives, Achaeans, and Danaans in the struggle for the possession of Helen: "He does not even use the word 'foreigners' [*barbaroi*], and this, in my opinion, is because in his time the Hellenes were not yet known by one name, and so marked off as something separate from the outside world."[36] The experience of travel, here armed and in force, engenders a collective self-consciousness as it acquaints travelers with the precise nature of their sameness and difference with respect to a world of others. As an experience of contrastive ethnic groups, travel entails the generation of a cultural self-image, and this is cultural change.

This is the argument of chapter 6, a discussion of Renaissance voyages and of how the encounter with unsuspected peoples required the mobilization of European traditions, generating a new cultural self-consciousness. From the sixteenth century on, Europeans encountered with increasing frequency a world of contrastive ethnicities, which allowed them to make comparisons between themselves and others. Out of these comparisons arose a self-image of a culture no longer merely the heir of ancient traditions, a periphery of ancient centers, but a center in its own right and a culmination of history on the cutting edge of the "modern." The history of travel sheds light on the cultural revolution of the Renaissance as well as upon subsequent revolutions of modernity.

The history of travel illuminates the history not only of the West but of the human species in general, suggesting that this is a story of the dispersal, aggregation, differentiation of the species and its adaptation to a variety of places, climates, soils, and topographies. In this, human history does not differ significantly from the history of other species that have evolved, preserved, and perpetuated variations that adapt a population to a "place," an ecological niche. Of course, human migrations are achieved not through "instinct" but through the imagination, through images of the mysterious and faraway, of sacred lands, lands of plenty and promises. The history of travel thus promises a unity of human and natural history, as well as a unified perspective from which to view the transformation of cultures. It suggests that it is not really paradoxical that the industrial era, in which the world's regions have been permanently linked through a world economy, is also the era of assertive nationalisms, flourishing tribalism, a growth of conscious individualities—collective and personal. In the encounters of travel, individuals as well as collectivities become conscious of their irreducible uniqueness and difference as well as of their generality, their sameness, the species being, humanity.

The history of travel is the study of a force—mobility—that has shaped human history and is observably at work in our present. Mobility is a force of change operating through distinctly different events that make up the structure of the journey: departure, passage, and arrival. The transformations of travel are an accumulation of effects derived from this sequence of distinctive situations: from departures that detach individuals from a familiar context; from passages that set them in motion across space; from arrivals that establish new bonds and identifications between strangers, creating a new union and coherence between self and context. Each of these events has its specific character and must be examined in its own right. Needs are a product of situations,* and each of these events, through many repetitions, produces and serves a particular set of needs. Departure may serve the need for detachment, purification, liberty, "individuality," escape, self-definition. Passage serves and generates a need for motion but may, in turn, generate other longings: for stability in a condition of disequilibrium, for fixed orientation in a world of flux, for immutability in the midst of transience. Arrivals serve a need for human association, for membership, definition, even confinement, and may, in turn, engender a growing desire for departure, liberty, and escape. In any one place and moment, these needs may be perceived as opposed and conflictual, but they are not when sequenced in the form of the journey. Here may lie the eternal appeal of travel—it resolves a logic of contradiction, a logic of place, into a logic of sequence, an order of change and transformation which serves and fosters a variety of human longings: for motion and rest, liberty and confinement, indeterminacy and definition.

*I thank anthropologist Janet Chernela for this suggestion.

I

THE STRUCTURE OF THE JOURNEY: DEPARTURE, PASSAGE, ARRIVAL

The departure of Gilgamesh
(Courtesy of the Bettmann Archive)

1

REACHING FOR ABROAD: DEPARTURES

The last belch from America had expired on the outer edge of the Venice lagoon, and moving through the still, sun-heavy Adriatic, I was now definitely gone. It was a refreshing feeling, somehow a sweet feeling, like a return to a very early youth; there was a sense of morning, and even of innocence about it. That was what travel did for me, but only in the furthest reaches of abroad.

—John Knowles, 1964

It is no small contradiction to human nature to leave one's home.

—Father Navarette, 1704

In every parting there is a latent germ of madness.

—Goethe, 1788

T he departure charters the journey, establishing its motives and first meanings. The departure also establishes the initial identity of the traveler. Ceremonious and public departures begin the heroic journeys of kings and would-be kings, while forced, surreptitious, or routine departures initiate the journeys and identities of captives, exiles, fugitives, and professional travelers. The four departures I will discuss in this chapter—of Gilgamesh, Adam and Eve,

Ywain, and Alexander Kinglake—suggest the motives activating all who have undertaken and suffered departures.

These specific departures also suggest a historical shift in the perception and definition of the meaningful journey and the heroic traveler. In the Middle Ages, certain features of ancient heroic and nonheroic journeys are combined to produce a new, ennobling species of journey which is both an exile and a search for fame. This redefinition is implicit in modern adventure-travels, such as those undertaken by Alexander Kinglake and generalized in modern tourism as an escape from civility and modernity.

Different ages and cultures may value the significant departure differently—as a beginning of selfhood, or a loss of self; as the beginning of freedom, or alienation—but the essence of departure does not change. Always, everywhere, it separates the individual from a defining social and cultural matrix. The subjective character of the events also remains remarkably consistent through the ages. In the earliest Western travel literature can be found the protest, despair, and detachment that John Bowlby (the authority on attachment and loss) describes as "separation anxiety." It is against these objective and subjective continuities of departure that a history may be seen, a history that is at once collective and personal.

JOURNEYS—HEROIC AND NONHEROIC

I have not established my name stamped on bricks as my destiny decreed; therefore I will go to the country where the cedar is felled. I will set up my name in the place where the names of famous men are written, and where no man's name is written yet I will raise a monument to the gods.
                                                        —Gilgamesh, c. 1900 B.C.

The heroic journey is designed to extend an identity across space and through time, to display power and status. Initially, a public and ceremonious departure establishes the identity of the leave-taker and affirms those relations in which this identity is rooted. The departure not only "excorporates" a member from a social body, it also "incorporates" and inaugurates the mobile body, whether an individual or a group. The heroic journey is a means of becoming known in the world, of garnering recognitions, and extending power. Fame, the extension of social being across space and time, is the chief characterizing motive of heroic travel: the mythical travels of Osiris, Dionysus, and Heracles; the legendary travels of Odysseus, Jason, Theseus, and Gilgamesh; the historical travels of Alexander and Caesar. The armed expedition was not only a way for an aspiring male to become known in the ancient world, but also a means of extending the boundaries of civility and of the world. Pliny assumed that the armed expedition was the chief means of gaining a knowledge of the world and this was why the sources of the Nile remained mysterious in his own day, having been "explored by unarmed investigators, without the wars that have discovered all other countries."[1] Heroic departures also characteristically assume a return, at least in their ancient form: they are round-trips, rather than exiles or migrations. The circular form of the heroic journey is implicit in its purpose—the geographical and temporal extension of identity. A journey undertaken to fix a persona in the sites of his deeds, in literature, in monuments, in human memory, assumes an observing public without whom there can be no fame. Passing strangers or the eye of the god may fulfill this function, but most often the role of the observing "third person" is filled by a place such as the one to which Gilgamesh returns to engrave on a stone the whole story of his journey.

In addition to asserting the identity of the traveler and establishing the purpose of the journey as a means of acquiring recognition, the heroic journey is voluntarily undertaken rather than forced. The willingness of Gilgamesh to depart is, of course, ambivalent, occurring as a result of a revelation by the god of the inevitability of death, the final departure and separation. But Gilgamesh does have a choice, as is clearly not the case in the nonheroic departures of exiles and fugitives. This element of choice becomes increasingly significant in the medieval heroic journey, and is essential to the conception of the journey as a means of asserting a "second," nonbiological nature.

The heroic journey in its ancient form is invariably a circuit, a form taken by modern tourism and adventure travels. But despite its prominence in the travel literature, this is not the only form of human mobility. The ritual tour, whether a pilgrimage, voyage, or parade, is clearly uncharacteristic of the vast majority of human travels which are undertaken by nomads, exiles, refugees, captives, colonists or fugitives. The nonheroic journey is a forced departure: the traveler is not moved by his own motives but propelled by necessity, chance, disaster, crime, or the violation of some norm. The forced departure initiates a journey that is suffering or penance rather than a campaign or a voyage. Often one-way or endless journeys, they muddle rather than define the persona of the traveler.

Gilgamesh: The Search for Fame

The earliest departure detailed in Western travel literature, that of Gilgamesh, a king of Uruk, upon his campaign against Lebanon c. 2500 B.C., is divinely ordained. It is initiated by Gilgamesh's god, Shamash, who revealed through a dream of Enkidu, Gilgamesh's follower, that the king's fate is to be death, not eternal life. Enkidu, originally a wildman of the hills who has been captured by trappers, conquered by Gilgamesh, and transformed into a follower and a servant, now eats the king's bread and drinks his wine. He has his own motives for a departure. His strength has been sapped on his civilizing journey, which brought him from the peripheral site of his bestial freedom to the densely ordered urban core, and he is bored: "I am weak, my arms have lost their strength, the cry of sorrow sticks in my throat, I am oppressed by idleness."[2] Gilgamesh's motives are different and characteristic of the heroic journey: he desires fame, and the journey is a means to this end.

The desire for fame, for extensions of the self in space and time, is a prominent motive of male, heroic travel and prestige trade.[3] Here this motive is generated by the presentiment of finality, of the terminability of human life, of death. Gilgamesh's journey is a circumvention of the god's incomprehensible decree denying immortality to mere men: the proximity of death supplies the chief motive for his departure, and for many departures of kings and would-be kings after him. The circumvention of death, too, is at the root of travel literature, those stories of journeys that seek to fix and perpetuate something as transient and impermanent as human action and mobility. The ideas of death and departure have long been linked historically. In Gilgamesh's text, the order of their occurrence is meant to suggest a causality: the idea of death awakens the idea of departure.

A variety of motives, however, conspire in this most ancient of recorded departures. Enkidu would regain his energy and freedom, scouting his childhood haunts and beyond. Gilgamesh would fix his image more permanently in the "bricks" and claim the briefer immortality granted by human memory: moreover, he would achieve this in spite of, even *through*, his death: "Then if I fall I leave behind me a name that endures; men will say of me, 'Gilgamesh has fallen in fight with ferocious Humbaba' [the guardian of the forest]. Long after the child has been born in my house they will say it and remember."[4] Gilgamesh's departure reveals the most ancient motives for a heroic journey: kings and would-be kings seek to circumvent death by achieving that extension of self we call fame; servants like Enkidu seek liberty; the king's subjects, relief from the oppressions of the state.

This departure contains the essence of all historical and observable departures. First of all, it separates an individual from a fixed social matrix—in this case, Uruk, Gilgamesh's home—and from that nest of relations that define identity. This detachment of the individual from the social matrix is an event that constructs one as an autonomous and self-contained social entity. Of course, the degree and the intensity of the departure vary with the strength and meaningfulness of the bonds that stretch or break in parting and with the usualness of partings. A departure from a "home," a space that conforms to the body and all its needs, evokes with great intensity those emotions characteristic of all partings: protest, grief, despair, mourning. Gilgamesh first mourns for himself, or for an image of himself as unaccommodated man wandering through an insecure world, and protests before his god: "The tears ran down his face and he said, 'Alas, it is a long journey that I must take to the Land of Humbaba. If this enterprise is not to be accomplished, why did you move me, Shamash, with the restless desire to perform it?' "[5] Gilgamesh's "sacrifice of tears" moves the god to provide him with numerous well-armed followers (a band of brothers), the aid of the winds, and good counsel about routes and objectives. The tears of the mother at this separation move the god to further assurances and provisions for the journey.

The subjective nature of the events of parting might be found in the sequence of emotions at Gilgamesh's departure—protest, despair, and detachment. This sequence, which psychoanalysts have termed "separation anxiety," occurs with an infant's loss of attachment to significant others. John Bowlby observed this sequence of affect in toddlers left by their mothers in a nursery: "At first he *protests* vigorously and tries by all means available to him to recover his mother. Later still he seems to *despair* of recovering her and is vigilant for her return. Later he seems to lose interest in his mother and to become emotionally *detached* from her" (italics in the original).[6] This sequence is typical of many historical departures. Detachment, the last phase of separation anxiety, is a persisting condition of repression, the result of many separations, a defense against the painful emotions of parting. As a "character trait" of the seasoned traveler, it may be called "objectivity," "distance," or "disinterestedness." The modern celebration of departures—the routine, unemotional departures that are the norm in a society of travelers—is a product of a history that resembles what Bowlby found in children who, in parting, gave no sign of protest or despair. "The only children ... who appear undisturbed have been those who have never had any figure to whom they can become attached, or who have experienced repeated and prolonged separations and have already become more or less permanently detached."[7] The emotional sequence inherent in separation anxiety may thus indicate repeated change, a loss whereby one gains detachment and separability.

One cannot read about ancient partings without feeling pity at the sorrow expressed. The event of parting and separation is a species of human suffering. This leads us to wonder about the strength of the motives causing the voluntary undertaking of an act that "is no small contradiction to human nature." Why do men, in great numbers and at great expense, undertake departures at all?

The answer to this question may be found in the emotional sequence just described. Each separation from place must be understood in terms both of the specific history of the individual and the specific breaks, ruptures, and severances that have made up that person's past. Because every departure, no matter how routine and unexceptional, is part of a history of separations, each may echo the primal departures from the mother and from other significant figures. Such associations are evident in a poem Olearius—court mathematician, librarian, and counselor to the Duke of Holstein—introduced into his travel journal upon his departure from his hometown for Russia in 1636:

> *Oh Germany! You draw away your sheltering hands.*
> *As you see me lured off to foreign lands.*
> *Now mother, good night, I shall not wet with tears*

The lap where happily I lay these many years.
Of myself I leave with you indeed the better part.[8]

Olearius's departure, like so many others, introduces a division
within the self, a self-reflective, often self-pitying contrast between
an accommodated and an unaccommodated identity—as in Gilgamesh's weeping for himself as traveler. The departure of Olearius,
like that of Gilgamesh and many heroic travelers, is voluntary, but
the journey may awaken memories of those involuntary earlier
separations and become the repetition of a history, the artful elaboration and celebration of a fate begun with the first departure—
birth—and terminated with death. Habitual travelers may celebrate
and require their departures, as neurotics may celebrate and require their symptoms, to ameliorate deep-seated conflicts. Departure is always a break, both an ending and a beginning: it evokes a
past and projects a future. In this we may find the "latent germ of
madness" inherent in every parting.

   Finally, Gilgamesh's departure both "excorporates" him from
those relations that make him an identifiable person, and "incorporates" the traveling body, the transportable social organism that
will serve as his armor against a dangerous and uncertain world. Just
how the departure creates a separable and transportable social body
within which Gilgamesh retains his social being is illustrated by the
act of Ninsun, who ritually incorporates into her womb Gilgamesh's
chief servant, Enkidu, making his servant also his brother. Gilgamesh
departs in company, surrounded by those armed men who will be
his chief support and instruments for the display and extension of
his identity across space and through time.

Adam and Eve: "Being No Longer There"

The pattern of the nonheroic journey is exemplified by the departure of the primal pair from the walled garden of their paradise.
This departure, like that of Gilgamesh, begins with the act of a god,
but here this is an act of prohibition rather than mere revelation:
"You may eat from every tree in the garden, but not from the tree
of knowledge of good and evil; for on the day that you eat from it,
you will certainly die."[9] Of course, they do eat from this fatal tree,

and the rest is history—a history of wanderings, settlements, captivities, and liberations.

From one point of view, Adam and Eve themselves bear the responsibility for their own deaths and separation from a condition of coherence with God and His creation, and their departure might be construed as voluntary. But from another point of view, God, not the devil, is the first tempter, and the creator of the taboo also creates the sin for which the wandering condition is a penance. However deserved the departure, it is not chosen, but a fate imposed, a rejection, the initiation of a condition of permanent exile.

By his prohibition, the biblical god creates the choice that severs the first pair from symbiosis with a nurturing and named world. By another prohibition, the god bars the way home, back to the point of origin:

> The Lord God made tunics of skins for Adam and his wife and clothed them. He said, "The man has become like one of us knowing good and evil; what if he now reaches out his hand and takes fruit from the tree of life also, eats it and lives forever?" So the Lord God drove him out of the garden of Eden to till the ground from which he had been taken. He cast him out, and to the east of the garden of Eden he stationed the Cherubim and a sword whirling and flashing to guard the way to the tree of life.[10]

In Genesis, the barring of the gates to immortality assures the finality of the first couple's departure, its unrepeatability. Because of the impossibility of return, this departure brings about a permanent condition of rootlessness, detachment, and exile. It marks the end of a "holy" condition and the beginning of an "unholy" one, all of which is implied in the word *exile* as Elie Wiesel uses it: "I cannot see any other exile but the real exile, and that exile is total. It envelopes all endeavours, all explorations, all illusions, all hopes, all triumphs, and this means that whatever we do is never complete. Our life is not complete, and lo and behold, our death is not complete: one does not die when one should or the way one should."[11] Here the journey is conceived almost wholly in terms of what is lost with departure: holiness, completeness, certainty, security, union, and coherence with others. The necessitated departure has been the norm in human history, which is a record of wars and displacements, migrations and relocations.

We must read the myth of Adam and Eve, as all myths, backward. It assumes the reality of the condition it charters, a condition within which the image of permanence and coherence ascribed to the "original" condition of humanity assumes its power as the antithesis of the reality of wandering, of necessitated travel. The myth assumes the human condition described by Pascal: "We are floating in a medium of vast extent, always drifting uncertainly, blown to and fro; whenever we think we have a fixed point to which we can cling and make fast, it shifts and leaves us behind. ... Nothing stands still for us. This is our natural state and yet the state most contrary to our inclinations."[12] This is the state, too, that breeds fantasies of stability, of home, security, and assurance—fantasies that the anonymous author of the Old English elegiac poem "The Wanderer" invested in the hope of a lord and a mead-hall:

> "He who is alone often lives to find favor, mildness of the Lord, even though he has long had to stir with his arms the frost-cold sea, troubled in heart over the water-way, he had to tread the tracks of exile. Fully fixed is his fate." So spoke the earth-walker, remembering hardships, fierce war-slaughters—the fall of dear kinsmen.
>
> "... I crossed the woven waves, winter-sad, downcast for want of a hall, sought a giver of treasure—a place, far or near, where I might find one in a mead-hall who should know of my people, or who would comfort me, friendless, receive me with gladness. He who has no beloved protectors, exile's path awaits him, not twisted gold—frozen thoughts in his heart-case, no joy of earth.... All delight has gone."[13]

The solitary and homeless condition of this traveler is a product of many departures and disconnections which can never again be joined. The injury suffered by this "stranger" who long before left his home and buried his "gold-friend in the darkness of the earth" is a peculiarly social deprivation. No one "knows" him or recognizes him; he exists in the world without any confirmation of his social being, that self generated and nurtured in the gaze of beloved others, the absence of whom he laments. The loss of home is a loss of self and a deep injury which awakens the growing sense of invisibility that may overcome any traveler in a foreign land but becomes particularly acute in the case of long-term exiles. Günther Anders, a refugee from Hitler's Germany, described his feeling of "being no longer there": "There was not one of us who had not felt, standing one day on a street corner in some city, that the noise and rush of the world suddenly sounded as if it was meant solely for others—not one of us who, in short, did not have the experience of being no longer there."[14] The author of "The Wanderer" and Günther Anders describe a social death that is real, not just metaphorical. In departure, the traveler is separated from those recognitions that confer social specificity—indeed, the self itself—for there is no self without an other.

The death of the social self suffered by exiles, the displaced, those to whom any return is barred, is precisely the phenomenon celebrated and enjoyed by many travelers like Pietro Della Valle— the seventeenth-century Roman traveler to the Near and Far East— and James Boswell, for whom separation from the home was an opportunity to re-create identity, to become someone else. The severance of the individual from defining recognitions and identifications is the source of the suffering of exiles, but it is also the source of the modern enjoyment of travel as escape and freedom: "Why is travel so exciting? Partly because it triggers the thrill of escape. . . . The escape is . . . from the traveler's domestic identity, and among strangers a new sense of selfhood can be tried on like a costume."[15] However negatively or positively a traveler may experience the ambiguity of departure, the source of this ambiguity always remains the same: one's separation from a defining context of recognitions.

The departure of Adam and Eve from coherence with God and His creation is echoed by the vast majority of travelers for whom travel is a way of life, an unchosen condition, a necessity. Members of the medieval society of travelers appear, for the most part, to have begun as abandoned children, ejected from their homes or homeless from the start. Travel for these people was a profession or a way of life, not an escape from a settled, domestic existence. It is extraordinary how easily attachments and detachments were accomplished in premodern society, and how permeable was the preindustrial household, so different from the fortress that is the modern private family. Of course, the travels of those who journeyed by necessity, or because there was no better alternative, were not exclusively dolorous. John MacDonald, an eighteenth-century Scottish coachman and gentleman's valet, remembered his first journey nostalgically. His mother had died giving him birth; his father ("a hot and quarrelsome man") had fallen in battle, leaving six children without support. His fourteen-year-old sister, Kitty, led the three youngest boys (aged seven, four, and two and a half years) from Inverness to Edinburgh, a distance of 150 miles, in two months. John, the youngest, "remem-bered" this journey through the stories of his sister, and he tells of the kindness shown to the orphans by people who would give them a handful of oatmeal or, having none, allow them to cook their cakes on their gridiron. He claimed to remember sleeping under tartans in the open air or in barns, the smell of heather and straw, the man who saved them from drowning in a river. It is perhaps from this first journey that John MacDonald caught the habit of travel, which ceased only in his forties when he settled in Spain, having acquired a wife and child there.[16] The historical frequency of involuntary travel counteracts the distortions caused by looking at the history of travel through its modern conception as tourism, liberation, and freedom. This conception occurred initially in the departure of Gilgamesh, but became general only for a social elite in the Middle Ages and as-sumed prominence only in the modern period.

Ywain: The Heroic Exile

Modern departures, with their notion of travel as liberation, may go back to Chretien de Troyes's twelfth-century epic poem, *Ywain, The Knight of the Lion*, where Ywain departs on the journey that ultimately gives him his appellation. This departure is precipitated by Ywain's cousin, Calogrenant, who describes an adventure to the knights of King Arthur's court, an adventure in which Calogrenant has been de-feated and which inspires the other knights to think they can do better. Ywain wishes to steal the march on his comrades in order to have this adventure for himself, necessitating a secret departure.

> *So lord Ywain stole off,*
> *Making sure that he met no one,*
> *And went to his lodgings, alone.*
> *His servants and attendants were there,*
> *And he ordered his saddle put on*
> *And spoke to his favorite squire,*
> *One from whom he hid nothing.*
> *"Now listen! Come after me,*
> *And bring my weapons and armor!*
> *I'm going out through that gate,*
> *Not on my warhorse, and only*

Walking him. Be careful, and hurry;
I've a long, long way to go.
I want new shoes on my warhorse,
And I want him brought to me, and quickly,
And I want you to bring back the other.
But be careful, I warn you, and if anyone
Asks where I've gone, be sure
To tell him nothing. You may
Have counted on me before,
But never again, if you fail me."[17]

Ywain rides out on his palfrey. His servant follows with Ywain's warhorse, armor, weapons, and plenty of horseshoes and nails. The exchange of horses is made, and Ywain departs upon the adventure that will win him a lady, lands, followers, and a noble estate.

The differences between the departures of Gilgamesh and Ywain and of Adam and Eve are obvious. There is no question of the voluntary nature of Ywain's departure. At the same time, it is explicitly nonpublic and nonceremonious, and much strategy is employed to keep it that way. Here, too, the knight departs alone rather than in company, for his purpose is to achieve the glory of the adventure for himself. The solitude of the traveler is a pervasive feature of knightly departures, as in the departure of Calogrenant who begins his story: "It happened seven years ago that, lonely as a countryman, I was making my way in search of adventures, fully armed as a knight should be."[18] The solitude of the departing knight is an incorporation of the traveling body, in this case an individual rather than a group. It is thus the feature that most clearly indicates that this is a new, modern version of the heroic journey, an individuating journey, one that defines the figure of the person undertaking it not as a member but as autonomous, separate, and detached.

The solitude of the traveler here represents not fate, as it does for the Wanderer, but choice. The contrast between the departure of Ywain and of Gilgamesh suggests certain alterations in the traditional heroic journey. The former is clearly a heroic journey, undertaken for fame and glory, but it assumes no return, for the court of peers, the agency that would provide some ratification of Ywain's achievements, was eminently mobile. Ywain's departure is remarkable for the complete absence of any sign of those connections to land and place in which self and status were anciently embedded.

All depends on the outcome of the journey in which these memberships are to be acquired—another reason for the surreptitiousness
of this departure. If no one knows that Ywain is essaying this adventure, he will not lose face (as Calogrenant does) should he fail. He
is under no illusion that he will be remembered should he fail, for
there is no house or child to remember him. Such immortality is the
object of the journey, not its origin or inspiration.

Ywain is a follower, a retainer, not a lord over lands or a prince
over men; thus, the journey is a means of achieving status, not just
of demonstrating or extending it. This distinction is all-important,
and implicit in the absence of those ceremonies that assert the identity of the traveler in the original heroic journeys. This identity, defined in terms of its freedom and autonomy, is, to begin with,
ambiguous. Ywain's identity is eminently mutable, proceeding as it
does through a series of disguises and transformations assumed in
the course of his journey.

The language of Calogrenant's departure has been superbly an-
alyzed by the German philologist Erich Auerbach in his classic *Mimesis*;[19] and Ywain's departure displays the same realism, the same
practicality, the same focus upon the doing rather than upon the
meaning or the emotions of departure. It is a description in what
the political theorist Jean Bethke Elshtain calls the "strategic voice,"
which is "cool, objective, scientific, and overwhelmingly male."[20] The
tone is peculiarly detached and "strangely dissociated," with no hint
of the emotions of protest, grief, and mourning usually surrounding
departure. This departure is clearly a routine event, distinguished
from other knightly departures only by the special security measures designed to maintain its secrecy. The flat emotional tone, the
routine nature of the procedures, would be appropriate to a modern departure on a business trip or for a day at work. Ywain has
already attained that detachment characteristic of professional travelers and of children "who have experienced repeated and prolonged separations and have already become more or less
permanently detached."

Ywain's journey is not so much a means to an end as an activity
intrinsic to the heroic character. As Gutierre Diaz de Gomez argues
in his tract on chivalry, the knight is defined by his mobility and is
one who rides a horse: "He who of custom rides upon another
mount, is no knight; but he who rides upon a horse is not for that
reason a knight; he only is a knight who makes it his calling."[21] This

conception of arms and mobility as a calling implies that deeds of arms and travel are not so much means of doing something as ways of *being* something, personifying rather than merely instrumental activities. In other words, travel and mobility have become symbolic of a new species of social being, defined as permanently detached and always in motion: the knight. The role travel plays in the construction of the very identity of the knight becomes clear in Ywain's second departure from the lands and wife he won as prizes for the successful completion of his first adventure. He is allowed to enjoy the estate he has acquired for only a few weeks before his comrades urge him to new departures. His friend Gwain argues that the settled life will make Ywain worthless, and that his wife will regret her love for him which she gave, after all, to an adventuring knight, not to some well-accommodated homebody:

> No one should be loved
> Who isn't worth it. And you,
> Surely you'll regret her love
> If it makes you worthless. For a woman
> Can just as easily fall out
> Of love—and there's nothing wrong
> In hating anyone who turns worthless
> As soon as he's lord of a realm.
> It's now that you need to prove
> Yourself! Take the bit in your teeth:
> We ought to go jousting, you
> And I, so no one can call you
> Jealous. You shouldn't be lazy,
> But throw yourself into tournaments,
> Take on the world, and with pleasure,
> Whatever it costs you! Lying
> Around will change you for the worse.[22]

This notion of love as a measure of worth, and worth as something that hinges upon its demonstration and performance in travels and deeds of arms, is the reason the "worthy" knight may not cease his journeys and adventures without ceasing to be a knight. His journey, because it is personifying, is endless.

Ywain's second parting is more difficult than the first, for now he has a wife to leave and defining bonds to break. This breach causes the grief and mourning normal in the severance of parting: "And now Ywain had his freedom, / But wept at the thought of taking it." In addition, this second departure initiates that "dividedness of self" experienced by many travelers who, as a result of departures, come to see themselves as solitary wanderers, through the lens of the stable home:

> How hard it was for my lord
> Ywain to leave his wife!
> He rode off without his heart.
> His body might follow the king,
> But his heart could not be led.
> She who held it, joined
> To her own, was she who stayed home.[23]

Ywain overstays his allotted year on the tournament circuit. He is repudiated by his wife and loses his home. His third departure, for the forest, is the final stage of his alienation, the completion of his solitude and freedom: "He withdrew from his fellow / Knights, and feared for his sanity. / And they ignored him, left him / Entirely alone, as he chose."[24] Ywain becomes a madman, wandering the forest until he meets a lion who befriends him. He allies himself with this lord of the forest and takes on the persona of his totem-animal, becoming the Knight of the Lion and continuing his adventuring.

The Altruistic Journey of the Middle Ages

The notion of the altruistic journey, one made for no other end than to "prove" the character of the person undertaking it, of the journey as a nonutilitarian activity voluntarily undertaken, is essentially medieval and defines a medieval ruling class. As late as the twelfth century, when Chrétien de Troyes composed *Ywain*, the concept of the altruistic journey, of the adventure, had apparently not yet filtered down to commoners. When Calogrenant identifies himself as a knight to the gigantic, ugly herdsman in the forest, he uses terms that are obviously unfamiliar to this bumpkin:

> "I am, as you see, a knight,
> Seeking what I cannot find:

I've hunted and I've found—nothing."
"And what are you trying to find?"
"Adventures, to test my bravery,
To prove my courage. And now
I ask you and beg you, if you can,
To counsel me, tell me—if you know one—
Of some adventure, some marvel."
"As for that," he said, "too bad.
I know nothing of any 'adventures.'
No one's ever told me
Any."

The ceaseless wanderings of the herdsman neither distinguish him nor make him an individual. When Calogrenant asks him to identify himself, he can only say, "I am a man . . . I am nothing but myself."[25] The travels of commoners remain economically motivated, necessitated travels, not adventures or self-referencing journeys.

This new concept of adventure contrasts significantly with ancient heroic travels in assigning a positive value to the risks and dangers of the journey. In *Ywain* this risk is a celebrated possibility. It is incarnated in the fabulous realm of the forest, where reside those possibilities excised from domestic order. Ancient heroic travelers suffered the risks and uncertainties of the path for the sake of the gains to be achieved through the journey. Michael Nerlich, in his work on adventure, notes that the medieval adventurer has a different attitude, and the knight is marked by an "acceptance of the unknown as a positive value; the deliberate leaving of the known for the unknown; desire for the new."[26]

Ywain's attitude toward risk is very different from Gilgamesh's. He chooses the forest as an appropriate domain of knightly activity, not as timber to be cut down and turned into roofbeams for palaces and temples. As the domain of chance, of the fabulous and wondrous, it is embraced and affirmed by one who would become himself through demonstrations of prowess. The medieval adventurer courts what the ancient adventurer suffers: the unexpected, the new, the alien. This attitude becomes characteristic of successive generations of adventurers and travelers and is noticeable in explorers, curious gentlemen naturalists, and indefatigable tourists who eschew the beaten track.

But Nerlich is wrong in regarding this conception as definitive of an already formed "class," the nobility in the Middle Ages, and, later, the "bourgeoisie." Rather, this concept of adventure in its successive approximations and appropriations is a way of achieving social status through territorial passage. Successive generations of "mere" men, sons of hewers of wood and drawers of water, appropriated this image and defined themselves in its terms, on the way to becoming free and noble men. The image codifies a connection between territorial and social mobilities, which persists in Western culture. One who would rise to the status of a free man could do so through the agency of travel, the solitary journey, done for purpose other than adventure and the demonstration of prowess.

In its medieval conception, the true adventure is always altruistic and disinterested, done for the sake of others or for its own sake. Providing a moral content to the medieval adventure, altruism continued to mark the truly ennobling journey and to demonstrate the traveler's transcendence of mundane necessities. Altruism enters into the Renaissance voyage, the voyage of discovery, humanistic travel—done for no other reason than curiosity and a desire to know the world. In this form, the chivalric journey—heroic travel—is intellectualized and given philosophical status.

Alexander Kinglake: The Escape from Civility

Modern departures assume a settled, articulated world—a fully elaborated, if onerous, civility. The contemporary departure acquires much of its meaning from what is left behind as the passenger enters into a contrasting moral and psychic condition. A striking example of the conception of departure as an escape from civility was the experience of the Englishman Alexander Kinglake when, in 1837, he left the Christian Europe that was his home, traveling to the border dividing Austria and Turkish Hungary. His escape from civilization began at this border when he met a "compromised" official, one who had had contact with plague areas. "We walked down to the precincts of the quarantine Establishment, and here awaited us a 'compromised' officer of the Austrian Government, who lives in a perpetual state of excommunication. The boats, with their 'compromised' rowers, were also in readiness." There on the banks of the Sava River, his friends left him and the compromised officer came forward to shake his hand. This was his parting: "I met it with mine, and there was an end to Christendom for many days to come."[27] Kinglake landed in Budapest, clearly an "other" world, where people wore turbans.

This departure was, as always, a separation. But for Kinglake the river was the boundary of a civilization. From his first glimpse of the quarantine station at the river's edge, Kinglake perceived himself to be separated from a zone of hygiene identified with Christendom, respectability, and machines, and entering one of pollution and disease. Kinglake experienced this passage from the holy to the unholy, from the clean to the unclean, not with grief or mourning but with relief and a sense of liberation. He recommended this form of departure as therapy to the unnamed friend who was the recipient of his travel letters: "It is sweet to find oneself free from the stale civilization of Europe ... and so remembering how many poor devils are living in a state of utter respectability, you will glory the more in your own delightful escape."[28]

Kinglake was thus liberated from a cultural order which has recognizable, identifiable features. Before crossing the line, while awaiting passage, he was still "encompassed by the scenes and sounds of familiar life: the din of a busy world still Vexed and Cheered me. . . . I had come . . . to the end of wheel-going Europe, and now my eyes would see the Splendour and Havoc of The East."[29] Kinglake, ironically, and knowing better, affirmed the "disorder" identified with the non-Christian East as an escape into a freer European past, an old regime in which people still spent months in the saddle. His departure was a rejection of the cleanliness and order that had nourished his identity as a European, and an escape into difference. It was a rejection of coherence, a sacred order, a secure if frenetic existence; a self-exile that, in a reverse of the exile of Adam and Eve, was chosen and celebrated as a liberation.

But the Europe Kinglake left behind was not a land or a city so much as a state of mind, extendable, ineffable, and, perhaps even in 1837, inescapable. Thus, as he stared over the outermost edge of his world, the river Jordan, the border between settled Palestine and the nomads of the desert, he wondered at the differences on either side of it:

You joyfully know that you are upon the very frontier of all accustomed respectabilities. There, on the other side of the river ... there

reigns the people that will be like to put you to death, for not being
a vagrant, for not being a robber, for not being armed and
houseless. There is comfort in that—health, comfort and strength
to one who is dying from very weariness of that poor, dear, middle-
aged, deserving, accomplished, pedantic and pains-taking govern-
ess Europe.[30]

The liberation Kinglake celebrated at the boundaries of his world
was from the watchful and judgmental eye that reinforces respectabilities, law, cleanliness, propriety. "Over there" is that other world,
the antithesis of the settled world, a land of lawlessness, mobility,
wilderness, and liberty. Kinglake is one of those many Victorians
who, a homosexual, suffered the tyranny of respectability by which
the bourgeoisie effected its cultural dominance over the laboring
classes and the aristocracy. The historian George Mosse, examining
the growth of this phenomenon in the eighteenth and nineteenth
centuries, noted that the Arabs and the desert provided a metaphor
for freedom, specifying a new noble savage, "whose mores were un-
conventional but who in his own setting made the abnormal clean.
Many Englishmen and women had fleshed out their fantasy life with
stories from Arabia, seeing in the Arabs the last remnants of both
chivalry and unabashed sexuality." (While the English and the French
tended to use the Arabs as a countervailing reality, German writers
based their images of freedom on the American Indian, who lived
and hunted outside "the prison civilized man calls his home," at the
very moment in history those Indians were being herded onto res-
ervations in their native land.)[31]

Kinglake's departure places a characteristically European and
modern emphasis upon departure as freedom, but with an added,
subjective significance. The captivity from which Kinglake sought his
release is from a set of internalized prohibitions and repressions that
produces the appearance of civility, normality, and respectability.
But these he carried with him, and his search for an escape from
modernity ultimately failed, his hopes scattered before the reality
of the world he encountered. By a series of misadventures he crossed
the Jordan and met up with a band of nomads who did not act in
the ways he had anticipated: "They did not offer me the bread and
salt, which I understood to be the pledge of peace amongst wandering tribes, but I fancied that they refrained from this act of hospi-

tality, not in consequence of any hostile determination, but in order that the notion of robbing me might remain for the present an 'open question.' " He later learned that these lords of the desert simply did not have bread, salt, or any other comestibles. A band of starving outcasts from the villages, they literally lived on grass and desperately desired a "passport" back to settled territory from which Kinglake had been released by his journey. Thus Kinglake, and many other contemporary travelers, learned that modernity is inescapable: "Wherever man wanders, he still remains tethered by the chain that links him to his kind."[32]

THE TRAVELING SELF, DIVIDED AND DEFINED

Thus it is that every country to which a man has grown accustomed holds a spell over him.

—Diodorus Siculus, 49 B.C.

The essence of departure as separation may be found not only in the anxiety of parting but also in the resulting dividedness of self as one takes leave of a localized identity. This dividedness is expressed by the tears of Gilgamesh, as he weeps for himself and pities that person wandering the roads and suffering the dangers and uncertainties of the journey. It is also apparent in the writing of Charles Moritz, an eighteenth-century German clergyman whose journals of travel in England are among the classics of travel literature. Wondering how he might appear, as a solitary wanderer in a foreign land, from the perspective of his best friend at home, Moritz put his finger on the notion of distance in the experience of seeing oneself: "When I was going on again, I thought of the place of my residence; and all my acquaintances, and not a little of you my friend, and imagined what you would think and say; if you were to see your friend thus wandering here all alone totally unknown, and in a foreign land, and at that moment I first seriously felt the idea of distance."[33]

In the conditions of settlement and rootedness, departure has observable social, psychic, and intellectual consequences. With separation from a context of recognitions, the social being of the traveler becomes ambiguous and malleable. Psychically, departure effects a kind of alienation that has been variously experienced as a suffering and penance by Adam and Eve; as an opportunity for the "objectification" of self by Gilgamesh; as the opportunity for self-definition by Ywain; and as therapeutic by Kinglake. Intellectually, the alienation of departure gives the seasoned traveler the character of "detachment" and "objectivity", the status of observer. The alienation of self implicit in departure accords with Karl Marx's use of this term. In departure the traveler is "objectified" and becomes a thing persisting outside those relations that identify him, an autonomous individuality. The world becomes an array of "objects," artifacts, and exemplars whose meaning is mysterious to the outsider and must be decoded from appearances. Through being removed, one may come to see one's native culture—which once provided the lenses and meanings through which one looked out upon the world—as an object, a thing, a unified, describable phenomenon.

The perceptual psychologist James Gibson has noted that when one is "outside" something, it is a substance; when inside it, it is a medium. Thus, water is a medium for fish; a substance for terrestrials; and both a medium and a substance, alternatively, for amphibians.[34] Many travelers experience this transition as a suddenly objective appreciation of home. Freya Stark, a modern adventurer and superb travel writer, valued her sojourn in Lebanon for the alienation and estrangement she felt: "One great interest in such a civilization is that it gives you a sudden fresh view of your own; the nearest in fact to getting out of the world and examining it as an object."[35]

Goethe was forced to mobilize the distinction between the truth of the traveler (the outsider) and the truth of the native (the insider) when he defended himself against a charge of being a spy after having been discovered making a sketch of the medieval castle above the town of Malcesine, on Lake Garda. At his hearing before the assembled townspeople, he delivered a speech on the value and aesthetics of medieval buildings, "though they could not be expected to recognize, as I did, the picturesque beauty of buildings which had been familiar to them since childhood." Goethe went on to describe the picturesque qualities of their locale, their medium, to an increasingly interested body of natives who ultimately released him after deciding that he was not a spy but an "honest and educated gentleman who is travelling to enlarge his knowledge."[36] Clearly, the "picturesque," at least within realistic and naturalistic traditions of painting, assumes a point of view outside the "frame," the point of view necessarily taken by the traveler who is in a context but not of it.

While there is no disagreement on the essential character of departure as separation and alienation, there is considerable variation in its experience. Many travelers feel the dividedness of self, the process of estrangement, and the ambiguity of identity as injury and suffering, an occasion for protest. Abd-Er-Razzak, an Arab clerk and scribe who with great reluctance accompanied an Arab embassy to India in 1413, felt his estrangement keenly: "At the remembrance of my mistress and of my country I weep so bitterly that I should deprive the whole world of the taste and habit of traveling. I am a native of the country of the Arabs and not of a strange region. Oh mighty God ... Vouchsafe to bring me back to the company of my friends."[37]

But others, with Alexander Kinglake, have celebrated this alienation and experienced it as a liberation, a positive gain. With departure, a dysfunctional relationship between self and context may be left behind: "In a very real sense, a psychoneurosis may have been left behind. . . . In the anonymity of travel feelings of self-hatred may slough off."[38] This separation from an emplaced self was a selling-point of educational travels in the seventeenth century. Richard Lassels, a traveling tutor of young English gentlemen on their European tours, found the morally improving features of travel in the alienations of departure: "At his embarking let him have a special care not to carry *Himselfe* abroad with Himselfe in travelling. Many men, sayeth Seneca, return home no better than when they went out, they take themselves along with themselves in travelling."[39]

With a place of origin might be left behind certain disreputable realities of the person: vices, bad manners, pride. Lassels recommends that the young lord plan on leaving behind "all willfulness and stubbornness; all tenderness and seeking his own ease too much, all effeminateness and delicateness; all boyish tricks with hands and mouth, all delighting in being the best man in company, all familiarity with servants and meane men."[40] In short, the separations of departure are a moral experiment determining which aspects of the self may be left behind in the context of their germination, and which are ineradicable features of it. It is in this sense that travel and departure are often regarded as a purge, a stripping of the accommodated self, which might improve and clarify a person's outlines. But this appreciation of travel as the occasion for personal change and improvement is merely a positive evaluation of that ambiguity of self, that plasticity of identity suffered by ancient exiles and involuntary travelers.

THE FREE KNIGHT: MOBILITY AND AUTONOMY

Locomotion was the behavioral sign which indicated most visibly to the observer the end of the "hatching process"; that is to say, psychological birth.
—Margaret Mahler, 1975

The shift of emphasis from the losses to the gains of departure occurred most clearly in the Middle Ages. This new concept of adventure and of the hero as free reflects underlying realities. The figure of the knight served the ruling military class of medieval society as a way of defining the criteria of membership. It legitimized an acquired power and status as a consequence not of violence and predation, but of intrinsic virtues revealed in the adventure, representing status as the reward of an altruistic acceptance of risk. The concept of knightly adventure was clearly functional within a medieval society in the stage of its crystallization as feudalism, for it assigned a function, a purpose and dignity to human elements increasingly anomalous within that social order.

The medieval chronicler Guibert de Nogent thought God introduced the crusade "so that the knighthood and the unstable people, who shed each other's blood in the way of pagans, might have a new way to win salvation;"[41] and Fulcher of Chartres—chaplain to Baldwin and chronicler of the expedition to Jerusalem of 1095—clearly understood that the crusade was a solution to internal disorder, a way of turning against "the pagans the fighting which up to now customarily went on among the Christians."[42] Baldric of Kol, himself a crusader, thought it a good piece of work to send against the heathen men who were so much like them. "oppressors of orphans and widows ... murderers ... temple-defilers ... law breakers who seek the rewards of rapacity from spilling Christian blood."[43]

This rationale for the promotion of armed adventure "outward" persisted through the *reconquista* in Iberia and its extension overseas to Africa, Asia, and the Americas in the period of discoveries. It continued to provide the rationale for Europe's primary export— young men. A panel of citizens responsible for determining whether it would weaken the colony of Mexico to send a large body of men on Coronado's expedition in 1540 were unanimous in their opinion that the discharge of these superfluous young men would positively benefit the colony. In the judgment of Pero Almidez, "it was very beneficial that those people who were going left Mexico, since they caused the residents more harm than good, for they were mostly idle young gentlemen without any occupation either in Mexico or in their homeland." Moreover, these men were observed to go voluntarily and with high hopes into the unknown to the north. Gonzalo de Salazo noted "that they all went very happy, and that they were the ones who had asked to go on the expedition and did not have to be persuaded."[44]

Here perhaps is a better explanation for the "expansiveness" of medieval and modern European society than some putatively Western will to conquer. It also suggests a coincidence of "expansion" through the export of superfluous human matter and the crystallization of the European social order which occurred in the late Middle Ages. The anthropologist Mary Douglas reminds us of the structural rule that "when something is firmly classed as anomalous the outline of the set in which it is not a member is clarified."[45] Placeless young men without families or any profession but arms were clearly anomalous within the increasingly ranked, aristocratic society of Europe until 1789. The export of these anomalies served the purpose of establishing peace and order, as the removal of such men removed the anomalous elements within that order. It is ironic that elements inimicable to social order were used to extend and defend the system.

The image of the knight as a free, autonomous person specifying his identity through travels effectively codified this anomaly and made it into a cultural ideal available to any young man with arms and a horse. This image also specified the appropriate direction of the un-attached knight's self-realizing journey as the *outward-bound* path toward a generalized realm of possibility, the forest and wilderness. The medieval period redefined freedom in practical terms, as the opposite of bondage to soil or household, a definition that persists today. All were free who enjoyed the right of free departure and could defend their autonomy. In England, the serf could alter his status by departing from the soil of his bondage and remaining away for a year; in deed, any man might attain free status by departure.

The association of mobility with autonomy, of departure with freedom, is thus historical, but it has also become a constituent element of modern Western culture. The importance of this association may be seen in our concept of the normal person as free person and in our notions of human development as progress toward autonomy, illustrated in the psychologist Margaret Mahler's interpretation of an infant's first steps:

> We had not expected and were surprised by the finding that the advent of the capacity of free, upright locomotion seemed to take place in a direction not *toward* but *away* from the mother.... This is, we feel, an indicator that the normal infant is endowed with an innate given that prompts him at a certain point of his autonomous maturation to separate from the mother—to further his own individuation. Walking makes possible for the toddler an enormous increase in reality discovery and the testing of the world through his own control, as a quasi-magical master. It coincides with the upsurge of goal-directed aggressiveness.[46]

Maturation is, by definition, the attainment of a norm, and here we may see this norm deployed: a notion of the person as autonomous, realized through processes of separation and motion which are validated as "discovery," a testing of self and the world, the attainment of "control" over contingency. Here the outward-bound trip, the motion away from the mother, is the significant action, not the return trip, as is likely in a classical context. Separation is construed not as suffering but as the "psychological birth" of the individual. Conversely, the inability to detach oneself from an original matrix and symbiosis is an indication of abnormality: "We become more and more convinced that the 'basic fault' in the psychotic was his inability to perceive the self and the mother as separate entities, and thus to use the mother as a 'beacon of orientation in the world of reality'; as his 'external logo.' "[47]

The status of the detached individual and the sanctification of the separations incurred in many departures create the domain of meaning in which modern departures occur, coloring our experience of travel. Each departure is meaningful as a recapitulation of a personal and cultural history, and may dissipate disgust with the all-too-familiar. Thus, novelist John Knowles writes:

> The last belch from America had expired on the outer edge of the
> Venice lagoon, and moving through the still, sun-heavy Adriatic, I
> was now definitely gone. It was a refreshing feeling, somehow a
> sweet feeling, like a return to very early youth; there was a sense of
> morning, and even of innocence about it. That was what travel did
> for me, but only in the furthest reaches of abroad, where the groove
> had not been deeply worn in advance by everyone from Benjamin
> Franklin and Henry James to Zelda Fitzgerald and Elizabeth Taylor,
> where the guideposts were few and ambiguous, and the accommo-
> dations simple or non-existent, where they didn't know quite what
> to make of me and I didn't know quite what to make of them, where
> I had to improvise in a new and unfamiliar world; in other words,
> to behave like someone very young.[48]

This experience of the journey as rejuvenating, as a return to early
childhood, assumes a periphery beyond which one may find the
"furthest reaches of abroad," a strange and unfamiliar world. But
the fulfillment of this expectation by many generations of European
travelers has left little of the world unexplored or unmarked and
reduced the strange to the familiar. The disillusionment of modern
travelers is a product of a history that has implanted as a norm the
need for "difference," for escape, while eradicating those realms of
difference into which the adventuring, self-realizing person can actually escape. Many modern travelers, experiencing this history as
irony, become like Leiris: "His attempted escape has been a complete failure, and anyway he no longer believes in the value of
escape."[49]

In modern journeys, the would-be individual, defined by modern circumstance, often learns that modernity is inescapable, that
there is no longer a boundary between the civilized and the uncivilized. Claude Lévi-Strauss bitterly elucidates the paradoxes encountered in the furthest reaches of abroad, where one may find the
flotsam and jetsam of an industrial civilization that has become a
global system:

> Now that the Polynesian islands have been smothered in concrete,
> and turned into aircraft carriers, . . . when the whole of Asia is be-
> ginning to look like a dingy suburb . . . what else can the so-called
> escapism of travelling do than confront us with the unfortunate
> aspects of our history? The first thing we see as we travel round the
> world is our own filth, thrown into the face of mankind.[50]

The modern traveler, seeking that forest in which Ywain found the constituents of self-defining adventure, finds only something "polluted," desecrated by the impress of modernity. The very inescapability of modernity requires the projection of the traditional *topos* outside the world, in fantasies of space travel and expectations of monsters arriving from beyond the boundaries of our global home. The need for escape and self-definition through detachments from the familiar is rooted in a history that has generated an ideology requiring a wilderness, a domain of alternative realities, in which the self can assume its uniqueness and recover its freedom in the climate of the new and unexpected—just when history has all but terminated the possibility of that alternative.

"Had every sail at command in the way, as if Neptune himself had been present, without any resistance or refusal or resisting" (William Sloan).

(Courtesy of the National Maritime Museum, London)

2

''SUCH SWEET WAYFARING'': THE SEDUCTIONS OF PASSAGE

About ten o'clock at night we got in about seven leagues to the windward of Cape Passado under the Line, and then it proved calm; and we lay and drove all night, being fatigued from the previous day. The eighteenth day we had little wind until the afternoon, and then we made sail standing along the shore to the Northward, having the wind at SSW and fair weather.

—William Dampier, 1906

These lines come down to us by virtue of a rule that became ironclad in the eighteenth century: any ambitious young seaman who wished to acquire the dignity of an observer recorded every day in his log, whether or not anything happened. William Dampier was one such, and this eighteenth-century English privateer, hydrographer, merchant, and habitual traveler filled his logs with facts and observations of interest to the gentlemen of the Royal Society (who published them).[1] His companions wondered at him when, having to cross a river with the Spanish colonial militia in hot pursuit and stripping himself of his other possessions, Dampier bore his logbooks, wrapped in an oilskin, across the river on his head. When he wrote the lines quoted above, he was cruising the Gulf of

Panama looking for targets of opportunity and heading in the general direction of the Isthmus.

But what does this passage mean and what does it describe? It appears to describe a period of motion—a day and two nights of passage, and passage to no particular purpose—but it does not really do so at all. The essence of passage—motion through space—is missing. The text fixes upon marks of orientation—a cape, the Equator, points of the compass, night and day, morning and evening. There are, during this period of serendipity, no remarkable incidents that might test these sailors and show what they are made of. This period of motion is narratable at all only because of the contrasts and changes of night and day, of direction, of the "state" of motion— laying hove-to and driving off a lee shore, calm and then fair sailing. Alterations in the kind and tempo of motion, the vicissitudes of motion, seem narratable but not so the motion itself. This cryptic passage leaves us to imagine all those movements that through the ages must have comprised the vast bulk of travel at sea, but that are unrecorded and, perhaps, unrecordable events: the rocking and swooping, flowing and streaming of the wind and water; the hypnotic, ever-moving but persisting pattern of the woven waves; the changing forms of clouds and light; the routines of passage and working a ship, going about, making the reach. There is no history here, except perhaps the history of technique.

Anyone who has attempted to investigate the effects of the passage experience upon human perceptions and mentality has encountered a frustrating paucity of text. In travel journals, logs, and diaries, periods of passage are entered briefly, for example: "On March 10 we came to ...," or, "after two days we arrived at...." Travelers most often write of where they are going or where they have been, about the sights, incidents, and vicissitudes of the journey, not about its unexceptional flows, motions, and pleasures. Periods of pleasant easy passage are unnarratable perhaps because they are unexceptional. Patrick Brydone, an eighteenth-century English traveler and writer, was thankful for the storm that punctuated an otherwise easy passage from Naples to Sicily: "A sea expedition is nothing without a storm. Our journal would never have been readable had it not been for this one."[2]

It is rare to find descriptions of fair passage before the eighteenth century, and particularly of pleasure in passage. One exception, William Sloan's description of a day of sailing down the coast

of Africa with Sir Francis Drake's expedition around the world, contains that characteristic "meaninglessness" and generality found in
Dampier's log, that curious absence of subjectivity that characterizes
many notices of passage: "Now we are coasting along to the Southward for Cape Blanko, ... had every sail at command in the way,
as if Neptune himself had been present, without any resistance or
refusal or resisting."[3] Here, Sloan highlighted what was lacking —
resistance, friction, choice—rather than the sheer irresistible motion
that must have surrounded him.

Thus, the very absence of data about passage is not only a problem for those who would understand the transformations of passage
but also the first indication of what those transformations are: easy,
pleasurable, unexceptional and apparently silencing. An equally telling and frustrating difficulty is that passage is the phase of the journey that seems to supply its own motives. People often travel for no
particular purpose, or, in fact, to escape purpose, going out for
drives, taking cruises, spending their surplus and even their substance on passage. And there are those inveterate and habitual travelers—Dampier among them—who do not travel in order to trade,
to acquire wealth or fame, but spend their wealth and become
strangers to their spouses and children, all for the sake of the passage. Passage is an end in itself for such travelers, who may often be
found in the transport trades and among the homeless. As a group,
they may be represented by the Yankee mate encountered by William Dean Howells in Venice—a man who, in one of the most lyrical
cities in the world, never went ashore during his three-week stay.
Howells, himself in love with the genius of place and an inveterate
tourist, admitted that such men were wholly alien to him: "What
curious people are these seafarers. They coast the whole world and
know nothing of it, being more ignorant and helpless than children
on the shore."[4]

Those for whom the end and motive of travel is the passage,
who are fixed in a state of transience, are often "marginal" members
of settled societies who have no single home, like the man of the
road who appeared from out of a hedge, unshaven and dirty, before
Thomas Gent, printer, on his way to London in the 1830s: "Upon
my asking him where he was going he said, 'to and fro upon the
earth for every place was alike to him.'"[5] But among these habitual
passengers are also the stellar travelers: Marco Polo, Charles Montagu Doughty, Freya Stark, Thomas Coryate, and many others like

them. Mark Twain, one of these travelers by disposition and vocation, admitted his addiction to passage to his brother before he left,
in 1867, on the pilgrimage to the Old World that was to produce
The Innocents Abroad: "You observe that under a cheerful exterior I
have got a spirit that is angry with me and gives me freely of its
contempt. I can get away from that at sea and be tranquil and
satisfied."[6]

Clearly, passage consumes motives extrinsic to it and generates
its own purposes; it tranquilizes and satisfies, consumes the conditions of narration, and provides a pleasure upon which habitual
travelers spend their wealth and lives as though it were some darling
lover. Travel exercises its seductions by changing the relation of the
traveler to place until motion itself mediates the passenger's perceptions of the world, the self, the other.

Passage is qualitatively different from both departure and arrival: it is an experience of motion across boundaries and through
space, while departure and arrival are experiences of detachment
from and attachment to places. In passage, motion becomes the medium of perception as well as the primary determinant of one's
physical condition. The passenger becomes more conscious of self
as a "viewer" or "observer" of a world flowing past, a world that
becomes a sequence of continuously unrolling pictures. As a Mrs.
Gordon said to Paul Theroux on a train passing through Scotland:
"Taking the train, to me, is like going to the cinema."[7]

But all passengers are not changed equally by their passage, and
a season of passage that changes one person's very identity may
change another not at all, or little, or only produce nausea and
motion sickness. Clearly, the attitude of the passenger toward the
period of passage is a significant variable in the degree to which
passage transforms and alters one's condition, mind, and character.
This, at least, is the observation of Alexander Kinglake:

> Day after day, perhaps week after week, and month after month,
> your foot is in the stirrup. To taste the cold breath of the earliest
> morn, and to lead, or follow your bright cavalcade till sunset
> through the forests, and mountain passes, through valleys, and des-
> olate plains, all this becomes your mode of life. . . . If you are wise,
> you will not look upon the longer period of time thus occupied in
> actual movement, as the mere gulf dividing you from the end of
> your journey, but rather as one of those rare and plastic seasons of
> your life, from which, perhaps, in after times, you may love to date

the moulding of your character—that is your very identity. Once feel this, and you will soon grow happy and contented in your saddle home.[8]

Kinglake's emphasis here is instructive. He treats passage as a sequence of motion that can transform character, even identity, in so far as it is chosen, and for its own sake, not for any extrinsic purposes or goals. It is similar in emphasis to Joan Didion's description of the "rapture-of-the-freeway" (see page 14), a communion in passage closed to those who are thinking about where they are going and where they have been, open only to those who surrender to the conditions of motion, something not possible for everybody.

Didion and Kinglake describe the pleasures of mobility as the onset of what the sociologist Mihaly Csikszentmihalyi calls a "flow state," a state triggered by entry into a situation in which "action follows action according to an internal logic that seems to need no conscious intervention by the actor."[9] The state and condition of the passenger who surrenders to that logic are "altered." The question is how we may understand these alterations.

In the discussion that follows, I suggest that we may read the nature of passage in the features of the traveler it shapes, in those traits of mind and character that remain so remarkably consistent through the ages. Of course, the character traits of the traveler must be regarded as the result of the choices one makes and of the defenses one constructs against the condition of flux and disequilibrium. The "mind of the traveler" is a product not of some imprint of an outside force upon the sentient being in passage, but rather of what the traveler does with the ideas, impressions, perceptions gathered in motion.

Thus we may learn something about the force of mobility from the human face it shapes; from the characteristics, traits, and defenses it necessitates; from the invariant masks and veils it imposes upon the passenger's vision. Certain invariant and persisting features of character and mind arise within the flux and change of passage. And the condition of motion produces a structure of experience with its own logic and order, distinct from the logic and order of place, locale, territoriality. In making these statements, particularly the last, I aim to counter the prejudices inherent in sessility, prejudices that have distorted our view of the figure and character produced by passage. This figure, observed by several socio-philosophers—in Georg Simmel's still reverberating depiction of "the stranger," in Robert Park's and Everett Stonequist's image of the "marginal man," in Victor Turner's description of the liminal state—is misapprehended because all describe the passenger from the position of those rooted within stable community. The stranger, the marginal person, the liminal figure is "betwixt and between" places, or communities or allegiances, and defined by the ambiguities of this "position" rather than by the experience of motion. The experience of motion is most often left out of considerations of the figure produced by travel who—in the form of the stranger, the marginal or liminal figure—is often treated as the product of his or her relation to a fixed "place" on or between the boundaries defining communities. But passage is not simply the experience of an "interstitial" zone; it is, as I have said, an experience with its own structure, logic, and consequences. Only by examining this experience through the character produced by it may we locate both the uniqueness of the phenomenon and the reasons why passage silences, tranquilizes, addicts, generates purposes and needs.

THE WANDERING PHILOSOPHER

He travels on, and in his face his step
His gait, is one expression: every limb
His look and bending figure; all bespeak
A man who does not move with pain, but moves
With thought.

—Wordsworth, "Old Man Travelling"

Then comes the time, who lives to see't
That going shall be us'd with feet.

—Shakespeare, *King Lear*, III.3.93–94

If the character of the traveler is both reaction and defense against the mobile condition, it is significant that these are traditionally spoken of as "intellectual" reactions and "conscious" defenses. From the very beginning of travel literature, passage was thought to extend the range of a passenger's knowledge across broader regions of difference, and thus to introduce a qualitative transformation in one's intellectual state. The notion that travel enhances the intelligence of the traveler is as old as Gilgamesh, who, through his travels, came to know "the countries of the world, he was wise, he saw mysteries and knew secret things."[10] In the ancient world, the state of passage was considered appropriate to philosophers. When Dio of Prusa was condemned by the Oracle of Delphi to travel, as expiation for his sins, to the ends of the earth until instructed otherwise, he did so "being taken by some for a vagabond, by others for a beggar, by others again for a philosopher."[11] Strabo, the widely traveled Greco-Roman geographer, included those "looking for the meaning of life" among those addicted to "mountain roaming," and he repeated what was already proverbial by the first century B.C.: "[T]he wisest heroes were those who visited many places and roamed over the world; for the poets regard it as a great achievement to have seen the cities and know the minds of men."[12] The identification of the philosopher with the wandering condition is an association formed in the ancient world which continues into our own.

This association suffuses Renaissance appreciations of the effects of travel upon the passenger, reviving and extending the ancient *topos*. In Renaissance treatises "in praise of travel," it was assumed that passage brings about a sharpening of the intelligence of the passenger. Thus, travel was increasingly recommended as a finish to an education and a means of "pleasant instruction":

> [A]ll wits, whatsoever naturall instinct of towardness they have, do wax dull and even die, being included within the narrow bounds of their domesticall seats and . . . there is no dullness of mind, no darkness so great which is not in a measure kindled with the course of travels, and in all respects made more cleere and vigorous.[13]

Richard Lassels, a seventeenth-century traveling tutor and guide, used what had been a commonplace for millennia in recommending his services to well-supplied gentlemen essaying their Grand Tour: traveling "makes a wise man wiser by making him see the good and bad in others. . . . It makes a man think himself at home everywhere, and smile at unjust exile."[14] Travel clearly extends the experience of the traveler over a broader range of differences, acquainting one with a greater variety of things, people, customs, flora, fauna, topographies, architecture, and so on. As Christopher Columbus said, "The further one goes the more one learns."[15]

To Renaissance promoters of the discipline and art of travel, it

seemed obvious that the transformations of travel were a direct result of the experience of a greater variety of people, customs, animals, plants, and topographies made available by passage. As Andreas
Francesius, the Italian Humanist, observed, "the result of seeing such
a variety of things and disparity of customs is that men of low intelligence soon become quickwitted and clever. In fact there can be
scarcely anyone who, by picking out the best and worst of all he sees,
will not quickly form sensible habits of life and improved virtues."[16]
Here the intellectual alterations of travel are related to the training
of judgment in comparing customs and things and "picking out the
best and worst." They are a result of the operations which the atten-
tive traveler performs on the broader range of experience made accessible through passage, rather than a product of that extension of
experience itself. Thus, this extension of experience alters "consciousness," that source of continuity within identity.

THE OBSERVER AND RECORDER

*I discovered, though unconsciously and insensibly, that the pleasure of observing
and reasoning was a much higher one than that of skill and sport. The primeval
instincts of the barbarian slowly yielded to the acquired tastes of the civilized man.*
                                                              —Darwin, 1878

In the sixteenth and seventeenth centuries, the intellectual transformations effected by passage were increasingly perceived to be a
result of the extent to which travel developed observational skills.
The consciousness specific to the traveler was the consciousness of
the observer; and philosophy, now reduced to science, was increasingly regarded as little more than disciplined and objective observation. The wandering philosopher of the ancient world became the
humanist traveler of the Renaissance and the scientific traveler of
the seventeenth and eighteenth centuries. The transformations that
passage worked in the character of the traveler were thought to be
a product of observation, comparison, the sharpening of judgment,
the ability to formulate a general picture or representation of the
world from observation. This became the standard conception of the
transformations of travel and remains so in the modern era.

In his four years aboard the *Beagle*, Darwin gave up his youthful obsession with shooting birds and concentrated on a less ultimate form of appropriating a world: observing, measuring, taking notes, collecting specimens. His association of observation with "civility" is itself a significant marker of the extent to which, in early modern Europe, the disciplined observer was endowed with a dignity hitherto not enjoyed.

Even more significant is the persistence, through successive eras, of the ancient insight that passage engenders a form of "reason," a "point of view," a self-consciousness rooted in the observation of the world and its several contexts and environments. The source of the intellectual effects long ascribed to travel may be perceived to lie not only in the extension of the passenger's experience over a greater range but in the limitations passage imposes upon the perceptions of the traveler, and in the attempt to overcome and compensate for these limitations.

Generations of travelers have understood these limitations. Mobility confines the traveler's view of the world to brief instants. It places a characteristic distance between the mobile observer and the world he or she observes. It limits those observations to surfaces, exteriors, lines, and figures quickly glimpsed in passing. Jean Cocteau, on his journey around the world, admitted these limitations on the traveler's perceptions and was grateful for the modern technology of photography which transcended them: "It is a method I advocate. Either live with things or just glance at them. I hardly look. I record. I load my camera obscura. I will develop the image at home."[17] This implicit distinction of status between a mere viewer and a "recorder"—one consuming the world and its sights, the other fixing and textualizing these sights in words and photos—is a distinction between the casual and the serious traveler. It assumes the dignity of the observer which was established with the new science of the seventeenth century. But this science of observation was founded in a clear understanding of the limits and distortions of all observation, particularly the observations of the passing stranger. This is the source of the legitimate charge that the traveler's view is necessarily superficial, external, and impoverished, lacking the richness or complexity available to the insider, who dwells amid those people and things the passenger merely glimpses.

In defending the traveler's view of the world from the charge of superficiality, Claude Lévi-Strauss sounds the ancient *topos*, and suggests that the limitations upon the traveler's observations may be the source of intellectual improvement: "I have learned ... what a useful training in observation ... short glimpses of a town, an area or a culture can provide and how—because of the intense concentration forced upon one by the brevity of the stay—one may even grasp certain features which, in other circumstances, might have remained hidden."[18] Here the character of the traveler as observer, philosopher, recorder of the world seems to be a compensation for those limitations, restrictions, and handicaps the conditions of passage place upon the conscious knowing of the observer. Motion connects the traveler to the world but also distances one from it. In overcoming this distancing, the serious traveler must develop techniques of reading from the surfaces of things and people to discover their interiors, relationships, functions, and meanings. A world is constituted through these operations of the observing and recording traveler, a world of knowledge, lore, and description of things that is marked by the observer's relationship to the observed. The truth of the learned and observing traveler is always the truth of the "outsider," not the truth of the "actor."

Bronislaw Malinowski recognized this distinction and understood that the system of Trobriand prestige trade, which he first described in *Argonauts of the Western Pacific*, was a product of the ethnographer's observations and characteristic activity; that this system did not appear as such to the native acting within it: "For the integral picture does not exist in his mind; he is in it, and cannot see the whole from the inside."[19] It may be that "wholes" and "systems" appear as such only from the outside, and this is a valuable advantage of the traveler's view. What to the native is a medium that defines the particularity of his or her situation is to the traveler an object, a part of a generality, which must be understood in terms of its relations to other parts of a system.

THE STRANGER

The stranger is an outsider in a world ... of ambiguity, inconsistency and flux.
                                                    —Dennison Nash, 1963

The twentieth-century sociological image of the traveler as the "stranger," the "marginal" or "liminal" person, still contains all that the ancients meant when they described the traveler as a philosopher, as well as what early moderns signified in designating the traveler of dignity as an objective observer and recorder of the world.

Simmel ascribes four characteristics to the stranger: freedom, objectivity, generality, and abstractness. "Freedom" and "objectivity" mean essentially the same thing: the stranger is "detached" from the community in which he resides by virtue of his mobility. Because of this freedom and detachment, the stranger may view "objectively" the conflicts and situations within which locals are mired; thus, strangers have often been welcomed into communities as judges, confessors, and confidants. As Simmel describes the stranger, "he is freer, practically and theoretically; he surveys conditions with less prejudice; his criteria for them are more general and more objective ideals; he is not tied down in his actions by habit, piety, and precedent."[20] By "generality" and "abstractness," Simmel means the way the stranger is viewed by the locale rather than the stranger's own point of view. Bearing a "general" and "abstract" character to the native, the stranger represents the merely human stripped of specificity, embodying all of those features the natives have in common with everybody else, those generalized features of the human against which natives pose their particularities.

Simmel's four features have long been associated with travelers, though traditionally described in different terms—as a "philosophical" disposition or the character of the "objective observer." To Stonequist, the traveler's position between communities is what enhances his intelligence: "To be poised between two groups demands mental agility. The individual is not permitted to come to rest and possibly vegetate. The necessity for continual adjustment prods the mental functions into swift activity." The increased quickness and intelligence of the marginal figure is a result, in this context, of bilingualism, the necessity of translating between different cultures, norms, groups, a product of the necessity of adaptation to a new context: "But migration involves more than an adaptation or adjustment of old customs and habits to new geographic and economic conditions: It results in a quickening of the mind, a stirring of the higher mental functions."[21] Both the stranger and the marginal man are social beings defined by the groups between which they mediate, and are peculiarly passive and static, products of the

interstitial position, the frontier between organized, rooted, territorial communities.

THE EFFECT OF MOTION ON PERCEPTION

*I come upon familiar objects in an unfamiliar world; everything is just as I
imagined it, yet everything is new. It is the same with my observations and ideas.
I have not had a single idea which was entirely new or surprising but my old
ideas have become so much more firm, vital and coherent that they could be called
new.*

—Goethe, 1786

For four thousand years, passage has been thought to stir the higher
mental functions and to create individuals who are outside of and
between communities, and thus, in some sense, "objective" observers
of differences within the human and natural landscape. But the features long attributed to the mentality of a passenger—freedom, objectivity, generality, and abstractness—are to some extent a
consequence of the activity of the traveler in the conditions of passage. Furthermore, motion both mediates the passenger's state and
condition quite independently of one's relations to those places one
departs from and arrives in, and shapes one's perception of world
and self. Travel is, in fact, only a specific form of human motion in
general, and the effects of days or weeks of passage differ only in
degree, not in kind, from the perceptual effects of driving from home
to work or walking across a room.

Particularly useful in understanding the role motion plays in
perception of the self and the world is James Gibson's insistence that
motion in general is an essential condition of "adequate" perception, and that perception itself must be regarded as a mobile and
active undertaking rather than a passively received "occurrence in
the theatre of consciousness":

> Moving from place to place is supposed to be "physical" whereas
> perceiving is supposed to be "mental," but this dichotomy is mis-
> leading. Locomotion is guided by visual perception. Not only does
> it depend on perception but perception depends on locomotion
> inasmuch as a moving point of observation is necessary for any

adequate acquaintance with the environment. So we must perceive in order to move, but we must also move in order to perceive.[22]

From Gibson's point of view, terms like "object" and "subject" derive their content from the relativities of motion. "Object" or "objective" refer to invariants or predictable variations perceived in the optical array, while "subject" and "subjective" refer to invariances within the conditions and frames of perception. Passage only intensifies that climate of motion and change in which objective and subjective persistencies are more easily perceived. One might expect, moreover, that the more we move, the more we perceive; that in the prolonged and intensified motions of passage, the world becomes more objective, an array of things stripped of their subjectivity, while the self becomes more subjective and invisible as it is subsumed in the activity of observation and defined in terms of this activity.

The objectification of the world and the subjectification of self as observer are mutually engendering processes in the experience of motion. These are at work on a historical and collective plane as the world is objectified in seventeenth- and eighteenth-century travel reports simultaneously with the "discovery of the subject" as a persisting point of view; and they are linked within an individual experience of passage, such as that Wordsworth describes in the poem "In a Carriage Along the Banks of the Rhine" (1790):

> Amid the dance of the objects sadness steals
> O'er the defrauded heart—which sweeping by,
> As in a fit of Thespian Jollity,
> Beneath her vine-leaf crown the green earth reels
> Backward, in rapid evanescence, wheels
> The venerable pageantry of time.
> . . .
> To muse, to creep, to halt at will to gaze—
> Such sweet wayfaring—of life's Spring the pride
> . . . that still is mine,
> And in fit measure cheers autumnal days.[23]

The mobility that choreographs the "dance of the objects," plays with the settled order of things, and sets the world into a "rapid evanescence," is the same that distances the passenger from the world through which he is passing. Here this distance is experienced with a sense of sadness, of being "defrauded" of content and excluded from interiors, relations and subjectivities that generate the observed.

The Objectivity of the Passenger

Much of what we mean by "objectivity" and the "objectification" of the world is a process that excludes the passenger from interiors, leaving only surfaces and forms to apprehend. This same forlorn sense of exclusion from domesticities overcame the travel writer Colin Thubron as he was driving, alone at night, across Russia in 1982. He noticed travelers' tents that "lay under the trees like dimlit pyramids. Their warmth and glow excluded me unbearably."[24] But such exclusion is implicit in the transformation of the observed phenomenon into a thing devoid of purpose, intention, subjectivity. The thing must be understood not in terms of its internalities, from which the passenger is excluded by the conditions of passage, but in terms of its form and function, its relations with other things that are observable and evident. In the condition of "ambiguity, inconsistency and flux," which is the state of the passenger, the "thing" may provide a fixed source of security and a beacon of orientation to ease a condition of transience and impermanence. But there is another source of permanence in the flows of passage. The very consciousness of the observer who muses, creeps, halts at will to gaze is, for Wordsworth and many other habitual travelers, a source of continuity, an identity that, persisting from youth to old age, may be actualized simply by setting forth on a journey.

Thus, the objectivity long ascribed to the traveler may be not simply a result of detachment from and attachment to context, but also a consequence of the conditions of motion, of the distance motion creates between observer and observed. This objectivity is best understood as a consequence of the methods a passenger uses to find continuity and predictability in a world in flux, while those other characteristics of the stranger, abstractness and generality, may be standard reactions of the passenger to a world that is flowing past as one moves through it.

Passage permits the passenger more easily to separate off the form of things from the sequence of their occurrences, familiarizing the observer with the abstract figure of a phenomenon that persists through a range of contexts. The context of motion furthers what William James called the "law of dissociation by varying concomitants": "What is associated now with one thing and now with another tends to become dissociated from either, and to grow into an object of abstract contemplation by the mind."[25] The sequential experience of individual objects—a house, a barn, a person, an animal—in a variety of contexts serves to isolate those objects from any *particular* context and to make the passenger aware of their persisting features, their formal and general characteristics, their identity independent of the accidents of their appearances. A traveler's version of Plato's allegory of the cave would emphasize the release of the observer from immobility and the entry into motion as the event that begins to acquaint one with the idea and form of things. This was the experience Goethe had continuously on his journey through Italy, as he came upon "familiar objects in an unfamiliar world," an experience in which everything was new and fresh.[26]

The apprehension of the form of things independent of their particular context is a product of continuous, ongoing comparison. The experienced traveler, whom Henry James called the "cosmopolite," is formed out of the habit of "comparing, of looking for points of difference and resemblance, for present and absent advantages." James was not certain whether this habit was good or bad; it was simply an apparently unavoidable consequence of the condition of the passenger:

> It is hard to say exactly what is the profit of comparing one race with another, and weighing in opposed groups the manners and customs of neighboring countries; but it is certain that as we move about the world we constantly indulge in this exercise. This is especially the case if we happen to be infected with the baleful spirit of the cosmopolite—that uncomfortable consequence of seeing many lands and feeling at home in none.[27]

This kind of comparison is perhaps the most common feature of travel reports, and the primary source of the knowledge derived from travel. The modern Italian historian of Renaissance voyages Antonello Gerbi notes that the comparison, the similitude, is the dominant schema of Renaissance voyage literature:

> And in fact this basic alternative, very simple and easily reversible, is extremely fruitful. Saying that a new—generally animal or plant—

species is "like in Europe" or "like in Spain" ... means accepting
it within one's mental horizons, appropriating it to the known and
familiar world, recognizing that it possesses the normality, tradi-
tionality, and rationality of the animals and plants of our own
climate.[28]

In the sixteenth and seventeenth centuries, travel was perceived as
a philosophical and scientific endeavor because it allowed the passenger to make comparisons. As a way of "picking out the best and
the worst," it allowed the passenger to formulate more universal
values independent of custom. For the French social scientist Joseph-
Marie Degerando, in his instructions to the scientists voyaging with
the explorer Nicholas-Thomas Baudin on his second expedition to
the South Seas in 1797, science was nothing more than observation
and comparison: Science "gathers facts to compare them and compares them to know them better. The natural sciences are in no way
more than a series of comparisons."[29] Clearly, the comparison is not
an invention of the traveler; equally clearly, travel thoroughly mo-
bilizes this mechanism as an instrument by which the flow of perception may be ordered, marked, rendered meaningful.

The comparison is the way in which the traveler calls up a base
of familiarity before the spectacle of the new and the strange, which
is perceived as such only in relationship to the known. In so doing,
one may diffuse the anxiety normally associated with the strange and
unusual. Travel in general, and "exploration" in particular, may be
motivated not by love of the strange and unfamiliar but by the desire
to reduce, by active and aggressive means, the uncertainty implicit
in the strange and unfamiliar. In this sense, the comparison, which
becomes the habit of the traveler, may be regarded as a defense
against the strange and unusual which differs only in direction, not
in motive, from retreat and avoidance. Exploration, which becomes
a culturally valued activity in the modern period, is triggered by the
unknown and terminated when the strange becomes familiar, and
this might be its purpose. "It is the special property of exploratory
behavior that it transforms an activating stimulus into a terminating
one," as Bowlby says.[30] One of the pleasures of travel, the joy of the
encounter with the different and the strange, may be nothing more
than a reduction of the tension and anxiety these properties evoke
from infancy on.

The comparison also may be identified as the mechanism that

produces the stranger, the cosmopolite, the person who, as a result of "seeing the world," is at home "nowhere." When the unfamiliar is rendered familiar by its comparison to the known, its difference defined and similarities established, the formerly strange may itself become the ground of the familiar, the base of future comparisons. An explorer may initially experience the Cordilleras of South America in terms of how they are like or unlike the mountains of Spain; but later compare other mountain ranges with the Cordilleras. Thus exploration, an aggressive way of dealing with the anxiety inherent in the unknown, by its very nature extends the experience over a range of things that become examples of increasingly clear general categories and forms. In a life of travels the original ground of comparison may be absorbed and replaced by a generalized consciousness of universal and general forms of which each particular thing is an exemplar. Passage produces the comparativist and the relativist, as Henry James noted:

> If you have lived about ... you have lost that sense of the absoluteness and the sanctity of the habits of your fellow patriots which once made you so happy in the midst of them. You have seen that there are a great many *patriae* in the world, and that each is filled with excellent people for whom the local idiosyncrasies are the only thing that is not rather barbarous.

Here the process of generalization occurring in a course of travels is the loss of absolutes, a diminished sense of the sanctity of the home, which comes from an activity that eradicates its separateness from other places. This encounter with a great many forms of excellence, a general appreciation of the worth implicit in all *patriae*, makes it impossible any longer for the person born through passage to pin his "faith to a chosen people."[91]

But the experience of passage may produce other absolutes. One of the "forms" derived from the invariances perceived by those in passage is "humanity," an idea that emerged during the great age of European travel and discovery and is not separable from the activity definitive of that age. Travel is a "generalizing" activity, both in confronting the passenger with many domains within which persistent forms are perceived and in giving the traveler a general character. Henry Blount, traveling to Turkey on a Venetian galley in 1637, found himself to be the only Christian passenger among Turks and

Jews, and learned of the freedom that comes with the company of strangers who know one not at all: "[T]hen I had a freedom of complying upon occasion of questions by them made, whereby I became all things to all men, which let me into the breasts of many."[32] In a sequence of strange lands, the passenger learns not only others', but also his own generality—that which he has in common with the other despite differences of language, culture, race, religion, diet. This was the most fundamental lesson Charles Doughty drew from his passage through Arabia: "A pleasure it is to listen to the cheerful, musing Beduin talk, a lesson in the traveller's school of mere humanity— and there is no land so perilous which by humanity he may not pass, for man is of one mind everywhere."[33]

Another source of the abstractness and generality of the passenger is the discovery of invariant relations *between* things in the flows of passage and within a range of contexts. These relations, as well as the form implicit in a variety of similar things, become a source of orientation for the passenger and an anchor in the flux of passage.

Darwin's years of passage acquainted him with a larger range of contexts and varieties of flora and fauna than were available to him in England. This larger range of variation compelled him to identify the species implicit in varieties and also to think hard about the *relation* of variation to the context of that variation. This became the problem that occupied him on his return to England, and the context of its solution—while Darwin was in passage—is relevant to the nature of that solution: "I can remember the very spot in the road, whilst in my carriage, when to my joy the solution occurred to me. . . . The solution, as I believe, is that the modified offspring of all dominant and increasing forms tend to become adapted to many and highly diversified places in the economy of nature."[34]

In his plastic season of passage aboard the *Beagle*, Darwin focused not only on an enormous variety of species but also on the role played by context in the change of species character. A traveler is required to adapt to many diverse contexts, and passage shows that there is great variety in the specific terms of relationships as well as a remarkable persistence in the character of a relationship despite the variety of its terms. Thus, although a pen may be "far" from my hand, and Japan may be "far" from Europe, the variety of these terms does not alter the relation of "farness." In experiencing

a continuous change of the terms of relations, the passenger is acquainted with the persistent features of those relations independent
of their terms. One who is, in passing through a variety of human
groups, liberated from a particular human group may be impelled
to think about the relations that constitute groups generally. It is
in this quality that Simmel found the objectivity of the stranger,
the ability to abstract relations from the local terms of those relations, beyond which locals cannot see. It is a quality engendered in
passage.

The Self of the Passenger

*The doctrine that vision is exteroceptive, that it obtains 'external' information
only, is simply false. Vision obtains information about* both *the environment* and
the self: In fact all the senses do.

—James Gibson, 1979

The self of the mobile observer is an alternative to a "social" self,
the identity woven in the consciousness of being observed, recognized, and categorized by others. One cannot function simultaneously as observer and observed. Those conflicts engendered by the
recognitions of others may be resolved in becoming, for a season,
more purely a concentrated observer of the world that passes. This
is the sense in which Darwin felt he had been transformed by his
voyage, a voyage that removed him from the expectations and
doubts of a powerful, demanding father, and made him an observer
of the world and its varieties, a role that was to become his vocation. Goethe undertook his journey to Italy with the expectation
that a close observation of a world of different objects and persons
would provide the conditions for the clarification of a "natural"
self subsisting beneath social attributions: "My purpose in making
this journey is not to delude myself but to discover myself in the
objects I see."[35]

The self discovered in the world of objects is the self of the
observer, which becomes a pole of attention and source of security
in a world in flux. Kinglake lamented that the truths of the world an
honest traveler is determined to tell may never be separated from

the subject who tells them or from the point of view of that subject: "His very selfishness—his habit of referring the whole external world to his own sensation, compels him as it were, in his writings, to observe the laws of perspective; he tells you of objects, not as he knows them to be, but as they seemed to him."[36]

The forms, relations, and patterns of recurrence that arise in the experience of passage become those "nonchanges in the midst of change" that orient the passenger in a world transformed by motion. Motion, in other words, seems to be a medium of perception that abstracts and generalizes form and relations out of things and terms. But the flows of passage not only provide information about the world; they provide information about the self of the passenger. Passage provides a prolonged and intensified context of change in which one may become aware of those invariant veils, frames, and screens mediating one's observations of the world. These become the components of a body, a gazing and observing self that persists through a variety of contexts, from one's childhood to one's later years. The mind of the traveler is not separate from the body of the traveler, and the changes registered as habits of mind, objectivity, abstractness, relativism, a comparative consciousness or generality, proceed from the body, from sensation, and from reactions to the sensations of motion. Darwin insists upon this in a peculiar passage of his autobiography in which he represents the transformations effected in his travels as at once mental and physical:

> That my mind became developed through my pursuits during this voyage is rendered probable by a remark made by my father, who was the most acute observer I ever saw, of a sceptical disposition and far from being a believer in phrenology; for on first seeing me after the voyage, he turned round to my sisters and exclaimed, "why, the shape of his head is quite altered."[37]

This, as I have argued, is more than a metaphor. The mental effects of passage—the development of observational skills, the concentration on forms and relations, the sense of distance between an observing self and a world of objects perceived first in their materiality, their externalities and surfaces, the subjectivity of the observer—are inseparable from the physical conditions of movement through space. These are the features of the human character crafted and shaped by mobility.

THE STRUCTURE OF PASSAGE

You cannot travel on the path before you have become the Path itself.
—Gautama Buddha

I have regarded the characteristics of the traveler thus far as a re-action to and defense against the disequilibriums and transforma-tions of passage. But passage itself imposes upon experience a particular form and structure to which inveterate travelers become habituated. In this structure we might find the source of the free-doms and pleasures peculiar to passage, which for some are tran-quilizing and addicting.

The order imposed upon experience by the condition of mo-bility is an order of sequence, an order of "one-thing-after-another," a "progress." Motion resolves all orders of space—topographies, po-sitions, scenes, containments, places—into an experiential order of continuously evolving appearances, an evolution with its own pe-culiar laws. The passage, the form of the path, willy-nilly imposes what the philosopher and anthropologist Gregory Bateson calls a "progressional ordering of reality" upon passengers—a method of organizing information in a sequence of occurrences which he dis-tinguishes from "selective" or categorical ordering of information. Individuals and cultures differ, Bateson suggests, in their preference for these forms of codification.

> It is clear . . . that persons differ in the relative importance of these two processes. Some will try to act selectively in contexts where time relations of actions would seem to demand progressional integra-tion, while others will let themselves be guided by a progressional psychological élan even in contexts where the alternatives could have been more conveniently evaluated in categories.[38]

Perhaps this is an expansion of the cryptic wisdom of Gautama Bud-dha quoted above. The sequences of the path give form to ancient itineraries and travel directions, which are little more than linear recitations of places, stations, cities, and distances between them, along a given route. The structure of the passage is an experience that gives rise to a structure of representation, the epic and journal form of one place, scene, thing after another connected only by the motions of the actor. The transitions between scenes in the *Iliad* are almost invariably accomplished through the territorial passage of some god, goddess, or hero. The linear and progressional order of passage is made concrete in the path-forms and road architecture that dominate modern landscapes. It is graven into texts as epic structure and as rhapsodic, stitched together, form. The journey sequence, the progressional order of egoistic passage, was the form of travel guides well into the nineteenth century, when it was replaced by the Baedeker—representations of "all possible" routes and places, the view from above, the geographer's rather than the traveler's view. But the progressional order native to travel literature contains categorical possibilities, exploited to the full by seventeenth- and eighteenth-century travel writers, who used the "place" as a handy category within which to file all that was known or written about that place, country, domain.

The skeletal remains of the progressional order of passage in road forms and architecture, in itineraries and epic, are missing what gives this order its life and animation: motion and change. The structure of passage is a structure of change, a structure that governs the *evolution* of appearances, not just their arrangement. The "dance of objects" is always organized in and through the motions of the observer. The use of motion both as a tool of perception and a way of dissolving permanence was clearly understood by Victor Sengalen, a late-nineteenth-century French traveler and aesthete who spent his life in journeys, in an "incomplete quest for self among others," dying in China in 1919. Sengalen perceived that the form of many Chinese monuments owed much to the nomadic condition, being tents in stone which could be returned to their original condition and reanimated through the motions of the observing traveler: "Palaces, immobile by accident ... it's I that will move toward you; and the undulation of my walking ... will return to you the shoulder's rhythms and oscillations by which you were once animated. I will walk to you."[39] The order of continuously changing appearances that is passage may be laid over stabilities, the dead accomplished forms, to imbue them with the traveler's own life and motion.

The notion of the structure of passage as a structure of change may confuse those who think of structure as the antithesis of change, as a source of rigidity and permanence rather than as a principle of growth or evolution. The laws governing the change of appearances in passage are the only things that, themselves, do not change. According to James Gibson, the experience of passage is organized around two invariants in a field of continuous transformation: the "aiming" point from which things originate, growing larger as the passenger approaches; and the "vanishing point" into which things diminish and disappear.[40] These mainstays in a flowing perceptual array give direction, the chief points of the passenger's orientation. The point of the outflow is the direction one is going toward; the point of inflow, the direction one is coming from. As the motion of the traveler superimposes this pattern of outflow and inflow upon an environment, one derives from it an idea of an objective world, of that which does not change as one changes. These points of divergence and convergence are obviously "egoistic," changing as the motion of the passenger changes, becoming more pronounced with an increase in the speed of passage. These are the nodes upon which is spun that perceptual envelope inhabited by the passenger during the season of passage, an envelope that elongates into a tunnel as the speed of passage increases.

All the knowledge gained in passage originates in this experience—a condition that clearly alters the passenger's perceptions of time as well as of space. The inner durations of consciousness we know as time are, through motion, mapped upon space and integrated into our experience of it. In passage, the future becomes that which is feeding through the aiming point, becoming larger as the passenger approaches. The present is that which is flowing by. The past is the other half of the optical array into which things diminish and disappear, to persist in the memory of forms and relations.

Paul Theroux asks, "What was it about train windows that made people remember? Train windows seem to mirror the past."[41] From the recorded beginnings of travel literature to the present, passage has been regarded as a way of "denying time by crossing space," a "symbolic way to stop growing old."[42] Gilgamesh undertook his journey in order to avoid that pattern of recurrence obvious from a stationary point of view, to escape mortality, and to replace the repeated cycles of birth, maturation, and death with the linear progress of occurrence vouchsafed in passage. A fictional and comic use of this idea occurs in Graham Greene's novel *Travels with My Aunt*, where one of the characters, an Uncle Jo, "wanted to make his life last longer. So he decided on a tour round the world."[43] When Uncle

Jo becomes too sick to travel, he asks for a house with many rooms so that he may be moved each day, continuing his life through the continuation of his motion.

A mathematical statement of this idea is contained in Einstein's special theory of relativity, which asserts that time and space, within the perceptual envelope woven in motion, are functions of each other and relative to each other, "in so far as they depend on the state of motion of the selected inertial system." The absoluteness of both time and space depend upon the stationary position: "According to the special theory of relativity, spatial coordinates and time still have an absolute character in so far as they are directly measurable by stationary clocks and bodies."[44] The integration of time and space through the linearities of motion, apparently a difficult concept for many people, is accessible mainly to travelers, physicists, children, and primitives. The child psychologist Jean Piaget notes that until the age of six or seven, the child has no conception of a "homogeneous" dimension of time: "The child acts as though each movement had its own time ... and that the time indigenous to certain movements can therefore not be coordinated."[45] The separateness of a continuous dimension of space and time is learned in the course of history and individual maturation—a learning dissolved in the experience of passage, which may call up an earlier, even a primal, integration of temporal and spatial dimensions.

The impact of this structure of passage upon the passenger depends upon one's ability to surrender to the conditions of motion and to the order of experience shaped by motion. It is only with this relaxation into the sequences of evolving appearances that, according to Didion, "a distortion of time" takes place and the mind "goes clean." This relaxation into the logic and inevitabilities of mobility may thus be the condition of the purifications of passage, what Kerouac called "the purity of the road." This surrender to the orders of motion is the condition that alters the state of the passenger. The condition of motion gives a positive and active content to the negative and passive character of liminality: "One finds in liminality both positive and active qualities, especially when that 'threshold' is protracted and becomes a 'tunnel,' when the 'liminal' becomes the 'cunicular.' "[46]

Insofar as travelers are able to place themselves within the conditions of motion and forget about those places external to that motion, passage absorbs them into its characteristic order, purifies, becomes addictive and a pleasure and motive in itself. With this relaxation into the structure imposed by motion, passage becomes an "autotelic" experience, rewarding in itself, and triggers the "flow state" studied by Csikszentmihalyi. Such states were reported by many of the participants in his study who engaged in sports, dance, sailing, and mountain-climbing. The term itself was taken from a mountain-climber's description of what he found intrinsically satisfying about his chosen activity—the feeling of continuity it induced in him: "The purpose of flow is to keep on flowing, not looking for a peak or utopia, but staying in the flow. It is not a moving up but a continuous flowing; you move only to keep the flow going. There is no possible reason for climbing except the climbing itself."[47]

The flow state, however it is induced, contains only one imperative—it must be perpetuated—and thus becomes, in itself, the source of motives and of needs. It is triggered by activity that has its own logic and progression, by a situation in which "[a]ction follows action according to an internal logic that seems to need no conscious intervention by the actor."[48] This quote perfectly describes the structure of passage, which imposes an inevitable and irresistible logic of sequence on those who commit themselves to a path. In passage, the actor is unable to see himself as such, for the ego is absorbed into the conditions of the action, to re-emerge only when there is danger and threat or when the ego becomes aware of being observed.

The peculiarities of autotelic motion may be a source of the peculiar inarticulateness induced by passage, a reason why pleasant passage silences and produces few texts and narrations. The activity of passage connects self and the world in a seamless sequence of predictably evolving transformations. It unifies those elements— actor, world, action, past, present, and future—that might otherwise be knit through words and narration. A storm, or the collapse of the observer's concentration on the flow with the awareness of being observed ("How am I doing?"), separates out those elements once more, creating the condition and necessity for words, a need for the connectivities of language and for narratable experience. Smooth, frictionless, and unresisted motion induces a flow state, a "unified flowing from one moment to the next ... in which there is little distinction between self and environment, between stimulus and response, or between past, present and future."[49] In this state, the pen drops from the hand; a period of hours and days in passage may be noted in a log as "in two days we came to . . ."—a period in which nothing happens worthy of record.

The reason the experience of motion is often productive of flow states appears to lie in the one property essential to motion in general: continuousness, continuity, inertia. As Zeno's paradoxes show, there is no reality to motion once its continuousness is denied, when it is articulated in discrete portions between points in space: Achilles will never catch the tortoise once the race-course is divided into a series of fixed points, for then the essential property of motion, continuity, is annihilated. Clearly, it is wrong to say that a moving body is at a place rather than moving through a place, for when it is at a place, it is no longer moving.[50] In other words, place and space are words that refer only to the relativities of motion. The continuousness of motion gives rise to an idea of space as endless, roomy, free. An interruption of the continuities of motion resolves space into place: "[I]f we think of space as that which allows movement then place is pause; each pause in movement makes it possible for location to be transformed into place."[51] We might resolve space into place by halting our motion, and transform place into space by taking it up once more. The continuity of motion is implicit in those connectivities between separate locales and moments formed in passage. It is assumed in the flow state entered into by those who surrender to the conditions of motion, a state in which things follow each other automatically with no conscious intervention of the observer. This connectivity that motion imposes upon experience explains something of its addictiveness, why the connectivities of motion can supplement or replace the connectives of person to place, producing the habitual wanderer who is at home nowhere but in motion.

THE LIBERATION OF PASSAGE

When I was a kid, to really move *was my delight. I felt released because I could move around anybody. I was free.*
                                 —Eric Nesterenko (from Studs Terkel, *Working*), 1974

So far as a man has the power to think or not to think, to move or not to move, according to the preference or direction of his own mind, so far is a man free.
—John Locke, 1689

The transformations of passage implicit in motion explain something of the "therapeutic" effects of travel upon even the occasional passenger. The onset of motion resolves boundaries into paths, makes thresholds into perceptual tunnels of continuously evolving appearances, converts limits into avenues. Passage, in short, dissolves the realities inseparable from place: the reality of boundaries, the recurrences of time and mortality, all inherited containments within the defining and confining orders of place. The freedom long attributed to travel begins with departure, the separation of the traveler from sources of definition. But this freedom from place begun with departure assumes a different, more positive and active form in passage, where it is associated with motion. As is implicit in the equation of freedom with motion by the hockey player Eric Nesterenko,[52] the freedom of passage involves moving "around" places and people, assuming an absence of contact, a distance and detachment now structured into the very conditions of motion. The freedom inherent in passage, while active, is also limited and bounded. It is channeled and contained within the linear frames of the road, the path, the course, as well as fixed by the permanent "coordinate system" supplied by the mode of conveyance—whether carriage, airplane, ship, or car. The sequence of evolving appearances, while possibly entered into voluntarily, negates volition—and this may be the source of the altered state, the rapture, tranquility, peace, and satisfaction experienced by those who resign themselves to the conditions of motion. While valued by moderns as the exercise of freedom, travel in the phase of passage negates the will by placing the passenger within an ordered sequence of appearances that are independent of the will. Passage is an ambiguous state of freedom, a form of motion often chosen because it allows the passenger not to think, or to think according to the order in which appearances present themselves. The freedom of the passenger is open-ended in two directions—that from which one is coming and that toward which one is going—while foreclosed on either side by the conditions of motion. The liberty of passage is that of action rather than will—a liberty like that of the

prisoner imagined by John Locke, who stands at the north wall of a
cell twenty foot square, and who "is at liberty to walk twenty feet
southward, because he can walk or not walk it; but is not, at the same
time, at liberty to do the contrary, i.e., to walk twenty feet northward."[53] The freedom of passage, in short, presumes the constraints
and channelings of the path.

The experience of passage transforms limits and boundaries into
"frames" passed through—a feature of passage that may contain the
psychic content of the notion that passage is "de-repressive" and
liberating. Passage may dissolve inherited containments and be experienced as a cure of the diseases and attributions acquired in place.
The boundary acquires its absoluteness from the position of those
situated outside or within it; and this absoluteness of the boundary,
as well as that absoluteness of time and space, is dissolved with the
onset of passage. Paul Theroux, on his tour around the coast of
Great Britain, noticed many, often elderly, Britons seated on deck-
chairs or in their cars, staring for hours across the expanse of the
ocean. Regarding this as an inexpensive, vicarious form of passage,
he commented: "They are symbolically leaving the country. Going
to the coast was as far as they could comfortably go. It was the poor
person's way of going abroad—standing at the seaside and staring
at the ocean."[54] But the onset of motion miraculously transforms
what has been a limit and a boundary into a path, an infinitely extended world which is both endless and bounded. Anyone, no matter
how poor, may experience this transformation by rising from a
seated position on one side of a boundary and walking that boundary, perhaps the one that separates ocean from land, which now
becomes a path, a channel of passage. What was a "betwixt and between" has become a corridor and an avenue along which the mobile
person may "halt and gaze at will." In its most specific meaning, the
Latin word *limen*, from which liminality is derived, referred not to a
threshold but to the outermost *road* of the Roman Empire. The extreme limit of the imperial domain was a pathway, and thus a world
in itself with its own logic, sequences, liberties, and constraints, not
simply a boundary between inner and outer space.

The "loss of integration" with environment effected by departure is structured in passage, a state of disequilibrium, transience,
and flux which induces its own species of "reflection." The force and
power of mobility, evident as "change," affects passengers in specific
ways. Here the mentality of the traveler has been interpreted as an

array both of defenses constructed against the disequilibriums of passage and of techniques utilized to transcend those limitations and distortions that mobility imposes upon one's perceptions. Although the condition of stability and sessility may produce a need for change that is acted upon in departures, the climate of change that is passage stimulates quite another array of needs—for permanence, predictability, invariance, stability, orientation. The peculiarities of the mentality of the traveler derive in large part from the service of these needs. The limitations passage imposes upon the perspective of the traveler were noted two thousand years ago by Strabo:

> All that is in front of us and behind us and on either side of us is presented to our minds as a plane surface and offers no varying aspects with reference to the celestial bodies or the movements and position of the stars relative to us. . . . The sailor on the open sea or the man who travels through a level country, is guided by certain popular notions . . . because he is unfamiliar with the heavenly bodies and ignorant of the varying aspect of things with reference to them.[55]

Although Strabo contrasts the "progressional" ordering of reality native to the traveler's perspective, confined within "a plane surface," to that categorical ordering of reality appropriate to the geographer with his climates, fixed points of orientation, and stars, one would seem to require the other. The egoism of the traveler's view and its confinement within the perceptual envelope woven of motion require an outside point of view, fixed points of orientation such as those stars that became the clues to Odysseus' passage from the island of Calypso to Phaecia: "he watched the Pleides, watched the Wagoner, slow to set, watched the Bear that some call the Wain, which turns forever in the same spot, with an anxious eye on Orion, which alone of all the constellations has no share in the baths of the ocean."[56] Navigation, the structuring of a world in terms of fixed, external points, is one of those techniques by which the passenger overcomes the limitations of passage and stabilizes its disequilibriums.

Other transformations of passage derive from the structure that the continuity of motion imposes upon the experience of the traveler—an order that supplies many of the pleasures, relaxations, and autotelic features of travel. The structure of passage connects and may, in replacing a passenger's connections to place, become an addiction. But the connectivities inherent in passage are more than an experiential or psychic reality. They construct a world. In the Renaissance, travel and trade were legitimated as a chief means by which men might through their own efforts reassemble that which God, in his unfathomable wisdom, had chosen to put asunder. The commercial or curious traveler was thus imposing his own order, the order of his motion, upon a dispersed creation. It was thought that the very dispersal and scattering of goods, rarities, products across the planet created the necessity for trade and the bartering traveler. The standard opening line of Elizabethan commercial treaties and letters of introduction sent to foreign potentates was: "Foreasmuch as God hath planted all realms and dominions in the whole world with sundry commodities of the other, so as the one hath need of the amity and commodities of the other, and by means thereof traffike is used from one to the other, and amity thereby increased. . . ."[57] The assumption here is that the traveler, through passage, creates a world order. More than a Renaissance *topos*, this is a fact of history.

Thus, a global reality, over and above domains, continents, topographies, and places, is knit through the structure of the journey and connected through the continuities of motion. It is this world, the world criss-crossed with paths, some of which have remained in use for thousands of years, that remains the native home of the traveler. The structure of the passage experience is graven in modern topographies, in the road forms, strip architecture, that dominate modern landscapes. It is implicit in the transformation of cities from closed and bounded into open structures, networks of roads, matrices of passage.

The entry of Cortéz into Mexico *(Courtesy of the Bettmann Archive)*

3

THE STRANGER AT THE
GATES: ARRIVALS

*The transition period caused by my emigration lasted nearly 20 years and was
retarded by the Great War. A return to normal emotional life showed itself by an
absence of dreams in which I saw myself back home again. . . . Now all my plans
and hopes centered in America and the desire for a permanent return to Europe
ceased. Also the fear of isolation in America ceased and a sentiment of coherence
with the new country and an identification developed.*

       —Austrian-German immigrant, to Robert E. Park, 1925

There is no precise moment of arrival. Arrival is a protracted
process—for the tourist, a matter of hours or days; for the
sojourner, weeks or months. It was twenty years before a German immigrant to the United States—Robert Park's informant—"arrived"
in the full sense of the word, before he ceased to dream of his former
home and to desire to return to it, before a "sentiment of coherence
with the new country and an identification developed."[1]

  No matter what level of entry a traveler seeks, arrival is always
a process of "identification," as the traveler identifies the place and
as the place identifies the species of traveler before its gates. Arrival
is a process, too, of incorporations that develop a sense of coherence
between person and place.

A moment of arrival would seem to occur when Ywain arrives in the castle of Esclados the Red, in pursuit of its owner, whose brains he has bashed in and from whom he seeks a token of his victory: a bladed portcullis falls and Ywain's horse is sliced through, though "Lord Ywain ... was barely touched, for the blade came level with his back, cutting off both his spurs, just even with his heels."[2] This might be taken for an "arrival": a dramatic and definitive passage over a threshold sealed in blood between an outside and an inside, an open and a contained world, between the forest and the castle. Yet Ywain's arrival actually begins with the battle that identifies him as a "true" knight and superior to the man he defeats. It ends only when he is wholly incorporated into the domestic domain, becoming its lord and defender. This process of incorporation proceeds—as so often in the history of travels—through the agency of women, in this case the Lady's maid, Lunette, who feeds and clothes Ywain, renders him as invisible as a stranger, and pleads his case in the court of love before the grieving Lady Laudine.

The procedures of identification and those of incorporation are often simultaneous events of arrival. The battle of entry that identifies Ywain's character is also an incorporation, killing being in some sense an ultimate method of appropriation.* The procedures that incorporate Ywain into place and appropriate his energy, strength, "Mana," for the use of the domestic order are clearly identifications as he, through his behavior and address, is matched against the image of the true, courtly and courageous knight, and found to be a worthy replacement of the former lord. The arrival procedure is complete only when he defeats his former comrades in defense of the Lady's spring and acts as host and lord in the ensuing entertainments.

The procedures of arrival are important not simply for what they reveal about the social bonds and identifications extended to the stranger, but because they create structures of place, and articulate and materialize domestic order. The events of arrival, over time, generate rules and procedures of inclusion and exclusion by which the membership of a group is defined and relative status articulated. Ultimately, these procedures of identification, definition, exclusion, and inclusion are materialized in walls and gates, corri-

*I thank Janet Chernela for this suggestion.

dors, and precincts within precincts. The architecture of a place reveals something about the humanity that has flowed through it over
the centuries, for this architecture is the material residue of the intrinsic reality of place—all of the relations, identities, behaviors, exchanges, and meetings that make it up. Arrival procedures, too,
reveal how ethnicities root themselves in the landscape, transforming kinship categories, ethnic and class distinctions into quarters,
walls, and rooms. But it should be clear that the walls, ramps, gates,
avenues that make up ancient ceremonial complexes, much as the
palisade of a native village, assume a world in contact. Peoples who
are not in contact do not need boundaries, walls, and gates, or procedures of identification and incorporation.

The events of arrival do not simply perform established harmonies and meanings of culture; they *create* those harmonies and
meanings. They are not merely the laying on of ritual but the creation of tests, ordeals, and proofs by means of which the unknown is
made known, membership defined, the "alien" excluded. In effect,
boundaries are made by those who cross them and are a legacy of a
history of arrivals. And the history of arrivals, which is the history
of social relations formed and perpetuated between strangers, tells
us something about why human history in general is a history of an
ever more precise articulation of human differences and varieties
rather than a process that makes the species more uniform. Eons of
arrivals have not erased the differences among cultures; on the contrary, these events have generated a consciousness of these differences, represented, and even celebrated them. Thus, the history of
travel shows us not one culture and one world, but many increasingly self-conscious national, ethnic, and cultural domains that assert their distinctiveness and integrity vis-à-vis a transnational regime
identical to the "society of travelers," examined in part III of this
study.

Mary Douglas, in her still reverberating 1970 essay on pollution,
power, and taboo, has argued that order in general, and certainly a
spatio-temporal order, is created by the human exaggeration of the
differences found in the human and natural world: "It is only by
exaggerating the differences between within and without, above and
below, male and female, with and against, that a semblance of order
is created."[3] The exaggeration of differences, which often transforms
a difference into an antithesis, is achieved by means of the repres-

sion of continuities, by the fashioning of boundaries that set apart and render contiguous what is, in experience, continuous: time and space. It is the taboo that creates the "sacred," and sets apart that which God joins. Moses thus created the "domain of the sacred," and performed an act of sacralization when he fenced around Mount Sinai and forbade contact with it to all but priests and the purified, according to the instructions of the Lord: "You must put barriers round the mountain and say, 'Take care not to go up to the mountain or even to touch the edge of it.' Any man who touches the mountain must be put to death. No hand shall touch him; he shall be stoned or shot dead; neither man nor beast may live."[4] And then God described the proper procedures of approach so that the divine power might be received as sacred law. Similarly, the procedures of arrival create sacred domains, and describe the proper means of entering them, so that the power of the stranger may be tapped and used.

The procedures of arrival—identification and incorporation— are thus all-important, for they distinguish a proper and rule-governed entry into place from an improper and rule-breaking one; and this is a distinction between *power* and *pollution*. Power is a result of the proper, rule-governed coming together of domains, people and things normally set apart by those taboos and boundaries that establish a given order; pollution is only the result of the improper contact between these separate and distinct realms: "In short, our pollution behavior is the reaction which condemns any object or idea likely to confuse or contradict our cherished classifications."[5] The stranger is a potential pollutant of the domestic order, as well as a potential source of strength within that order. The procedures of arrival effectively establish this distinction. The identity of the stranger is often determined by the manner of his entry. In the Gospel of John, "the man who does not enter the sheepfold by the door, but climbs in some other way, is nothing but a thief or a robber. The man who enters by the door is the shepherd in charge of the sheep."[6] The unorthodox entry of the robber identifies him and his entry as a pollution, a violation of the domestic order. The entry of the shepherd through the door identifies him as the proper ruler of the sheep. Christ, in this same parable, speaks of himself as a "door" and gateway, characterizing himself as the proper channel of association between the world and the deity, and thus a channel of power. The unpurified man who touches the mountain pollutes it and himself, incurring the penalty of death. The purified man or priest who approaches the mountain in the proper way is the recipient of divine power and law, the foundations of order.

Insofar as the traveler enters a place properly, he or she is a source of power, good, reputation, health, and the augmentation of social being. Insofar as one enters improperly, one is a pollutant and a danger, a source of contagion who deranges a sacred order of differentials materialized in walls, partitions, and corridors. The procedures of identification and incorporation are the means by which the stranger is cleansed of the pollutions acquired in passing through unknown domains and over countless borders. His power is identified, integrated within a spatial and temporal order, which establishes lawful and rule-governed relations between antitheses.

The power of the stranger is a product of events that establish one's relations to a place, events in which battle enjoys an original prominence. Before becoming a mythic attribute, the power of the stranger is a fact of history established in battle, and this power is evident in the walls and portcullises, gates and defenses, that have been erected against the stranger. Thus, the arrival of strangers, armed and in company, is a primary source of historical change and may contain the origins of certain political and social structures. Powerful outsiders founded ruling clans in Hawaii, Fiji, ancient Latium, Athens, Russia, and many African kingdoms. In the mid-ninth century, the Slavic tribes around Lake Ladoga invited Rurik and his brothers in, according to the Primary Chronicle, because there was war between the tribes: "They said to themselves: 'Let us seek a prince who may rule over us, and judge us according to the law.' "[7] The Alur, a people residing on the borders between modern Uganda, Zaire, and the Sudan, traditionally brought their chiefs in from outside because they assumed that such men were more powerful than the local chiefs and able to control the weather, to ensure fertility of the soil, and to exercise potent magic: "The kingship makes its appearance from outside the society. Initially a stranger and something of a terror, the king is absorbed and domesticated by the indigenous people, a process that passes by way of his symbolic death and consequent rebirth as a local god."[8]

This is the scenario anthropologist Marshall Sahlins found in the myths detailing the founding of ruling dynasties in Hawaii and Fiji. Typically, the founding king is a stranger, a prince in his native land who, through crime or misfortune, is banished. With his companions he "takes power in another place, and through a woman: princess of the native people whom he gains by a marvelous exploit involving feats of strength, ruse, rape, athletic prowess and/or the murder of his predecessor.... Before it was a fairy tale it was a theory of society."[9] If we were to consider the countless examples of such military conquest in formulating an image of historical change, we would have to conclude that the state is an ingrowth, an importation into territorialized societies, rather than an outgrowth from them necessitated by social contradictions; and that historical change is more often a process that substitutes one thing for another (the Chinese definition of change) than it is an organic growth, the evolution of some inherent potential espied in retrospect.

The discussion that follows is organized around the topics of battles of entry and the mediations of women, an idiosyncratic approach to the literature of travel and to premodern arrivals. I leave out modern arrivals and many of those exchanges—of food, gifts, objects of trade, recognitions—prominent in premodern arrivals, in order to penetrate more deeply into the first terms of the history of hospitality, the terms and languages of violence which in time are replaced by symbols, rituals, other languages of exchange, and more peaceful reciprocities. My focus upon the mediations of women in premodern procedures of incorporation was dictated by the frequency with which these mediations occur in the travel literature and by the fact that it allows me to consider the role of gender and sexuality in the history of human travels, a much-neglected issue. Travel literature largely describes the mobilities of men and assumes the sessility of women. Much nonrecreational travel is the travel of unattached young men looking for a home, a home almost invariably associated with the mediations of women. Arrivals, in the deeper sense of symbiosis between person and place, are often an achievement of relations between the sexes that specify certain gender characteristics. In conditions of civility and settlement, travel becomes a "gendering" activity, specifying a difference between the mobile male and the sessile female. The latter embodies place, inhabits the walls and containments built by men, and inducts strangers into the relations of kinship and food giving.

THE BATTLE OF ENTRY

I have come to change the old order, I am he who was born in the hills, I am he who is strongest of all.

— Enkidu, in *The Epic of Gilgamesh*, c.1900 B.C.

The first recorded arrival in Western travel literature is that of Enkidu into the city of Uruk, portrayed in *The Epic of Gilgamesh*. Enkidu begins his journey toward the city as a wildman, identified with the wilderness and its inhabitants; and he begins by accident, frightening a trapper so badly that the man's face was "altered like that of one who has made a long journey." The trapper conceives a plan for capturing this man of the hills. Procuring a prostitute from the city, "a harlot and wanton from the temple of love," he places her beside the stream from which Enkidu usually drinks and instructs her: "When he comes near, uncover yourself and lie with him: teach him, the savage man, your woman's art. For when he murmurs love to you the wild beasts that shared his life in the hills will reject him." The prostitute erases Enkidu's former identity in six days and seven nights, alienating him from his former companions who run from him. This joining of opposites, of wildman and woman of the city, reduces Enkidu's characteristic strength and deprives him of his animal agility. After seeking his former friends, he returns to the prostitute who tells him of his destiny; clothes, bathes, and feeds him; teaches him, guides him. She makes him human by offering him the characteristic goods of civilization, saying, "Enkidu, eat bread, it is the staff of life; drink the wine, it is the custom of the land." Enkidu eats and drinks and his transition is complete: "Enkidu had become a man."[10]

He conceives of his entry into the city in a way characteristic of his time and place—as a military campaign. Standing before the city walls, he challenges to battle the chief representative of the civic order, Gilgamesh, identifies himself, and asserts his intention of changing the "old order." But in the ensuing wrestling match, Enkidu is defeated, once more transformed by the order into which he is inducted: he becomes a client of the king he intended to replace. His transformation into a servant of the civic order is completed when Gilgamesh's mother adopts him into the temple of love over

which she reigns as priestess and from which was taken the prostitute, his initial guide, teacher, and inductress into the precincts of
civilization.

The battle of entry, here as in the arrival of Ywain, is an act that
asserts a boundary and determines the relation of this stranger to
the place he enters. The act of violence is often, in history, a
boundary-marking act that decrees the distinction between "us" and
"them" as the line that one may not cross without the permission of
the bounded ethnicity. Even when boundaries are symbolized and
sacralized, marked with stones and walls, emblazoned with the sig-
natures of sovereignty, the experiential origins of the boundary in
acts of violence are evident and may be traced. This was clear to the
ancients and explicit in the inscriptions on the pillars set up by
Ursurtasen III (twelfth dynasty) to mark the southernmost boundaries of Egypt, inscriptions that called upon his sons and their sons
to defend these boundaries, sacralized with the blood of thousands
of soldiers expended in the great king's conquests: "But if he aban-
dons it, so that he does not fight upon it, he is not my son, he is not
then born of me. I have caused my own image to be set up, on this
boundary which I have fixed, not only that ye may worship it . . . but
that ye may fight upon it."[11] The act that establishes boundaries is
committed again and again in the history of travels, perhaps nowhere more clearly than in the landing of the Portuguese navigator
Pedro Fernandez de Quiros on the island of Espirito Sancto four
hundred years ago, when he was confronted by a body of armed
natives: "The native king, making a line along the ground with his
bow, said that no one was to pass beyond it. Louis Vaez [a gentleman-
at-arms], considering that it would be cowardly not to do so, crossed
the line."[12] A shower of arrows immediately followed, to which the
Spanish replied with a volley of arquebus fire, establishing relations
of war between hosts and guests. The Spanish had to leave this island
upon which they had planned to found a colony.

The historical roots, and the meaning of the threshold, were
evident to Marco Polo when he entered the throne room of Kublai
Khan and found two gigantic men armed with staves on either side
of the doorway, ready to punish those who stepped on rather than
over the threshold: "They think, in fact, that it brings bad luck if
anyone touches the threshold. They strip the offender of his clothes
and he must either pay a fine or suffer a number of blows with the

staves."[13]* It is clear, or was to those who lived before the age of industrialized and atomic warfare, that violence is an instrument of sociation rather than dissociation, that it establishes rather than severs relations between distinct ethnic entities, that it resolves dualities and oppositions just as it asserts them.

The anthropologist Franz Boas saw how, in the rite of entry practiced by the Central Eskimo tribes, the contained and framed act of violence can forge relations where none had existed before:

> If a stranger unknown to the inhabitants of a settlement arrives on a visit he is welcomed by the celebration of a great feast. Among the south-Eastern tribes the natives arrange themselves in a row, one man standing in front of it. The stranger approaches slowly, his arms folded and his head inclined to the right side, then the native strikes him with all his strength on the right cheek and in turn inclines his head awaiting the stranger's blow.... Thus they continue until one of the contestants is vanquished.[15]

According to natives, the meaning of this duel is that "two men in meeting wish to know which of them is the better man." The duel establishes relations of dominance and subordination, normally translated into host/guest. In his discussion of this rite, the anthropologist Julian Pitt-Rivers ingeniously explains how this transformation is accomplished: the right of the victor to the life of the defeated exists to be waived, establishing subsequent relations as those between one who owes his life to another: "This fact would surely find some social recognition in a kind of bond; when one has fought for one's life against someone, lost and been spared, one can hardly resume the relationship of mere acquaintances."[16] If the stranger wins the duel, the community is honored by the visit of a man who is clearly superior to the local champion. If he loses, he becomes "some kind of client to the man who conquered him," who in turn becomes the patron and the host. In either eventuality, the

---

*In this context it is difficult to sustain H. Clay Trumbull's thesis that the frequent use of blood, dismemberment, sacrifice, in the marking of thresholds in traditional circumstances is due to the inherent sacrality of blood. Rather it would appear that blood becomes sacred because it is so often used to mark boundaries. That which sacralizes, that is, "sets apart," is often itself deemed sacred. This does not explain, however, the puzzling frequency with which one finds sacrifice and dismemberment rituals in the myths of arrival—from the killing and dismemberment of Osiris upon his return from his civilizing journey, to the frequent occurrence of fears of cannibalism in early modern travel reports.[14]

battle establishes the status of the stranger and his relation to the community. This is certainly the case for Enkidu, who becomes client and servant of the king who defeats him; and for Ywain, who through his victory and wooing becomes lord of the territory he enters.

Athletic contests, a common feature of ancient rites greeting significant strangers, may be seen as a framing and containment of the battle of entry which, when institutionalized in periodic games, continued to serve as a mechanism of linkage between separate cities. The real and ritualized battle is the initial term of the history of hospitality, and occasionally appears in modern arrivals as well. The first encounter of a teenaged Serbian immigrant with the New World in the first decade of the twentieth century repeats the most ancient forms of arrival and identification. As soon as he had set foot on the docks of New York, he was surrounded by a crowd of newsboys and bootblacks who jeered at the red fez the foreigner was wearing:

> Presently one of the bigger fellows walked up to me and knocked the fez off my head. I punched him on the nose and we clinched. My wrestling experiences on the pasturelands of Ilvas came to my rescue. The bully was down in a jiffy and his chums gave a loud cheer of ringing laughter. I thought it was the signal for a general attack, but they did not touch me or interfere in any way. They acted like impartial spectators anxious to see that the best man won. Suddenly I felt a powerful hand pulling me up by the collar, and when I looked up I saw a big official with a club in his hand and a fierce expression in his eye. He looked decidedly unfriendly, and after listening to the appeals of the newsboys and bootblacks who witnessed the fight he softened and handed me my fez. The boys who a little while before had jeered and tried to guy me evidently appealed in my behalf when the policeman interfered. They had actually become my friends. When I walked away toward the Castle Garden, with my red fez proudly cocked on my head, the boys cheered. I thought to myself that the unpleasant incident was worth my while, because it taught me that I was in a country where even among the street urchins there was a strong sentiment in favor of fair play, even to a Serbian Greenhorn.[17]

This ritual battle is not only an induction of a stranger but also a means by which that stranger learns the "moral" order of the place he is entering. Here, as in Boas's description of the ritual welcoming battles of the Central Eskimo and in Enkidu's battle with Gilgamesh, violence is a clearly a language—the first language—in which boundaries are marked and crossed.

THE ORDEALS OF CIVILITY

When I came, General . . . , you lined the walls and filled the gates with thousands of arms and shields, masses of pennants fluttered. Gongs and drums rumbled. . . . I am a stranger, we have not been acquainted a day. Yet you have shown me your might, treated me generously, and taken leave of me kindly.

—Ch'oe Pu, 1492

In the history of travel the blood of animals spilled in ceremonies of arrival substitutes for the blood of men shed in battles of entry; identifications, examinations, an exchange of documents, interrogations replace the simple options of battle. As successive generations of arrivals knit the bonds between peoples the instruments of violence become symbols of a preponderance of strength whose display honors the guest rather than challenging him to battle. When Ch'oe Pu, a fifteenth-century Korean official cast away on the coast of China, left a city on the road to Peking, he thanked the governing general for honoring him with a display of power.

Of course by this time Ch'oe Pu's status and identity had already been established in a series of rigorous examinations and exchanges. Upon his arrival on the Chinese coast, he had been identified as a pirate and scourged by the villagers. Not until he was brought to Ning Po was he able to establish his real identity before a panel of prefects, who instructed him as follows: "If you are Korean, write and bring to us a statement of the historical periods of your country, its changes of rule, the capital cities, the geography, the people, the customs, sacrifices, rules for mourning, population, military system, land tax and style of dress. We shall compare it with the histories and find out what is and what is not so."[18] This not-so-simple request assumes much: it is a definition of civility. It assumes literacy and mastery not just of letters but also of a history, a literature, a domain of knowledge covering the extent of Chinese civilization.

Successfully complying with the prefect's request furthered Ch'oe Pu's arrival into ordered space but did not end it. He was given food

to distribute to his secondary officials and soldiers, and passage to
Hang Chow was arranged. There he was again questioned, this time
by the Grand Defending Overseer and the Three Resplendent Authorities, who asked him about the civil service examinations used
in Korea, and tested his knowledge of the classics. In Peking he performed brilliantly, writing a quatrain on the subject of the shadow
of a Japanese pagoda and an eight-line poem in the Tang style on
the subject of "crossing the sea," quoting an appropriate passage
from Chang Ning's "On Leaving the Golden Pavilion."

> Light plays on the boat
> With the Haw-finch prow.
> As I look into the distance—
> Do I see the end of the world?
> I am airborne;
> The earth floats under me.[19]

Ch'oe Pu's entry into the center of the world from its periphery,
from the point at which "water and sky meet in endless space," was
a process not just of official but also of unofficial examinations that
tested his mastery of the idioms of status, those criteria by which a
person's relative value is measured within the precincts of civilization. In Chien T'iao he got involved in a bragging match with a local
official who claimed that he was on the civil service examination list
for 1486, received a public stipend of rice sufficient for a large
household, and had a banner-gate (an entry gate bearing the name
of the owner of a residence) of two stories. Ch'oe Pu retorted that
he had been placed on the Korean list twice, once receiving second,
received a much larger stipend of rice, and had a banner-gate of
three stories. The official knelt at Ch'oe Pu's feet and said, "I am not
at all your equal."

But the tests and examinations that replace the trials of battle
in the procedures of arrival may be of considerable subtlety, tests of
civility, of consciousness of the rules governing exchanges and incorporations. Ch'oe Pu revealed a knowledge of the rules of exchange that surpasses an ordinary understanding when he refused a
man's gift of a book and request for a poem. When a friend chided
him that even Confucius accepted something in such circumstances,
he replied: "That man did not want to give away the book, his mind
was on getting the poem. Thus the exchange would not have ac-

corded with the Way, and the meeting would not have accorded with etiquette. Once I accepted it would have been receiving payment for a poem I had sold. That is why I refused him."[20] The implication of "trade" would have reduced the status of a member of the ruling class, whose material relations to others were supposed to be of unilateral rather than reciprocal exchange, of gift rather than barter. The journey that began with the accident of a storm won Ch'oe Pu considerable fame and elevation of status upon his return home, but in some sense this status had been "achieved" in successive examinations on his journey into the core of civility.

THE ATTRIBUTION OF DIVINITY

Gods often take upon themselves the likeness of strangers from far countries; they assume this shape and that, wander about our towns and observe both outrage and righteous dealing among mankind.

—Homer, the *Odyssey*

The procedures of identification might be more adequately portrayed as a presentation of a series of options and choices rather than a laying on of images. The first option presented to arriving strangers is that of "friend" or "enemy," potential help or potential harm. While listing the taboos on intercourse with strangers, the pioneering student of myth James G. Frazer noted that these were "an elementary dictate of savage prudence,"[21] which dictated those techniques of "silent trade" which the anthropologist P. J. Hamilton-Grierson exhaustively itemizes in his classic work on the origins of hospitality and trade.[22] The stranger was an enemy until proven otherwise. As the old English proverb states, "The stranger, if not a trader, is an enemy." The option here is the same one presented to arriving strangers in the *Odyssey* in the form of a question: "Are you bound on some trading errand, or are you random adventurers roving the seas as pirates do, hazarding life and limb and bringing havoc on men of another stock?"[23] By an unauthorized passage over the precincts of place, the option of enmity is actualized.

Another primal option is often presented to strangers, particularly novel species of strangers, in premodern arrivals: God-Man. The Greeks justified the extension of hospitality to strangers, even

beggars, by this formula: the stranger could be a god or the messenger of a god. As the epigraph above implies, much of the power of
the stranger derives from his communicational function, from the
fact that he is a witness who will leave and carry the news of this
place with him, establishing its reputation and collective honor in
relationship to other communities. But the godlike power of the
stranger often proceeds from whence he comes, from the fact that
he arrives from the outside world, the world upon which seated societies project all that is impossible within their domestic arrangements. The stranger is thus a creature of fantasy who may resolve
repressions, alleviate the boredom inherent in the familiar, and represent wonders and powers unknown to those whose horizons are
set by the boundaries of place. The attribution of godhood to the
stranger is logical, flexible, and prudent, absorbing the stranger into
existing relationships, ceremonies, and practices designed to structure relations between a place and those forces external to it.

These projections almost invariably lead to elevated expectations of the stranger which he, as a mere man, cannot help but
disappoint. W. B. Grubb, a merchant traveler and the first white man
to dwell among the Lenguas of the Grand Chaco, was a beneficiary
of these attributions of power to the stranger:

> The most marvellous powers have been attributed to me . . . I have
> been supposed to be able to hypnotize men and animals, to bring
> up the storms and the south-winds at will, to drive off sickness when
> I feel so inclined. . . . They believed that I had the power of the evil
> eye, and knowledge of the future, that I was able to discover all
> secrets and to know the movements of people in different parts of
> the country . . . to drive off the game, and to speak with the dead.[24]

Alfred Russel Wallace, collecting zoological specimens in the primitive Aru Islands, was regarded by the natives as having similar powers: "They already believe that all the animals I preserve will come
alive again; and to their children it will be related that they actually
did so. An unusual spell of fine weather setting in just at my arrival
has made them believe I control the seasons. . . . every confession of
ignorance on my part is thought to be a blind, a mere excuse to
avoid telling them too much."[25] Such expectations of the stranger
result from a presumption, and from evidence, of his difference vis-

à-vis the natives. Lord MacCartney, the first ambassador sent by England to the Emperor of China, in 1793 to 1794, noted that the Tientsin *Gazette* reported that the gifts brought by the English included several dwarfs not over twelve inches high, an elephant smaller than a cat, a hen the size of a mouse, a singing bird as big as a hen that ate fifty pounds of charcoal a day, and "an enchanted pillow, on which whoever lays his head immediately falls asleep, and if he dreams of any distant place ... is instantly transported thither without the fatigue of travelling."[26] Here the stranger embodies fictions, expectations, impossibilities, which derive their energies from the constraints and limits of rootedness in place. If the power of place derives in large part from the imagination of the passenger, the power of the stranger is, in large part, a projection of place, and a consequence of the repressions, delineations, and rules necessary in its creation.

Such projections of divinity upon the stranger are initial designations and by no means final. Of necessity, the progressive identification of the stranger-god is often a disillusionment. A Reverend Moffat, a nineteenth-century missionary in South Africa, was assigned an arid spot for his mission by native authorities who believed he would make it verdant by his power over the weather. When he complained to the local chief, explaining that only God could make the rain and that he was not God, the chief did not believe him: "Why do you talk to me about God? You yourselves are God: do give us rain."[27]

In polytheistic cultures, the category *god* is almost infinitely expandable. Which god, spirit, or devil the stranger embodies is often a matter of his own behavior or accident. When Christian missionaries first landed, in the 1880s, in the Banks Islands, New Hebrides, they were regarded as spirits, but exactly which spirits was unclear until this was resolved by the strangers themselves:

> When Mr. Patterson first landed at Mota, the mission party having seen the previous year at Vauna Lava, there was a division of opinion among the natives; some said that the brothers of Jat had returned, certain supernatural beings of whom stories are told; others maintained that they were ghosts. Mr. Patterson retired from the heat into an empty house, the owner of which had lately died; this settled the question, he was the ghost of the late householder and knew his home.[28]

One may imagine that had Mr. Patterson arrived, for example, in the cool of the evening, he would have borne a different set of attributes. This arrival, projected beyond his initial identification, would also introduce some changes within the host culture, requiring a new category of otherness, that of "white man." Captain Cook was initially a beneficiary of the accident that his arrival in Hawaii coincided with the feast of the native god, Lomo, whose identity he was assigned, establishing appropriate relations between strangers and hosts. But the fact that Captain Cook's men ate with women, thereby violating a fundamental taboo, raised doubts in the minds of the natives; and Cook's unscheduled return to the island to repair a broken rudder was not in the ritual script. He was killed—not the first god to suffer this fate.

Many travelers have not been reluctant to make use of the attribution of divinity. Since gods and spirits are assumed to be immortal, the Spanish, on first arriving in Mexico, were careful to preserve this character, burying their casualties of the Tlascalan campaign in underground corn cribs "so that they [the Indians] should not see we were mortal but believe that we were indeed *teules* [gods or devils] as they called us."[29] Hernando de Alarcons, the first explorer of the Colorado River and a man much more adept than many of his compatriots at establishing friendly relations with the natives, was careful to find out the names of their gods: "Through signs I learned that what those natives worshipped and revered most was the sun. I leave them to understand that I come from the sun, at which they were very amazed. They stared at me from head to foot, and showed me greater respect than before." Here Alarcons casts himself in an identity that the natives projected on the outside world and on strangers coming from that world. This role was to govern his subsequent relations with these natives, who often came to him seeking advice and complaining of their "past and present troubles and their good or bad disposition toward one another." Alarcons was able to persist and function in this role, whereas many other Spanish *teules* were quickly revealed to be mere men and predators. When some Indians wanted to kill Alarcons, an old chief defended him: "This one is a son of the sun, and our lord. He is doing good; he will not enter our houses even when we ask him; he does not take anything away from us; he does not seek our women."[30] Alarcons remained a god because he was a good guest, respecting the boundaries of the place, bringing something more than he extracted, and, above all, refraining from unauthorized contact with the native women.

Identifying the stranger with a god is a way of making him known and familiar. The god is not an utter stranger, but a being whose relationship to the community is fixed and established through ritual, drama, prayer, and ceremony. The stranger who fits into these relationships may benefit from the sacred economy, as Cook's men did from the offerings of the Hawaiians: "They gave him [Cook] pigs, taro, tapa and all kinds of things the way these are given to the gods; they bargained not."[31] Gods are familiars in premodern cultures, and their treatment may differ considerably from our notions of hospitality. They may be killed and eaten so that their power is retained within the domestic order. They may be enshrined and presented to the populace as a representation of the power of authorities.

Gregory Bateson tells the story he got from Doctor Stutterheim, an archeologist in Java, of an event that took place before the arrival of Europeans. After a storm on the Javanese coast near one of the capitals, the people found washed up on the beach a large white monkey, half alive and of an unknown species. The religious experts identified him as a member of the court of Beroena, the sea god, and speculated that he had been cast out for some transgression. The raja ordered that the monkey be kept alive and chained to a stone in the marketplace, where for years he entertained locals who fed and cared for him. When the Europeans arrived they were shown this stone, upon which was scratched, in Latin, Dutch, and English, the name of a sailor and the story of his shipwreck. By this time the "white monkey" had become a stock character in Javanese puppet plays.[32]

THE WAITING PERIOD

In approaching the house of a stranger, it is usual to follow several little points of etiquette: riding up slowly to the door the salutation of the Ave Maria is given, and until somebody comes out and asks you to alight, it is not customary to get off your horse.

—Charles Darwin, 1839

Since the further specification of these universal categories of otherness depends much upon the behavior and appearances of potential guests, their power and address, it is difficult to regard the procedures of arrival as a ritual laying on of identities. The arriving stranger is presented with options—friend/enemy, god/man, pollutant/power—which he activates through his own behaviors and choices. The alternative to enmity—guestship—is first actualized by the potential guest's halting and waiting outside the boundaries of place, those boundaries that are mobilized by the arrival. Anthropologist Arnold van Gennep gives an excellent description of the procedures of identification in premodern circumstances:

> The actions which follow an arrival of strangers in large numbers tends to reinforce local social cohesion: the inhabitants all leave the village and take refuge in a well-protected place such as a hill or a forest; or they close their doors, arm themselves and send out signals for a gathering . . . ; or the chief, alone or with his warriors, goes before the strangers as a representative of his society, . . . foreigners cannot immediately enter the territory of the tribe or the village; they must prove their intentions from afar and undergo a stage best known in the form of the tedious African palaver. This preliminary stage, whose duration varies, is followed by a transitional period consisting in such events as an exchange of gifts, an offer of food by the inhabitants, or the provision of lodging. The ceremonies terminate in rites of incorporation—a formal entrance, a meal in common, an exchange of handclasps.[33]

The period of waiting outside the borders to be crossed is an essential indication of peaceful or hostile intent. This is followed by an exchange of words, interrogations, tests that more firmly fix the character and potentials of the guests.

The waiting period is almost universally recognized as a necessary preliminary to the status of guestship. It is this period that allows for initial identifications, normally based upon the appearance and manner of transport used by the guest. It may be extended into a period of quarantine, during which the guest may be purged of the pollutions and dangers he bears by virtue of having passed through distinct domains. This is a period of recognitions, and it may be waived to honor a guest whose status is already known, as Darwin observed of the rules of travel across the pampas of Argentina.

More than mere etiquette, the waiting period gives the possessor of the ground an occasion to examine the guest, to judge his appearance, and to decide whether he represents a danger or an opportunity, whether to greet, how to greet. This presentation of self to the mercy of the place is a prerequisite to the nonviolent forms of arrival, and precedes the granting of guest status along with its privileges. An aboriginal messenger in Australia was normally given a passport (a "bullroarer") to identify him, but was still required to observe a waiting period before entering the camp to which he was bringing a message:

> On approaching a camp he sits down waiting until the local men choose to take notice of him, which may not be until after an hour or so. They all go on meanwhile quite unconcernedly, as if he did not exist, and then one or two of the older men will go over to him; he will show them his credentials and deliver his message, after which he is brought into the camp, made free of the special men's camp and provided with food.[34]

THE TRAVELER'S TALE

Tell me and answer truly. Who are you? Where are your city and your parents? What kind of ship did you travel by . . . ? How did the sailors bring you here, and what name did they give themselves? These are all things I long to know.

Wandering men tell lies for a night's lodging, for fresh clothing; truth does not interest them.

—Homer, the *Odyssey*

If the visitor begins his knowledge of a place from its appearance, so too the place judges the stranger according to his appearance: his equipage; the manner of his coming; whether he has followers, those symbols of rank and actualities of power. The stranger who comes alone and on foot, unless he belongs to a special category (among the Mandingo of West Africa and very many ancient societies, orators, seers, minstrels, and blacksmiths were accorded rights of free passage even in time of war), is often treated with contempt and installed in the lower positions within the social order. Charles Moritz, a young eighteenth-century German clergyman who decided to tour England on foot, often had cause to repent this decision. He was viewed with suspicion, refused accommodations at inns that had room, and often shown to the kitchen or told to use the back door.

By a change of linen, he could become a gentleman once more and remain one so long as it stayed clean. Moritz clearly understood the source of his loss of status when he was refused a room in an empty inn by an innkeeper, who grudgingly allowed him to sleep beside a stove at the kitchen table:

> When the people in the kitchen thought that I was asleep, I heard them talking about me, and guessing who or what, I might be. One woman alone seemed to take my part, and said, "I dare say, he is a well-bred gentleman"; another scanted that notion, merely, as she said because I had come on foot; and "depend on it" said she "he is some poor travelling creature!" My ears yet ring with the contemptuous tone. . . . It seems to express all the wretchedness of one who neither has house, nor home; a vagabond, and an outcast of society.[35]

The modern means of establishing the identity of the guest is the interrogation, the "examination," which assumes a variety of forms. Words and documents substitute for more forceful transitions across boundaries.

The etiquette of interviewing the stranger varies from culture to culture and over time. Among the ancient Greeks, themselves a traveling and trading people, it was customary to reserve the questioning until the physical needs of the stranger had been met, until he had been bathed, fed, rested. Often, the questioning raised delicate questions of etiquette. When Telemachus goes into the Peloponnesus to gain news of his errant father, his host, Menelaus, wonders whether "he ought to leave him to utter his father's name or if he himself should question him and put all his answers to the test"[36]—a quandary resolved with Helen's recognition in Telemachus of the image of his father, Odysseus.

Darwin noted the different rules governing interrogations of strangers that operated in the Argentine, and contrasted them with the norms among the settlers in South Africa:

> The difference, however, between the character of the Spaniard and that of the Dutch Boor is shown by the former never asking his guest a single question beyond the strictest rules of politeness, while the honest Dutchman demands where he has been, where he is going, what is his business, and even how many brothers, sisters, or children he may happen to have.[37]

The degree of interrogation depends upon the extent of the danger posed by the stranger, upon the isolation and hunger for news of the place, and upon the norms that govern the satisfaction of local curiosity. The reticence or loquaciousness of the stranger is often an indication of credibility, and the stranger is in many instances not believed to the extent that he offers more than is asked of him. It was an old rule among Nordic peoples that to ask a stranger's name was an insult. A man was expected to offer it freely, whereupon the other, if he chose, could offer his. Thus, when Mykjartan, a king in Ireland, asks the recently arrived Olaf the Peacock about his background, Olaf's reticence is an indication of his pride, self-confidence, and dignity.

> Then the king asked him the news and Olaf dealt skillfully with all his questions. Then the king asked where they had sailed from and whose men they were; and after that he questioned Olaf more closely about his lineage than he had done before, for he realized that this man was proud and would not answer more than he was asked.[38]

Not surprisingly in countries where there are many travelers, and particularly in nomadic and traveling societies, the etiquette of questioning and answering is particularly delicate. Sociologist Nels Anderson, in his pioneering study of hoboes, notes that among homeless men there is a taboo on personal questions, except in the case of the very young, the sick, or the very old: "They live closed lives and grant others the same privilege."[39] Firmly rooted and implanted places, on the other hand, construct elaborate and detailed interrogations of strangers, interrogations such as those which inducted Ch'oe Pu into China and that differed little from ordeals.

The importance of the exchange of words, the examination and interrogation of travelers, goes far beyond matters of security and the necessity of making the unknown known, of removing the dangers associated with the stranger and mobilizing his powers and possessions for use by the place. Travelers—particularly before the modern era of print and electronic media—were a primary source of news and information about the outer world, and journalism begins in the journeys and journals of seventeenth-century travelers. The traveler, too, was a source of entertainment, of novelties, of comic relief, as well as of new conceits and designs. Certain species of travelers—singers of tales, bards (called *griots* in Africa), minstrels, comic actors, mountebanks—specialized in these functions and were welcome and honored guests. Among the Mandingo of West Africa, as among the ancient Greeks and Celts, bards were assumed to be protected by the gods and enjoyed rights of free passage through territory, even in times of war. But the ambiguities inherent in the stranger, present in his designation as god or enemy, extend also to his words, which are demanded of him but not necessarily believed: "The essence of the stranger is ... that he is unknown. He remains potentially anything: valiant or worthless, well-born, well-connected, wealthy or the contrary, and since his assertions regarding himself cannot be checked he is above all not to be trusted."[40]

The stranger may lie, represent himself as something he is not, re-create his identity in the uncertainty of arrival. Travelers have long had the reputation of fabulists, "bullshitters," fictionalizers. In the ambivalence that attends the traveler's tale may lie the origin of the *fiction*—a story or an image that, assumed to be neither true nor false, functions in a climate of suspended belief. In the *Odyssey*, the swineherd Eumaeus welcomes his lord Odysseus, disguised as a beggar, with the usual interrogations. Odysseus takes this opportunity to create a fictional persona and to make up adventures. But Eumaeus, once a captive and a traveler himself, and knowing that "wandering men tell lies for a night's lodging," *expects* him to lie. The ambiguity of the traveler's status, his "truth," creates a role and a function, reporting on a world that is assumed to contain all those strange and marvelous things excluded by a domestic reality that creates order through the repression of anomalies. The stranger is expected to be an anomaly, and to tell of those impossibilities that define an outer world.

Indeed, this becomes a convention within traditional travel literature: "[A]ny traveler's tale that claims to be a faithful report must contain a category of *Thoma* (marvels and curiosities)."[41] Travel literature long fulfilled the function of specifying alternative worlds, their reality at best problematical to those whose view of the world was limited by walls and channeled through gates. Seventeenth- and eighteenth-century travel writers were much disturbed by the traditional role of travelers as fictionalizers of the world and took great pains to establish a narrative style of description, which we have come to know as nonfiction—a narrative of truths, observations, and facts. Many modern travelers, though, were resigned to not being believed: "I shall not marvel if they that read this history will not believe my report of them; especially such as have not travelled, for they that have seen little believe not much, whereas they that have seen much believe the more."[42]

The characteristic double-bind of the traveler whose truths are uttered in a climate of nonbelief was particularly excruciating to modern travelers. They often found themselves accused of being dull and unentertaining when they told the truth about the world. Each novelty they offered, while entertaining the homebound, reinforced their reputation as liars. Lady Mary Wortley Montagu delighted in the activity of exposing the errors and fictions of (male) travel writers: "I am more inclined, out of a true female spirit of contradiction, to tell you the falsehood of a greater part of what you find in authors."[43] And yet she found herself in exactly the same position as male travel writers:

> We travellers are in very hard circumstances: if we say nothing but what has been said before us, we are dull, and we have observed nothing. If we tell anything new, we are laughed at as fabulous and romantic, not allowing either for the difference of ranks which affords difference of company, or mere curiosity, or the change of customs that happens every twenty years in every country. . . . For my part, if I live to return amongst you, I am so well acquainted with the morals of all my dear friends and acquaintances that I am resolved to tell them nothing at all, to avoid the imputation . . . of telling too much.[44]

Of course, Montagu was not silent, having put so much of her observations into letters to her friends. It is through her efforts and those of travel writers of the seventeenth and eighteenth centuries that the canons of nonfiction were formed, and that travel began to be regarded as a means of gaining access to the "truth" rather than as stories of an invented world.

The identifications of arrival are something more than a culture's imposition of templates on living, sentient matter. They are recognitions, the matching of image against the observed, out of which identities are actualized. The arrival has provided an opportunity for many travelers to become "someone else," to re-create identity, to assume disguises and personae that would be forbidden or impossible at home—all in the name of the necessity to "adapt" to foreign circumstances. François Pyrard, a seventeenth-century

French merchant marooned in the Maldive Islands, understood with many other generations of travelers that this adaptation to emplaced expectations was the condition of his well-being: "I became somewhat rich, according to the notions of the country, to which I conformed in every possible way, as well as to their habits and customs, so as to be better received among them."[45] Indeed, many travelers, such as James Boswell and Pietro Della Valle, have found a principal gratification of travel to lie in the possibilities of changing shape, transforming identity, trying on a variety of personae in performances before a variety of audiences. I will examine this re-creation with identity, the adaptations of persona, the shape-changing traveler, in chapter 10, for what it tells us about the nature of human sociation and the powers it generates.

Penelope with her women *(Courtesy of the Bettmann Archive)*

CHAPTER

4

SPACE AND GENDER: WOMEN'S MEDIATIONS

Masculine activity in general tends to be more mobile and to regularly engage a wider spatial domain than that of women; in particular, it is more directly associated with the sea and external domains of Gawan physical space. Thus according to one man, land ... is feminine ... because it stays in one place, whereas the canoe is masculine ... because it travels.

—Nancy Munn, 1986

In terminal arrivals—the arrival home, or anywhere that creates the ties between person and place we call "home"—the traveler forms what are in some sense permanent bonds, which presumably redefine the social and even the biological self and make the traveler a "native." François Pyrard, shipwrecked in the Maldive Islands in 1601, felt he had arrived when he survived the Maldive fever that attacks most recent arrivals and from which many of his shipmates died:

> [W]hen one gets over it one may feel sure he will recover from the other maladies to which the climate will subject him; for a man changes by habit with the climate and the manner of living, and this malady, as it were, makes him a new body, and he feels quite inured. And, indeed, if a stranger, whom in their language they call

111

pouradde ("voyage man") recovers from it, they say that he is *diues*, as we should say, naturalized and is no longer a stranger.[1]

Thus is the stranger and guest transformed into a native through transfers of substance—air, water, food, germs, even physical contacts—which make the passenger a new social body within the niche of a particular locale. These procedures of "incorporation" are processes of acclimatization, nativization, adaptation, which reveal something about the methods of human territorialization, the ways in which human groups establish fixed psychosomatic bonds to land, soil, and topography. These transfers of substance are the source of the "spell" Diodorus Siculus regarded as cast by "every country to which a man has grown accustomed."[2]

Alexander von Humboldt, upon leaving Teneriffe in the Canary Islands in 1799 after only a two-week stay, marveled at the power of tropical nature ("so rich, so various, and so majestic") to create a feeling of coherence, of home: "we withdrew from the island as if it had been our home."[3] The procedures of incorporation obviously require the traveler to spend a longer period of time in a place than would the typical visitor, tourist, or guest. This time varies, depending on locale. It has been set at two nights and the day between in Arabia (the period of time the host's food is assumed to remain in the guest's body), old Germany, Morocco, and Senegal. In ancient Ireland, Russia, and among the Anglo-Saxons, the period was three days and two nights—a time fixed in the Southern Slav saying, "A guest and a fish smell on the third day," and even more pertinently in the Anglo-Saxon proverb, "Two nights a guest, the third night one of the household" (meaning a servant).[4]

A thorough exploration of the procedures of incorporation—the exchange of gifts, food, substances, recognitions—would require many volumes and amount to a history of how human groups absorb strangers and form lasting bonds to territory and to other groups. Therefore I limit myself here to a consideration of the agency of women in these procedures, a subject that assumes an unexpected prominence in the history of travel. I have already touched on the central part of women in the arrivals of Enkidu, Ywain, and generations of powerful strangers, founders of ruling lineages and states. Indeed, anthropologists have long known and studied how, in all traditional societies, relations among men are mediated through women and through the exchange of women. Lévi-Strauss takes it as a universal fact: "the relationship of reciprocity which is at the basis of marriage is not established between men and women, but between men by means of women, who are merely the occasion of this relationship"—or, rather, the "medium" of this relationship that bonds men.[5] The agency of women may be found throughout the history of arrivals and almost-arrivals, and yet this history shows not a fixed and pre-established set of relations so much as a range of options and contingencies channeled through certain historical assumptions about the mobility of men and the rootedness of women.

THE EROTICS OF ARRIVAL

She told me the way to Minehead—not the shortest but the prettiest way, she said. She had light hair and dark eyes. I said her house was beautiful. She said it was a guest house; then she laughed. "Why don't you stay tonight?" She meant it and seemed eager, and then I was not sure what she was offering. I stood there and smiled back at her.... It was not even one o'clock and I had never stopped at a place this early in the day.
I said, "Maybe I'll come back some time."
"I'll still be here," she said.

—Paul Theroux, *The Kingdom by the Sea,* 1983

The erotics of arrival are predicated on certain realities in the history of travel: the sessility of women; the mobility of men; the uncertainty and contingency of the relations formed between them in arrival; uncertainty about what is being "offered," what gained, and what lost in the incorporations of a new member.

In the conditions of settlement and civility, travel is "genderized" and becomes a "gendering" activity, underlining a difference between men and women. Historically, men have traveled and women have not, or have traveled only under the aegis of men, an arrangement that has defined the sexual relations in arrivals as the absorption of the stranger—often young, often male—within a nativizing female ground. Pyrard noted that a vast number of the Portuguese colonists peopling the new empire were young men sent out as soldiers "to the Indies in exile for their misdeeds," who could not return before their sentence was expired. "Most of them marry and remain there all their lives."[6] Even noble native families would not be disgraced by giving their daughters to a soldier; in the colonies, that title was most honorable. Gonzalo Guerro, a Spanish sailor from Palos cast away on the Yucatán coast in the first decade of the sixteenth century, explained to a comrade who came to bring him back to civilization why he could not return, could not undo the procedures of his arrival: "Brother Aguilar, I am married and have three children, and they look on me as a Cacique [chief] here, and a captain in time of war. Go, and God's blessing be with you. But my face is tattooed and my ears are pierced. What would the Spaniards say if they saw me like this? And look how handsome these children of mine are!"[7] These terms of arrival are frequent enough in civilized travel to make it likely that much travel is stimulated by a male reproductive motive, a search for temporal extensions of self in children, only achievable through the agency of women. This spermatic journey has its classical form in the myths of the traveling gods, heroes, and patriarchs.

With the genderization of travel characteristic of civilities and settlement, travel assumes a particular "sexual economy." In departing on a kula-trading expedition (in the prestige trade of the Trobriand Islands), the commodore's customary last words to those on shore state this economy most succinctly: "Women, we others sail; you remain in the village and look after the gardens and the houses; you must keep chaste."[8] A married woman's inchastity would cause her husband's canoe to be slow and heavy, contributing to his failure in the kula trade and causing recriminations upon his return.

Fynes Moryson, a habitual traveler of the seventeenth century, enunciated the consensus of patriarchal civility when he suggested that travel is especially inappropriate for virtuous women, and masculinizing for the female traders of the Netherlands: "First, women for suspition of chastity are most unfit for this course, howsoever the masculine women of the Low Countries use to make Voyages for traffike."[9] With its inherent promiscuities, travel serves the spermatic journey: it broadcasts male seed that founds lineages, and, by extension, the walls, paths, precincts, and boundaries that contain women and control the access of other men to women. Penelope's chastity in refusing her suitors is the condition of Odysseus' ultimate arrival, for it preserves the relations that define the home within which is rooted Odysseus' identity as king, husband, father, son.

This repeated act of excluding other men was by no means normal, even in the world of Odysseus. The *Odyssey* was originally part of a larger, lost epic cycle called *Nostoi* ["Returns"] which described the homecomings of the heroes of the Trojan campaign: Agamemnon, who was killed by his wife, Clytemnestra, and her lover, Aegisthus; Diomedes who reached his home in Argos, but found that his wife had taken a lover (he subsequently wandered the Mediterranean and founded several cities in Italy); and Idomeneus, whose wife had also committed adultery but who was killed by her lover, who made himself king of Crete. One need not wonder for long why the *Odyssey* rather than the record of other returns comes down to us, for in this work we find a successful, rather than failed, arrival and thus a completed and terminated, rather than an endless, journey.

In contrast to the virtue of Penelope, that of Odysseus lies in the fact that he does not forget his home, even while captive to Calypso and to Circe:

> There was a time when divine Calypso kept me within her arching caverns and would have had me to be her husband, and another time when subtle Aegean Circe confined me in her palace and would have had me for her husband also. Yet neither of them could win the heart within me: so true is it that nothing is sweeter to a man than his own country and his own parents, even though he were given a sumptuous dwelling-place elsewhere, in a strange land.[10]

The "double standard" constructs the spatial domains of interiority (female) and exteriority (male) as domains of, respectively, sexual constraint and sexual freedom. The chastity of women is a technique of inclusion and exclusion, which decrees memberships, rights, and relations between males as well as sanctifying the male line of descent.

Women's identification with place in conditions of settlement has been regarded as "natural," a result of reproductive necessities that require stability and protection by men: thus, the genderization of space. The anthropologist Nancy Munn finds this duality structured into Gawan culture, where, as in all the Trobriand Islands, trading and traveling are sources of masculine prestige and women are expected to stay home. In Gawa, women are associated with immobility, permanence, heaviness, soil, renewals of time, gardens, in-

teriors, bounded space, security, and lack of freedom. Men are associated with exteriors, unbounded space, danger and insecurity,
light things—sea and air—and abnegations of time in speed (which
Munn calls the "concentrated potency" of the male). In Gawa, wom-
en's travels are fantasy travels, the nightflights of witches, and are
feared as undercutting the established order, that collective honor
projected outward, wearing a masculine mask. This antithesis rests
in the persuasive analogy that male potencies are excorporative while
female potencies are incorporative, interiorizing, and hidden.[11]

The antithesis between the exteriorizations of men and the in-
teriorizations of women, the superfluity of the sperm and the par-
simony of the ovum, has been mapped upon human mobility and
come to be considered an element of human nature. But the immobilization of women is a historical achievement, repeated in successive generations, and one of the chief means (along with, for
example, the implantation of gods, spirits, human deeds in a place,
the architecturalization of space) by which human groups achieve
permanent relations to territory, relations that subsequently define
needs, passions, articulations of gender characteristics, visions of nature itself. It is this territorialization that makes travel a gendering
activity.

Among nomads women, men, and children travel together, and
the migratory path gives rise to the structure and cohesion of the
group. Similarly, in our own industrial civilization, travel is no
longer a purely masculinizing activity. But during a long and significant period of human history, a period of the growth of patriarchal
civilizations, travel was thought to demonstrate a particularly male
character, antithetical to a femininity rooted in place, in soil and gardens, in the very maternal qualities of the earth.

With the genderization of travel, the arrival is eroticized and
stimulates hopes and fears that appear to define the masculine psy-
che—hopes of integration and connectivity, fears of captivity and
retention. We may read the hopes in the possibilities awakened in
Paul Theroux's arrivals: "I was often warmed by a small thrill in
following the younger landladies up four flights to the tiny room at
the top of the house. We would enter, breathless from the climb, and
stand next to the bed somewhat flustered, until she remembered to
ask for the £5 in advance—but even that was ambiguous and erotic."[12]
The male fears awakened by female incorporations—of unfreedom,
captivity, retention, and absorption, are implicit in Ywain's accep-

tance (see chapter 3) of the terms in which Lady Laudine demands his surrender:

> *"She wants you to be her prisoner,*
> *She wishes to have your body*
> *For herself, not even your heart*
> *To be free."*
> *"Surely," he answered,*
> *"I agree, I've no objections.*
> *I want to be her prisoner."*
> *"And so you'll be, by this hand*
> *I lay on your shoulder!" . . . And so she led him off,*
> *Worrying him a bit . . . and giving him hints*
> *Of the prison he was going to.*
> *What lover escapes his prison?*
> *She was right, calling it a prison:*
> *Whoever's in love is no longer free.*[13]

SEXUAL HOSPITALITY AND PROSTITUTION

Prostitution—that is, sexual intercourse for hire—is not a primitive practice; it is a product of civilization. . . . Where bands of "harlots" were allotted to a temple their earnings probably went to swell the temple funds out of which they were supported. It may well be suggested that the hire was not an essential part of the rite, but merely an aftergrowth in the process of adapting an older custom to the changing manners and religious ideas of a growing civilization.

—E. Sidney Hartland, 1907

The incorporations of arrival may mean different things for those who negotiate their relations through sexual exchanges. If for the male stranger sexual hospitality may be the final terms of arrival, awakening the fear/hope of inclusion, for the woman active in these exchanges it may be the first act of a departure, an act of exogamy. In traditional settings, the woman who offers herself to a stranger is often using the only means of female mobility. Dowry-prostitution— practiced in Cyprus, on the island of Chios, among the Lydians, the Etruscans, the Natchez Indians of Louisiana, the Indians of Nicaragua and Guatemala, as well as in Japan—was a way for a woman to accumulate enough money to contract herself in marriage to whom she wished, thereby escaping the domination of kin. In Cyprus, dowry-prostitution was practiced by women of the lower classes with sailors on the seashore, risking exile if caught. Queen Dido, on her way to Carthage, shipped aboard eighty of these women to serve as brides for her colonists.

Female travel has traditionally been specifically "unfree," of the sort envisioned by Hector for his wife after his own demise:

> I see you there in Argos, toiling for some other woman at the loom, or carrying water from an alien well, a helpless drudge with no will of your own. "There goes the wife of Hector," they will say when they see your tears. "He was the champion of the horse-taming Trojans when Ilium was besieged." And every time they say it, you will feel another pang at the loss of the one man who might have kept you free.[14]

In territorialized societies, the woman is the embodiment and the content of "place," and her relations to an outside world, her very freedom, are conditional upon her relations to men.

The territorialization of human groups and the immobilization of women are part of a historical cycle that transforms the tenor of women's mediations between groups, though it does not create those mediations. In nomadic circumstances, the woman of the tribe may be used as an avenue of entry into place, as Sarah was by Abraham to acquire grazing rights in the land of Gerar, ruled by King Abimalech. This practice exploited the options of the endogamous, polygamous marriages characteristic of nomadic peoples, for Abraham claimed Sarah at once as wife and "sister" (though they were not of the same mother): "And when God caused me to wander from my father's house, I said to her, 'This is the kindness you must do me: at every place to which we come say of me, he is my brother.' "[15] Abraham offers Sarah to King Abimalech, saying "she is my sister," and Abimalech sleeps with her for a night during which, in a dream, it is revealed by God that Sarah is actually Abraham's wife and that, in coupling with her, he would sin against marriage and patriarchy. Whether or not this sin was committed (the text is ambiguous on this point), Abimalech grants Abraham rights to the land and, to Sarah, a purse of silver as well: "And Abimalech said, 'Behold, my land is before you; dwell where it pleases you.' And to Sarah he said, 'Behold, I have given your brother a thousand pieces of silver; it is your vindication in the eyes of all who are with you; and before everyone you are righted.' "[16]

The offering of money, which vindicates Sarah and removes any stain incurred in this transaction, would in modern circumstances imply instead prostitution and commercialized sexuality. Sarah is a medium and instrument of connectivity to possessed ground, through whom is established Abraham's relationship to Abimalech and his realm.

This sexual exchange, repeated by Abraham in Egypt and by subsequent generations of patriarchs, may be a mythic compression of the events that territorialize nomadic peoples. It is the woman who is mobile in these circumstances, and she may prefer her mobility to sessility. This, at least, is the implication of Sheikh Sidi Ahmed el Beshir Hammadi's answer to the modern travel writer Bruce Chatwin's question about the pleasures of nomadic existence, when he found the Sheik camped in the desert with his family: "Bah! I'd like nothing better than to live in a house in town. Here in the desert you can't keep clean, you can't take a shower! It is the women who make us live in the desert. They say the desert brings health and happiness, to them and to the children."[17] Such a preference is understandable: although sessility offers showers, this very cleanliness and order also secures the confinement and emplacement of women—their unfreedom.

In the conditions of settlement, the mediations of women acquire a variety of different meanings. Sexual hospitality, the loan of a woman, is a method of incorporating a stranger into a settled and emplaced group. It is institutionalized in the practice of prostitution, the history of which is one of arrivals and of civilization itself. Its basic form, as "ritual," is described by Arnold van Gennep:

> If the rite is unilateral, a woman is loaned (a wife, daughter, sister, relative, wife of the host, or woman of the same clan as the host). Although in some cases the purpose of the loan is to obtain more gifted and powerful children (because of the mana inherent in all strangers), usually the rite is clearly intended to incorporate the stranger into a more or less restricted group of which the woman lent to him is a member. In fact, the loan is an equivalent of a shared meal.[18]

Arnold van Gennep's equation of sexual hospitality with a "shared meal" is more than a metaphor: women often function as food growers, food preparers, and food givers in traditional societies, functions that make women central to routines of hospitality and, with reproduction, are a source of female power. In many cultures, a prominent man is one who feeds visitors and entertains foreign guests. Offering native food to foreigners is a way not only of "naturalizing" the strange and alien but also of transforming items of consumption into the more permanent coin of fame and reputation. In Gawa the definition of a "big man," a *guyaw*, is "one who feeds visitors," and eating foreign foods is one of the chief pleasures of the constant visiting that goes on under the form of prestige (kula) trade:

> When we give food ... to someone else, when an overseas visitor eats pig, vegetable food, chews betel, then he will take away its noise ... its fame. If we ourselves eat, there is no noise, no fame, it will disappear ..., rubbish, it will default. If we give to visitors, they praise us, it is fine. If not there is no fame; Gawa would have no kula shells, no *guyaw*, no kula fame.[19]

The association of women with food giving and hospitality joins the two primary means by which the identity and substance of the visitor is believed to be transformed. Women's association with these practices is assumed in the magic spells the Trobriand kula trader uses to ensure his welcome in the village of his trading partners: "The great woman befriends me, where the pots are boiling; the good woman befriends me, on the sitting platform. . . . No more it is my mother, my mother art thou, O woman of Dobu! No more it is my father, my father art thou, O man of Dobu."[20] Among the Circassians, if an enemy attempts to make off with a guest, "the host's wife will give him milk from her breast. He thus becomes her son, and his brethren are bound to defend him and to avenge his blood."[21]

A similar inversion of an original association may be found to be the root of sexual hospitality. It is assumed that those who issue from the wombs of the women of the group are related by law and by blood. Thus men, even though they may originally be strangers, who enter into the bodies of the women of the group become, by this act, kin to the men of the group, in law and fiction if not by blood. In other words, a blood relationship is a relationship of identity mediated through sexuality and reproduction. Insofar as a stranger engages in the relations of sexuality and reproduction that define the group, he is conceived to have altered his identity and to have become "kin," entering into a relationship with place that is unlike relations of blood—terminable, legal, a fiction born of the friction of sexuality. Negating the fictions of kinship and obligation normally associated with sexual intercourse is what we mean by prostitution, sexuality pure and simple. It may be a peculiarly modern concept.

Sexual hospitality is one of the staple items of travelers' tales. It is related by Herodotus of the Babylonians, by Strabo of the Massegetae, by Eusebius of the Geli and the Bactrians, by Marco Polo of many peoples of the East, by many travelers of the Ladrone Islanders, the Eskimos, and the Pacific Islanders. Throughout the world and throughout history, women have been the medium of connection between men of different groups, as institutionalized in the practices of exogamy and prostitution.

Even when Christianized in medieval nunneries, and when dedicated to chastity rather than sexuality, temples of women preserved the original idea of a "marriage to a god" (who may be a stranger) as an alternative to marriage to a familiar man. The forms of institutionalized sexual hospitality in the ancient world are almost always found to be alternatives to, preparations for, marriage. Eusebius reports on such a use of prostitution among the Armenians:

> The most illustrious men of the tribe actually consecrate to her their daughters while maidens; and it is the custom for those first to be prostituted in the temples of the goddess for a long time and after this to be given in marriage; and no one disdains to live in wedlock with such a woman ... and they are also so kindly disposed towards their paramours that they not only entertain them hospitably but also exchange presents with them, after giving more than they receive.... However, they do not admit any man who comes along, but preferably those of equal rank with themselves.[22]

In the rite reported by Herodotus—the "sacrifice of chastity" required of Babylonian women at the temple of Mylitta—every woman was required, once in her life, to sit in the temple and wait until a stranger threw a coin into her lap and summoned her with ritual words, in the name of the goddess, to follow him. She was obliged to go with him. Herodotus also mentions this as a custom in Cyprus, and it is reported in Lydia. The women of Lydia, like those of Cyprus, accumulated their dowries through prostitution, saving enough to contract themselves in marriage.

Sexual exchanges served a variety of purposes in traditional hospitality, for sexuality is a *medium* of relations, not necessarily a fixed and established relationship. Sexual exchanges incorporate the stranger into the group, remove taboos on virginity, make attractive certain commercial centers, extract the stranger's mana (often in the form of money and goods), and offer a means of mobility to women entering such exchanges. This variety makes it difficult to conceptualize a history of prostitution or sexuality, for what we understand as prostitution is often a commercialized form of sexual exchange intended to extract something from the stranger. Prostitution as a form of extraction through the mediation of local women is often found in host societies, those that survive on trade and thus depend on travelers. Of Marco Polo's many accounts of prostitution in his travels, particularly telling is his description of the customs of a people in the province of Camul, west of the Gobi Desert along the Old Silk Road:

> They are a gay folk, who give no thought to anything but making music, singing and dancing, and reading and writing according to their own usage, and taking great delight in the pleasures of the body. I give you my word that if a stranger comes to a house here to seek hospitality he receives a very warm welcome. The host bids his wife do everything that his guest wishes. Then he leaves the house and goes about his own business and stays away two or three days. Meanwhile the guest stays with his wife in the house and does what he will with her, lying with her in one bed, just as if she were his own wife; and they lead a gay life together. All of the men of this city and province are thus cuckolded by their wives; but they are not the least ashamed of it.

Mangu Khan prohibited this shocking custom by decree; but, after a period of drought, these people petitioned him to allow them their customary usage, "for their ancestors had declared that by the pleasure they gave to guests with their wives and goods they won the favor of their idols and multiplied the yield of their crops and tillage." This is little different from the magical use by a sessile society of the stranger's power to ensure fertility, rain, or domestic production. In another province in Tibet, Marco Polo found that the local men considered the stranger to be a god whose potency could be extracted for domestic use if they offered their wives to him: "For they say that by this act the gods and idols are propitiated, and so enrich them with temporal blessings in great abundance."[23]

In yet another instance, prostitution to strangers would seem to have the function of setting a market price on prospective brides by creating differences among young marriageable women that could rebound to the credit or discredit of their future husbands. Among a people in the foothills of the Himalayas, Marco Polo noted the following custom: "When it happens that men from a foreign land are passing through this country and have pitched their tents and made camp, the matrons from the neighboring villages and hamlets bring their daughters to these camps to the number of twenty and forty, and beg the travelers to take them and lie with them." Every girl was given a suitable token by her lover, and the girl who had accumulated the most tokens was the most esteemed and valued as a wife, "for they say that she is the most favored of the gods. Obviously the country is a fine one to visit for a lad of from sixteen to twenty-four."[24]

The mana of the stranger may be extracted in purely monetary form, differing hardly at all from modern, commercialized prostitution. On the road leading into India through the Himalayas, Marco Polo encountered men who offered their wives to passing strangers in exchange for cloth or trinkets, often mocking the strangers as they rode away: "Let us see, ne'er-do-well, what profit you have made. We have got this of yours, you poor fool, and you have nothing to show for it."[25] The courtesans of Corinth were famous throughout the ancient world for their ability to extract the mana from the stranger in the form of goods and money. Their skills gave rise to a proverb: "Not for every sailor is the voyage to Corinth." Camana, the main market town in Cappadocia, was termed by Strabo a "lesser Corinth, for there too, on account of the multitude of courtesans who were sacred to Aphrodite, outsiders resorted in great numbers and kept holiday."[26] Here it is clear that the use of the woman by the community is less a formal attachment of the stranger to the place than an extraction from the stranger of what the community most desires: money, goods, wealth, and substance.

Strangers, since they are polluted anyway, have often been used to break local taboos on the shedding of hymenal blood, which would pollute native men. In cultures where virginity is more problematical than prized, and where hymenal blood marks a sacred boundary that may not be breached without danger, strangers are often utilized for this function. This need may have been the origin of the practice of premarital prostitution among the Babylonians and the Armenians. When the sixteenth-century Italian traveler and writer Lodovico di Varthema arrived in the city of Tarnassari on the Coromandel coast, he and his companions were met by four local merchants, self-declared "friends of strangers." One of Varthema's party was approached and told: "Fifteen days hence I wish to bring home my wife, and one of you shall sleep with her the first night and deflower her for me." Varthema's companion, from a land in which the virginity of the bride was prized as a guarantee of paternity and of the honor of both the bride's and husband's families, was ashamed for the man until he learned that it was the custom of the land. He fulfilled what was requested of him and then was told to leave—that "it would have been at the peril of his life if he had returned again."[27]

The variety of functions illustrates the two-way nature of sexual hospitality, which provides means for the integration of men into groups and for the detachment of women from defining, traditional social relations. In the ancient world, the temples of Aphrodite, the precincts of sacred prostitution, were essentially women's institutions, which mobilized women's value to men for the use of women themselves and for the community at large. In its first forms, institutionalized prostitution was a coining for domestic use of the contradiction noted by Claude Lévi-Strauss, "the contradiction by which the same woman was seen under two, incompatible aspects: on the one hand, as the object of personal desire, thus exciting sexual and proprietorial instincts; and, on the other, as the subject of the desire of others, and seen as such, i.e., as the means of binding others through alliance with them."[28]

The lenses supplied by patriarchal cultures require us to regard women as essentially passive in the construction of "gender structure," and to see these structures as the creation of "dominant" men in the service of their own sexual and reproductive interests. This view, a militant assertion of patriarchal norms strangely present in modern feminism, fails to comprehend the agency of women in the negotiations of membership and exclusion. The institution of sacred prostitution is strange to moderns, who live in a world where prostitution is anything but sacred. But something of its ancient functions can be glimpsed in its modern survivals on the fringes of Western culture.

Among the Ewe people of West Africa, the most ancient form of prostitution, sacred prostitution, is still practiced in the temple of the python-god. This temple, like ancient temples of Aphrodite, is a purely female institution; and any woman—old or young, married or unmarried, free or enslaved—may dedicate herself to the god. The only requirement for her entry is the public display of possession by the god in the form of an ecstatic trance. Her person is inviolable; and during the three years of her novitiate, she is strictly forbidden to enter the house of her parents or, if married, the house of her husband. This cult is often used as a means of escaping family constraints or attaining sexual freedom:

> A priestess belongs to the god she serves, and therefore cannot become the property of any man, as would be the case if she married one. This prohibition extends to marriage only, and a priestess is not debarred from sexual commerce. . . . Priestesses are ordinarily most licentious, and custom allows them to gratify their passions with any man who may chance to take their fancy.[29]

Jean La Fontaine's study of the "free woman" of Kinshasa, Zaire, stresses the role that prostitution plays in traditional settings as an alternative to kinship and marriage. The prostitute of Kinshasa is a free woman in the sense that she controls her own life and has escaped the restrictions of tradition. These women consider themselves to be free of the traditional subordination to men that is the norm within marriage. Yet, by leaving the traditional bonds of kinship, Kinshasa prostitutes also forfeit the advantages and protections implicit in these relations:

> The femme libre ... has deprived both her kin and her potential husband of the social profits which might be obtained from an official relationship. In so doing, she attacks the basic structure of the kinship system by denying the authority of men over women, of seniors over juniors. In refusing to be the vehicle for the creation of official ties, she deprives any children she may have of full kinship status, as they will have no paternal kinsmen.[30]

Erik Cohen, in his study of Thailand prostitutes, has found similar departures from Western practices. Thai prostitutes are most often women who have left marriages and relationships with Thai men and profess a strong aversion to them and a preference for foreigners (*farang*). They are motivated by "the interest and excitement of meeting strange and often attractive foreigners with a respected status and cultural background; and the hope of marrying a farang, [and] emigrating from the country."[31] Thai prostitutes often seek to transform a temporary and ephemeral relationship into something permanent, frequently acting as guides to foreign men in the hope that this may provide them with a way out of Thailand.

Sexual hospitality is thus traditionally a medium of intercultural relations rather than a fixed relationship in itself. I hope in this brief discussion of a complex situation to have made clear that in the context of the incorporative procedures of arrival, there is no established or predictable conclusion to be drawn from these sexual practices. We should grant as much awareness of contingency and possibility to these past actors negotiating their arrivals as we grant to strangers meeting in a modern singles bar. The deeper inductions into place, those that construct the identities we understand by "home," are commonly found in preindustrial arrivals, less and less commonly in the wheel-borne world of the modern machine age. Most modern travelers neither seek nor desire those more terminal incorporations within an environment: "settlement," or making a "home." Or do they, and it is only that we do not recognize these as incorporations because they are negotiated between individuals, in pairings, rather than between collectivities?

The incorporations and transfers of substance often found in premodern arrivals were acts of settlement which founded a coherence between population and topography that historically defined and articulated the world we inhabit. Such ritual incorporations are premodern because they are thought to involve a mutual transfer of personality, as the self of the passenger incorporates a landscape and as that social landscape incorporates the passenger. In modern circumstances, such transfers would be perceived as a pollution, an erosion of the boundaries that create the "individual," the autonomous and free person. Those deeper associations between peoples, biological and genetic links, have been forged in exchanges mediated through intercultural languages—gifts, sexuality, daily recognitions—which have been imprinted on the world we inhabit. In modern practice, travelers rarely "arrive" in the full, premodern sense of the word. We have become a society of travelers. The stranger—that autonomous, often anonymous, permanently detached figure—has entered into our definitions of the modern native.

''THE FORCE THAT MOVES NATIONS''

Power is the relation of a given person to other individuals in which the more this person expresses opinions, predictions and justifications of the collective action that is performed, the less is his participation in that action.... Morally the wielder of power appears to cause the event, physically it is those who submit to the power. But as moral activity is inconceivable without the physical, the cause of the event is neither in the one nor in the other but in the union of the two.
—Tolstoy, *War and Peace*, 1869

Tolstoy saw political power as resulting from relations established between different species of actors: those who specialize in communicational action ("express opinions," justify, legitimate, and delegitimate), and those who specialize in nonverbal action, specifically physical in its limitations. The rules governing the relations between these different spheres of behavior are what we mean by political structure. Tolstoy's view is, in other words, that power comes not out of the barrel of a gun but out of the relations established between those who have guns and those who have no, or fewer, guns. This view, that power is inherent in human relations rather than in those who enter into relations, clarifies the source of the power of mobilities, the force generated in the movements of individuals, groups, nations.

The energies palpable in arrivals—in battles, feasts, greetings, and entertainments—are generated by the essence of these events, which generate human associations through procedures of identification and incorporation. The power traditionally attributed to the stranger, and the power of place which I will examine next, are merely embodiments and symbols of that energy released in the coming together of differences normally kept distinct by our most cherished and traditional categories and boundaries. This association of what is culturally dissociated, the encounter between "strangers," must be regarded as one source of the energy generated in human travel and an origin of significant human powers. The emotions of arrival, the fears and hopes generated in meetings between antitheses—the strange and the familiar, the mobile male and the territorialized female, the solitary stranger and "society"—testify to the power inherent in these events and tell us of their nature: asserting and making conscious distinctions even as they are reconciled.

This explanation provides some clues to a mystery that has long baffled students of human affairs: Why did humans go out of their way to associate in the first place, and why do they do so in ever larger numbers? This mystery is also the mystery of exogamy and the genderization of human mobility, a question of the profits of human association. One could argue that there are more and more arrivals in history because people become addicted to the energies and transformations of state they generate.

But as boundaries are crossed more and more often, they are desacralized and internalized, effaced and made ambiguous; the power experienced in their crossing becomes less altering and more routine. By his first induction into civilization, Enkidu's strength is dramatically diminished; this is a metaphor for the operations of a system in which labor recruitment was a source of "power," as well as an explanation of what occurs at the junctures of distinctions joined in passage and realized in arrivals. Tolstoy's penetrating but generally overlooked insight into the nature of human power, the "force that moves nations," suggests a cycle and a dynamic, that certain species of power come out of particular events of human association, which itself becomes a reason for the repetition of these events and their evolution into rituals, routines, ordeals of civility. But arrival is only one event, the final term, of the structure of the journey.

In discussing the identifiable events that make up the structure of the journey, any journey—departure, passage, and arrival—I have tried to suggest that the force exercised by mobility in human history is composed of different species of events, each of which has its characteristic features and effects upon the passenger. Departures separate passengers from a defining matrix and strip life of everything immovable. The fatigues as well as the pleasures of passage simplify and reduce. One of the puzzles of the transformations effected by departures and passages is how a force traditionally described as causing a loss of substance, coherence, identity has been for so long regarded as a source of the positive gains of travel: liberty, wisdom, and fame. Whatever the differences between ancient and modern evaluations of the sufferings of the traveler, they also show remarkable consistency about the nature of the changes produced by departure and passage. In its first phase, the force of travel might best be compared to the force of erosion in geological processes. Stripping away the softer and more recent sedimentations of needs, travel sculpts and reveals more primal needs, earlier and harder layers of personal and cultural history. Departures evoke the earliest separations of childhood; passage, those experiences of early flight and physical freedom; arrivals, the magic of a return to beginnings and an achievement of coherence with others.

The wastings of travel persist through the stage of passage, as the world is objectified and made fluid through motion, and as the passenger—stripped of a sense of belonging—becomes an observer of the world that flows past. There is not yet a psychology of travel, but if there were it would have to focus upon the pleasures inherent, for some, in motion: its autotelic characteristics, the manner in which passage through space shapes the experience of time and perception in general. The period of passage is the distinctive feature of travel and, I suspect, the source of its novelties, the new features of mind and character that distinguish the traveler from the sedentary being. It is this experience that gives somatic content to the modern designation of travel as "freedom." In addition, the progressional structure that passage lends to experience obviously shapes our world, designed as it is around road structures, with strip architectures, presentations of information keyed to the passing eye, a world of transient but strangely mannered and civil relations. The forces that transform traditional societies, with their closed and highly rigid structures, into modern society—its structure open, its partitions permeable, its doors of communication wide—are those of passage, the erosions of mobility, the events of entry and arrival.

PART

II

PHILOSOPHICAL
TRAVEL

Self-portrait of a palmer (professional pilgrim) in twelfth-century France
(From the author's collection)

5

TRAVELING IN TIME: ANCIENT AND MEDIEVAL TRADITIONS

Sailing to the ends of the earth, is in fact traveling in time.
—Joseph-Marie Degerando, 1797

P hilosophical travel is travel in time, a journey to the sites of the beginnings of one's cultural order. As a search for roots and beginnings, it might equally be called "historical travel," for in this sort of journey the traveler often attempts to retrace the paths of ancestors and founders in all their circuits and returns. Clearly there is a fine line between philosophical travel and ritual journeys to reaffirm identities, pilgrimages to old sacred sites, and tours to newly hallowed ground. The philosophical traveler may be distinguished from travelers on these similar journeys in that the former often creates the beginnings that are subsequently the goal of pilgrims and tourists, becoming the originator of new cultural tracks and itineraries.

In part II, I will discuss the reorientation of Western traditions of philosophical travel from the ancient and sacred centers of Western civilization—Egypt, Palestine, Greece, Rome—to the peripheries of the world newly found by Renaissance voyagers. This world provided a wealth of material—new flora, fauna, and peoples—

which seventeenth- and eighteenth-century Europeans used to define their culture as secular and specifically "modern." This reorientation began with the Renaissance voyages and was completed by the time Joseph-Marie Degerando wrote his instructions on "The Observation of Savage Peoples" to scientists traveling with Nicolas Baudin's second expedition around the world in 1797 (see page 171). It was in the farthest limit of the Western world, in southwestern Australia, and not in its ancient and sacred centers, that Degerando expected

> ... to find the material needed to construct an exact scale of the various degrees of civilization, and to assign each its characteristic properties; we shall come to know what needs, what ideas, what habits are produced in each era of human society. Here, since the development of the passions and of the intellectual faculties is much more limited, it will be much easier for us to penetrate their nature and to determine their fundamental laws. Here, since different generations have exercised only the slightest influence on each other, we shall in a way be taken back to the first periods of our own history—we shall be able to set up secure experiments on the origin and generation of ideas, on the formation and development of language, and on the relations between these two processes. The philosophical traveller, sailing to the ends of the earth, is in fact travelling in time; he is exploring the past; every step he makes is the passage of an age. Those unknown islands that he reaches are for him the cradle of human society. Those peoples whom our ignorant vanity scorns are displayed to him as ancient and majestic monuments of the origin of ages: monuments infinitely more worthy of our admiration and respect than those famous pyramids by the banks of the Nile.[1]

Though filtered through Rousseauvian ideas, eighteenth-century notions, and the history of three hundred years of European voyages, the assumptions that long underlay philosophical travel are stated clearly and precisely here. The philosophical traveler, voyaging through space, "is in fact travelling in time," journeying back to the "infancy" of a civil and intellectual order. What makes Degerando's definition of philosophical travel characteristically modern is that he places this infancy in the peripheries of Western civilization. Here, in unknown islands and among savage peoples, Degerando found the orienting monuments of the "origin of ages," which he specifically contrasts with the pyramids of Egypt.

In chapter 6 I will examine the manner and method by which the
newfound peripheries became the site of cultural origins, in contrast
to which Europeans defined themselves and crystallized a cultural
self-image. Chapter 7 explores the consequences of this reorientation,
the way in which the peripheries produced a flood of novel species
of flora, fauna, and humanity. The assimilation of this information,
assiduously collected by curious European travelers, ultimately transformed ancient categories of order and even the image of the traveling philosopher who became first the humanist traveler and then the
mobile scientist, observer and collector of a world. This historical
instance of a cultural reorientation requires close examination not
because of the dominance of Europe, nor because of the fact that it
became a new world center with its history becoming world history.
For our purposes, rather, the reorientation of philosophical travel
from the ancient centers to the peripheries of modernity is important
because it provides a specific example of how travel transforms a
cultural order and alters persisting patterns of meaning.

TOWARD THE ANCIENT CENTERS OF ORDER

*We wish to know about those parts of the world where tradition places more deeds
of action, political constitutions, arts and everything else that contributes to practical wisdom, and our needs draw us to those places that are under government,
or rather under good government.*

Things tend toward the center.

—Strabo, c. 19 A.D.

The ancients had been intellectually indifferent or hostile to the
peripheries of their civilization. It was assumed that the barbaric and
nomadic tribes beyond their borders had nothing to show them but
an animal nature and the confusion of those things carefully kept
distinct within the precincts of ordered civilization. Strabo, in his
geography, unapologetically treats the Germans and Britons super-
ficially: "[T]here would be no advantage in knowing such countries
and their inhabitants, and particularly if the people live in islands

which are of such a nature that they can neither injure nor benefit us because of their isolation."[2] Civilized space here is clearly centered on places of order and good government, founded by the deeds of great men. The peripheries were places of cosmological convenience, providing, according to Pliny, "the hinges on which the firmament turns and the extreme limits of the revolutions of the stars." The ancient views of ordered space may also be found in the home-centered epic travels of Odysseus, in ancient cosmographies, and in Pliny's apology for treating Rome so briefly on his geographical tour of the fabulous Mediterranean Basin, "a land which is at once the nursling and mother of all other lands, chosen by . . . providence . . . to unite scattered empires, to make manners gentle, to draw together in converse by community of language the jarring and uncouth tongues of so many nations, and in a word to become throughout the world the single fatherland of all races."[3]

Diodorus Siculus also assumed that civility was identical with a community of language, and that those Ethiopians south of the zone of cities had the nature "of a wild beast" not only because they kept their nails long and were unkind to each other, but because "speaking as they do with a shrill voice and cultivating none of the practices of civilized life as these are found among the rest of mankind, they present a striking contrast when considered in the light of our own customs."[4] To Strabo, the remoter tribes of Lusitania (Portugal) were "wild" not simply because they were violent and warlike, but because "they are difficult to communicate with [and] have lost the instinct for sociability and humanity."[5] The peripheries presented only confusions of civilized categories, so that Diodorus reported the existence of "animals which are of double form and mingled in their natures" on the borders of Syria and Arabia.[6]

The Philosophical Traveler in Egypt

To the ancient Greeks and Romans, the origins of civilization lay in Egypt; there was even a belief that life had been generated spontaneously from the mud of the Nile River Valley. The ancients were essentially diffusionists, believing that all arts, order, government, and civilized practices originated in Egypt and spread from there throughout the Mediterranean. The agents of this diffusion were the originating and founding gods; the means, their civilizing journeys and ordering expeditions. Osiris, the mythical founder of Egypt who invented language and gave names to "unnamed things" just as Adam did in that other tale of origins, invented the alphabet and installed the ordinances governing the proper worship of the gods. On his paradigmatic civilizing journey, he spread the characteristic goods of civilized life—wheat, the vine, and barley—over the world and thereby made it "knowable" and familiar. He was the first to observe the orderly arrangement of the heavens, founding astrology, astronomy, mathematics, and music—disciplines that were regarded as intrinsically ordering and universal in their applications. By inventing the lyre and harmony, Osiris invented a means of playing the seasons, "for he adopted three tones, a high, a low and a medium; the high for Summer, the low for the Winter and the medium for the Spring."[7]

According to Diodorus Siculus, after this ordering of space, the Egyptian kings sent out colonies to Crete, Argos, Babylon, Cyprus, Palestine, Syria, and Athens. It was from the Egyptians that the Greeks believed they inherited the characteristically Indo-European arrangement of society into three orders: the *Eupatrids*, noble, educated priests and rulers of society; the *Geomori*, "holders of a share of the land," who were also expected to bear arms and defend the state; and the *Demiurgoi*, "workers for the people"—farmers and craftsmen. The very life of the Egyptian ruler embodied the ordered space of Egypt, "for there was a set time not only for his holding audiences or rendering judgments, but even for his taking a walk, bathing, and sleeping with his wife, and, in a word, for every act of his life."[8] The ceremonies presided over by the Pharaoh were considered the necessary ritual actions that guaranteed the pulsation of Egypt's lifeblood, the periodic inundations of the Nile.

Egypt was the first center of philosophical pilgrimage for those peoples who considered themselves members of Mediterranean civilization. Generations of Greek heroes and legislators visited Egypt in order to drink at the fount of wisdom. Orpheus, Daedalus, Homer, Lycurgus, Solon, Plato, Pythagoras, and Eudoxus were reputed to have visited Egypt and to have admired its ancient administration and strictly regulated life: "And for that reason those men who have won the greatest repute in intellectual things have been eager to visit Egypt in order to acquaint themselves with its laws and institutions."[9] In a pattern repeated continually in the history of travel, the philosophical travelers to Egypt were followed by pilgrims and then by tourists. Egypt remained a place of lasting power and significance within Western civilization, a significance perpetuated in literature, photography, souvenirs, histories, and tales.

Here, in the cultural reproduction of a significant cultural site, we may find the source of the magic of place sought by the philosophical traveler. The icons of place, like the Pyramids, furnish a store of unconscious images of the long ago and far away, which may be triggered and become conscious upon the traveler's arrival at that site. This occurred to Alexander Kinglake in 1838, upon his first view of the Pyramids:

> I had no print, no picture before me, and yet the old shapes were there; there was no change; they were just as I had always known them. . . . Strange to say, the bigness of the distinct blocks of stone was the first sign by which I attained to feel the immensity of the whole pile. . . . Almost suddenly a cold sense and understanding of the pyramid's enormity came down overcasting my brain.[10]

This cold feeling of immensity opened a channel of memory in Kinglake, recalling to him a nightmare that had continually recurred between his third and fifth year, but that he had forgotten. There was no image in this nightmare, only "the idea of solid immensity." Encountering a significant center or site can call up both a personal and a historical past within the frame of a present.

The frisson of the tourist, often reported by travelers encountering an emplaced cultural icon for the first time, might be seen as an experience of meaning, a sudden coherence felt between the fictive and the real, the imagined and the actual. Marking the conjuncture of dreamed, unconscious landscapes with an observed reality in a present time, it is an experience of the continuities of time and space that underlie the contiguities of eras and constructed boundaries. This climax of touristic desire came to one Monsieur de la Guillietière, a typical romantic Hellenist of the eighteenth century, upon his first arrival in Athens:

> And here I cannot but acknowledge my own weakness, you may call it folly if you please: at the first sight of this Famous Town (struck as it were by a sentiment of Veneration for those miracles of antiquity which were Recorded of it) I started immediately, and was taken with a universal shivering all over my body. Nor was I singular in

my emotion-commotion, we all of us stared, but could see nothing,
our imaginations were too full of the Great men which that city had
produced.[11]

It was not the sight of the city (which was shrouded in fog) that
triggered the universal shivering, the touristic orgasm, but its mere
actuality. Here as elsewhere, the origin of the power of place is clearly
in the imagination of the traveler, stocked with a literature and a
world of images. As Kinglake observed, "The superior Veneration
so often excited by objects that are distant and unknown shews not
perhaps the wrong-headedness of man, but rather the transcendant
power of his imagination."[12] The experience of the power of place
is apparently the product of a felt linkage between domains kept
separate: the literary and the real, the representation and the observed, the ancient past and the experienced present.

Goethe experienced his most memorable frisson as a traveler
while standing on a bridge over the Tiber gazing, for the first time,
at that other ancient center, the city of Rome. He was puzzled by
the peculiar feeling that he had seen these scenes before: "Now I
feel, not that I am seeing them for the first time, but that I am seeing
them again." Then he remembered that, as a child, every morning
on his way to breakfast he had passed down a hall hung with Roman
scenes his father had gathered on some previous Grand Tour. The
sense of the coming together of layers of the past in an experienced
instant was not entirely pleasant for Goethe, who was of an age
concerned with individuality and modernity, and who bore a con-
flicted relationship to the classical norms worshiped by his father's
Voltairean generation. He admits that, from his childhood on, he
did not "dare look into a Latin author or at anything which evoked
an image of Italy," and that he felt "acute discomfort" in reading
Christoph Martin Wieland's translation of Horace's *Satires.* When
touring the ruins at Paestum, and noting the contrast between the
"stumpy conical columns" and his imagination of the classical bred
by the Renaissance and its "more slender style of architecture,"
Goethe acknowledged that he found these masses of stone "offen-
sive and even terrifying."[13] But in general his tour of Italy was like
a return to childhood and to a primal scene associated with the
accoutrements of the ancient world and the more phallic classical
forms.

The Philosophical Traveler in India

Within ancient traditions of philosophical travel, there was an alternative to Egypt as a site of cultural origins, which reflected the prehistorical origins of Indo-European peoples: India and the East. To
ancient Greeks and Romans, India had almost exactly the same characteristics as Egypt. It was a land of unexampled fertility and wealth,
the home of a strictly hierarchical social order, and a land famous
for its wisdom:

> For India is a land of unusual beauty. . . . And it is said that because
> of the favourable climate in those parts the country has never ex-
> perienced a famine or a destruction of crops. It also has an unbe-
> lievable multitude of Elephants ... and likewise gold, silver, iron
> and copper; furthermore, within its borders are to be found great
> quantities of precious stones of every kind and of practically all
> other things which contribute to luxury and wealth.[14]

India's social order was more complex (consisting of seven rather than
three orders) and more "just" than that of Egypt. The highest grade of
society was an order of philosophers and priests who offered sacrifices
and performed rites for the dead. Next in order of dignity was not the
political class but the farmers, who were exempt from all taxes and
protected by all the others, for they were benefactors of the whole of
society whom they provided with food. Ranked under farmers, in de-
scending order of their importance to the well-being of the whole,
came herders and hunters, artisans, soldiers and the military, inspec-
tors and officials, and, in the last group, kings, magistrates, counselors,
and judges. The rule of philosophers over kings, of priests over magistrates, struck Greeks as an interesting and significant variation on
the theme of hierarchy. Alexander the Great's encounter with the philosophers of India, the Indian sophists, was the central episode the
Anabasis of Alexander, a life of Alexander written by the second-century
B.C. Greek historian Flavius Arrian. Alexander sent his emissary, One-
sicritus, to Colonus, chief of the Indian sophists, and received the story
of the beginnings of the world:

> In olden times the world was as full of barley-meal and wheaten-
> meal, as now of dust; and the fountains then flowed, some with
> water, others with milk and likewise with honey, and others with

wine and some with olive oil; but by reason of his gluttony and luxury man fell into arrogance beyond bounds. But Zeus, hating this state of things, destroyed everything and appointed for a man a life of toil, and when self-control and other virtues in general reappeared, there came again an abundance of blessings. But the condition of man is already close to satiety and arrogance again, and there is danger of the destruction of everything that exists.[15]

This conception of history being governed by cycles of destruction and reconstruction keyed to the moral condition of man reappears throughout ancient texts. It also appears in the "story of the days before the flood" brought home by Gilgamesh from his travels, as well as in the story of Noah. Nineteenth-century geologists turned back to this concept in order to give classical weight to the modern notion of change as an endless process of degradation and uplifting. To this end, lines from the Roman rhetorician Seneca were often quoted: "Every animal shall be generated anew, and men free from guilt shall be given to the earth."[16] To the Indian sophists addressing Alexander's emissaries, the presence of the conquerer itself signified the growing old of time and the immanence of a new period of destruction. It was in the mouths of these philosophical others, who were, paradoxically, ancestors, that the Greeks received an objective view of themselves. One of the Indian philosophers, Mondonis, when asked what he thought of the Greeks, replied that he "regarded the Greeks as sound-minded in general but that they were wrong in one respect, in that they preferred custom to nature, and were thus unacquainted with a life of frugality and prudence."[17] When the Indian wise men congregated in a meadow to greet the conqueror, they beat their feet on the earth to signify that no one really possesses any more of the earth than that upon which they walk. And Mondonis asserted his superiority to Alexander, noting that he had subdued his needs while the conqueror had subdued only the earth.

HOLY LANDS, SACRED TEXTS, AND PILGRIMAGE

[T]he chief men in Gaul hasten hither [to Palestine]; the Briton, remote from our world, if he advance in the faith, forsakes the setting sun and seeks the spot he knows by fame and from the scriptures. What shall we say of the Armenians, of

Persians, of the tribes of India and Ethiopia, of Egypt herself hard by, so rich in
monks, of Pontus and Cappadocia, of Calle-Syria and Mesopotamia and all the
swarms of the East? They all hasten to these places and show diverse types of
virtues.

—St. Paula, c. 370 A.D.

Beginnings are always constructed retrospectively; something needs
to exist before its "beginnings" can be discovered. The manufacture
of beginnings and traditions is thus an ongoing process within history and a crucial means by which individuals within a present define, legitimate, become conscious of the external "order" that
defines them. Thus, beginnings were manufactured in the Christianization of the Roman World that occurred in the fourth and fifth
centuries: ancient traditions were expunged, edited, and repackaged;
a "Holy Land" was created as a new center of philosophical travel,
subsequently becoming the goal of pilgrims and tourists. As a result
of processes I will discuss in the following pages, new gods were
emplaced and a new totemic landscape was imposed upon an old,
densely layered classical topography.

Simultaneous with the creation of a new holy ground, a more
fundamental process was transforming the character of philosophical travel by liberating the concepts of "beginnings," "wisdom," and
"order" from place in general; this process invested sacred authority
in text, particularly in a canonical work—whether Bible or Koran.
The creation of holy sites and a sacred literature occurred simultaneously from the fourth century on. The sacred sites demonstrated
the truth of the text, while the text supplied meaning to the sacred
site. A sacred reality is created through its representation, through
its reproduction in literature, artifacts, relics, and souvenirs, just as
it is materialized in chambers, precincts, temples, and itineraries.
The "true" and "authentic" is created with the reproduction. It is
the reproduction that furnishes the conscious and unconscious mind
of the traveler with a vision of place essential to an experience of
its "power" and magic. We may see the creation of sacred sites in
our own present, in our Disney Worlds, as well as in the past, in the
creation of Holy Lands. The processes are the same but for the fact
that newer constructions have not been hallowed by time.

The liberation of philosophical travel from place in general and
its refocusing upon text was anticipated by Socrates, himself a clas-

sically homebound philosopher. When mocked by Phaedrus for his apparent uneasiness and disorientation outside the walls of Athens, Socrates replied:

> I am a lover of knowledge, and the men who dwell in the city are
> my teachers, and not the trees or the country. Though I do believe
> that you have found a spell with which to draw me out of the city
> into the country, like a hungry animal before whom a bough or a
> bunch of fruit is waved. For only hold up before me, in like manner,
> a book, and you may lead me all around Attica, and over the wide
> world.[18]

The "book" here constitutes a means for the deterritorialization of centers of order. With the Christian era, Scripture and the commentaries of the Church fathers came to constitute the chief symbolic system in which meaning was anchored. Here, in the text, one might find the history of beginnings and laws, the emergence and growth of a moral order. Throughout the Middle Ages, the Book and those who knew books became themselves the objects of philosophical travel. The text itself, no longer merely a reproduction, representation, fixation of acts and deeds, became a potent sacred object. In the fourth century, philosophical travel evolved along two distinct but intertwined paths: the creation of a holy land and the development of scholarly travel in pursuit of text.

The creation of holy sites and a sacred topography differs little from the creation of any touristic site, as this process has been described by the sociologist Dean MacCannel in his pioneering work on tourism. First, the site itself is purified of associations extraneous to those being framed and marked. It is then "sacralized"—marked off and separated from its surroundings, isolated from similar objects. Then it is architecturally "framed," contained within walls and boundaries. Avenues of entry, fees, guardians, and so on are established. The site is then mechanically reproduced in effigies, pictures, models, relics, souvenirs, and icons, by means of which its fame and reputation are spatially extended. Finally, there is the stage of the "social reproduction" of the site, which, if successful, gathers a community around it and makes it a self-sufficing economic entity. The site continues, so long as it is sacred, to generate a literature, texts, guidebooks, testimonies, miracles, and travel accounts that perpetuate its now framed and contained power. This literature generates an audience to consume the site in and through travel, to encounter the actuality implicit in its reproductions and representations.

By the fourth century Palestine had already become a magnet to ascetics and those who took seriously Christ's injunction to cast off the attachments of family, property, and nativity and to follow him. In the third century, numerous convent communities had grown up to provide a haven for those who left their established homes. Women were especially prominent among the early pilgrims. The original attraction of Palestine to such as St. Paula, who left Rome and moved there in the last half of the fourth century, was not so much the original site of Christ's life and teaching as the saintly and holy men who congregated there from all over the world—Gaul, Britain, Armenia, India—and made it a destination to all who would "advance in the faith."

The marking off, framing, and elaboration of the sacred sites, the grounding in space of Christ's life, and the hallowing of the places given meaning by his footsteps, birth, life, and death began with the visit to Palestine of the Empress Helena, Emperor Constantine's mother, in A.D. 326, almost simultaneous with the acceptance of Christianity as the official religion of the Roman Empire. She was encouraged by Bishop Macarius of Aelia Capitolina (as Jerusalem had been called since its destruction and rebuilding by Hadrian two hundred years earlier) who, during the Council of Nicea in 325, had told her that nothing had been done to localize, preserve, or commemorate Christ's passion. On her visit to Jerusalem, she identified the sites of Calvary, the Holy Sepulcher, and, in Bethlehem, the site of Christ's birth. In making this journey, Helena was engaging in "footprint worship"—a reenactment of the paradigmatic journeys of the founder that characterizes many of the world's religions and constitutes the underlying logic of pilgrimage: "And when she had bestowed fitting worship on the footprints of the Saviour in accordance with the prophetic word which says, 'Let us worship at the places where his feet have stood,' she immediately bequeathed to those who were to come after the fruit of her personal piety."[19]

The process of building up those sites sanctified by the life of the founder began with the clearing of the ground, which was conceived as the eradication of extraneous and defiling associations. The clearing of the ground was identical with clarifying the meaning of a place, recovering its pure essence: "It seemed to him [Constantine] to be a duty to make conspicuous, and an object of veneration to all, the most blessed place of the Saviour's resurrection." The ungodly men who had determined to hide the light emanating from Christ's resurrection had built a temple to Aphrodite upon the spot of the sepulcher, which had to be cleared away. Constantine ordered the temple leveled and its materials, even the landfill, carried to a distant spot and scattered. In this process, the holy cave was uncovered: "For after its descent into darkness it again came forth into light, and afforded to those who came to see a clear insight into the history of the wonders which had been wrought." With the erection of a basilica over the site of the holy cave, the power impacted by history into the site was contained and framed. Empress Helena also had churches built at the original cave, at the site of the nativity in Bethlehem, and on the Mount of Ascension (Mount of Olives), establishing an itinerary for pilgrims to pace from Christ's birth to his death, burial, resurrection, and ascension. Constantine also ordered Macarius to undertake similar operations at the site of the Oak of Mamre, where God conversed with Abraham and where the Saviour appeared, with two angels, after his resurrection. Constantine spoke as if he believed that these operations would undo the corruptions and pollutions of time and restore the site to its original meaning: "truly it is a very great impiety that the holy places should be defiled with unhallowed pollutions."[20]

The construction of the churches in Palestine was a conscious effort to purify, sacralize, and frame a history in stone, topography, and territory. Eusebius, the theologian of Caesarea, mentions in his life of Constantine that St. Cyril used these sites as a way of removing any doubts the faithful might have about the reality of the life of Christ: "Should you be disposed to doubt it [the crucifixion] the very place which everyone can see proves you are wrong, this blessed Golgotha ... on which we are now assembled. ... Deny not the crucified ... Gethsemane bears him witness where the betrayal took place."[21]

Thus does the grounding and "siting" of myth demonstrate its truth and objectivity. The creation of the Holy Land was the architecturalization of text, which in turn "proved" that text. The Christian ceremonial centers, often built upon ancient sites of pilgrimage, thus constructed a new set of objects within which the suppositions of the faith, with its paradigmatic history of the founder, were rooted, incorporated, and rendered permanent.

The purification, hallowing, and framing of the site were immediately followed by its reproduction. Tradition established that Helena, while on her pilgrimage to Palestine, had uncovered the true cross and the nails used in the crucifixion. Reproductions of these items immediately began to be distributed. St. Cyril complained in 347 that so many pieces of the true cross were taken as relics that they could fill up the whole world, suggesting the tension that immediately springs up between the reproduction and the authentic item, a tension resolved in the philosophical journey to the site of origins. Especially after the second Nicene Council decreed in 787 that no church could be consecrated without relics, the market for the reproduction of these material furnishings of the story of Christ flourished. The fundamental motive of pilgrimage—the search for the true and original beginnings of a sacred world order—was intensified with the reproduction of its sacred elements. The Church declared that relics could multiply themselves by virtue of their essential sacred qualities—as Christ had multiplied the five fishes and the two loaves of bread to feed thousands—and that this miracle was no more or less wondrous than the ability of these objects to cure diseased spiritual and physical states. Reproductions of relics were installed in native churches and accumulated there, turning them into centers of pilgrimages in their own right: "Not only did the hope of successful relic-hunting send more and more pilgrims to the East, but also the arrival and possession of a relic of some Eastern saint in their home town would inspire western citizens to visit the lands where their new patron saint had lived."[22]

In the fourth century, too, the main itineraries of Christian pilgrimage were established. The anonymous Bordeaux Pilgrim made a journey in 333 and recorded the distances, stages, and stopping places of his route from Bordeaux through Toulouse, Narbonne, Milan, Padua, Belgrade, Sofia, Adrianople, Constantinople, and down the military road through Syria to Jerusalem, which remained the primary route for the generations to follow. The Bordeaux Pilgrim was followed by St. Silvia in 370 to 388, and by Paula, Eustochium, and Egeria in the 380s. Egeria, in her itinerary, left a complete description of the sites that were particularly sacred and worthy of visiting. By the close of the fourth century, not only had the true cross and nails been discovered and reproduced in great quantities, but also the reed and sponge with which Christ took his last drink, the lance that took his life, the cup used in the last supper, and the "charger" upon which John the Baptist's head had been presented by Herod to Salome.

Despite the Arab conquest of Palestine, pilgrimage became a standard form of ritual travel in the ninth and tenth centuries and was particularly fashionable among the Irish and the English. The Celtic Church was the first to consider pilgrimage a penance. In the tenth century, the monks of the Monastery at Cluny in southern France were particularly active in organizing pilgrim tours and in building hospices along the main routes and in Palestine itself. In this pre-Crusade period, the rules for pilgrims and their distinctive garb were fixed. They were to carry no weapons and to journey barefoot, clothed with the simple, rough robe, broad-brimmed hat, and wallet that soon became their identifying costume. They were encouraged to fast, to abstain from meat, and never to spend more than one night in any one location. In addition, pilgrims were admonished to avoid iron utensils, to neglect caring for the hair and fingernails, and to shun warm baths and soft beds. The poverty of the pilgrims, besides being a holy state, also made them unprofitable prey for the lords and warbands who infested the roads. Pilgrimage was encouraged, despite the doubts of many fathers of the Church, by the privileges accorded those who made the journey to the Holy Land, privileges later extended to the Crusaders. If a priest, the pilgrim continued to draw his stipend for three years while on the road. The layperson was freed from taxes and immune from arrest, trial, and confiscation of his property by creditors during the period of the journey.

In the eleventh century, pilgrimage was often undertaken on a grand scale. A pilgrimage led by German bishops in 1064 was said to have included around seven thousand men and women. In 1049 the citizens of Narni, France, reported having seen a multitude of pilgrims in glowing robes pass through their town, one of whom declared that they were souls who won everlasting life so long as they continued the holy journey to the sacred ground. Legendary heroes such as King Arthur, and historical kings such as Charlemagne who had acquired the aura of legend, were posthumously enrolled in the ranks of pilgrims, lending the authorization of heroes to a journey that was already commended by the Church, privileged by immunities, and a means of winning penance. All the established powers of medieval society, clerical and secular, combined to validate journeys to Palestine, Rome, St. James Compostela in Galicia (in northwestern Iberia), and other holy centers. Pilgrimage to a holy place became a method of suspending everyday life, gaining eternal glory, linking together Christendom as a territorial reality, and winning individual grace through territorial passage.

From the first Crusade, declared by Urban II in the Council of Claremont of 1095, the journey to the Holy Land ceased to be philosophical travel and became military tourism. The Crusades, as the historian Carl Erdmann argues in *The Origin of the Idea of the Crusade*, constituted a new combination of old forms of the journey, an "armed pilgrimage," which at once sanctified the soldierly profession and provided an appropriate destination for anomalous social elements.[23]

In the history of geography, the Christianization of the classical world is often lamented as an end to rational and mathematical geographies and a regression to myth, fable, fantastic and imaginative topography. Thus, the East was absorbed into images of Paradise, and Gog and Magog stood at the Iron Gates of Alexander. Ancient fictions—the Amazons, Giants, pygmies, Cyclopes, dog-faced or dog-headed men, hermaphrodites, happy-landers, and people who used their feet as umbrellas, all creatures of ancient travel lore and evidence of *thoma* (marvels or curiosities; see page 106)—were absorbed into Catholic Christianity and projected upon the fringes and borders of the known world. This "mythicization" of landscape testifies to the importance of text in the creation of meaningful topography and to the fact that myth and fable are both instruments in the creation of a meaningful world, as well as conditions for actual and authentic experience.

THE WANDERING SCHOLARS OF THE MIDDLE AGES

For what is unknown to the French schools will be revealed across the Alps; and what you cannot learn among the Latins, fluent Greece will teach you.
                                        —Abelard, twelfth century

Philosophical travel, in the Middle Ages, increasingly became travel-organized and targeted to text rather than to any specific locale. Often, this pursuit of text went hand in hand with pilgrimage, for books were considered, quite independent of their contents or meaning, sacred objects that were necessary in establishing the sanctity and centrality of provincial churches. The English scholar St. Bede (known as the Venerable Bede) records in his life of St. Benedict several journeys to Rome: the first to extract the "sweetness of wholesome learning"; the second more strictly a pilgrimage to the church of St. Peter and the city "hallowed by his remains"; the third for books and relics; and the fourth for more abundant supplies of spiritual merchandise (during which he arranged for a cantor, John, to teach him the Roman manner of chant), a title of privilege, and pictures of sacred scenes. The "Carmen de Transmarine Itinères," by the seventh-century poet Aethelwald, describes the departure of pilgrims from Rome and the booty they carried off with them:

> Then they carried off the volumes
> In their numerous battalions
> Written by the Manifold
> And secret tribal protocols
> Which the prophets and Apostles,
> Learned-Speaking oracles,
> Transferred to the willing parchment
> Inspired by the Holy Spirit.

Here the book is an icon, containing secrets and powers that may not be fully understood by those who bear it away, a vehicle through which the sacred may be contagious. Alcuin, as Charlemagne's cultural agent, traveled twice to Rome, in 766 and again in 780: "Now he travelled praying; led by the love of wisdom, through many foreign lands by a foreign road, looking in hope for the new in books and studies, looking to bring back with him his finds in those lands."[24]

Philosophical travel centered upon the book, and the search for the complete book was not exclusively a Western development but a phenomenon attendant upon the founding and dissemination of the world religions: Christianity, Islam, Buddhism. The search for the complete book and the concept that contradiction is a product of incomplete knowledge, of the imperfect dispersal of wisdom, of the corruptions inherent in reproducing authorized texts, was a deeply ingrained idea within Christendom as well as in the East. The greatest of Chinese travelers, Hsüan Tsang or Tripitaka, who lived in the seventh century, was compelled to journey by his sense that the Buddhist texts that had penetrated into China were corrupt, incomplete, and full of contradictions that could be resolved only by going to India, the place where sacred text had originated: "He finally understood that the holy books themselves had important differences, differences so great that he knew not which to follow. It was then that he resolved to go to the Western world in order to ask about doubtful passages." Tripitaka's journey was also a pilgrimage; he visited all the places "made holy by the Buddha's birth and death, his preaching and his miracle working." His visit to the site of Gautama Buddha's enlightenment, the Bodhi tree, was a traumatic confrontation with alternative pasts and possibilities:

> When Tripitaka had gazed on the Bodhi-tree and thought of the moment of perfect enlightenment, he threw himself face down at the holy site. Aware of his own shortcomings, he wept. To him it was inescapably clear that, had he not been sinful in his previous existence, he might have won the right to have lived in the golden days when Buddha walked the earth and would not have been condemned to this present baser age. "I wonder," he thought, "in what troubled whirl of birth and death I was caught when Buddha achieved enlightenment."

Tripitaka's journey is the recovery of a conjectural past that reached back beyond his own birth and into the domain of possibilities unrealized yet regretted. His journey, like the journeys of medieval scholars in the West, was also an education, as he stocked his mind with ancient texts. During his five years in Nalanda (633–37), he studied the Vedas, logic, grammar, medicine, mathematics, and astronomy, attending daily lectures and traveling to holy sites during academic breaks. After completing his course of study, he debated whether to remain in the land of learning or to return to China. It was clear that he would become more famous and learned if he stayed to drink at the founts of accumulated wisdom; yet he decided to return "so that he might dispel the darkness in his native land": "In India I have visited the sacred sites and learned the hidden meaning of the different schools. I desired now to go back and translate the texts and explanations to others so that they will know what I have heard."[25]

After returning to China, Tripitaka himself became the object of philosophical pilgrimage by young men who desired to learn what he had learned. Tripitaka's journey is a new species of philosophical travel in the sense that it is keyed to texts, which were the essential vehicles of wisdom and learning, coherence, and tradition; but it echoes the old species in being directed toward the source of a tradition.

In the West, the pursuit of learning, of the books and the men who knew them, was necessitated by the dispersal and destruction of texts during the barbarian invasions from the fifth through the ninth centuries. It became the sacred and defining duty of monks and monasteries to collect, preserve, copy, and broadcast those sources of authority that seemed to be vanishing. In the sixth century, books were collected in the monastery of Bobio in northern Italy, in the Papal Library in the Lateran, in Ireland, and in the Venerable Bede's library in the monastery of Jarrow in England. The Irish were particularly prominent among the learned travelers and missionaries of the sixth and seventh centuries, both as hosts of those who traveled in pursuit of learning and as travelers themselves. As the Venerable Bede states in his *Historia Ecclesiastica*:

> Many of the nobles of the English nation and lesser men also had set out thither, forsaking their native island either for the grace of sacred learning or a more austere life. And some of them indeed soon dedicated themselves faithfully to the monastic life, others rejoiced rather to give themselves to learning, going about from one master's cell to another. All these the Irish willingly received, and saw to it to supply them with food by day without cost, and books for their studies, and teaching, free of charge.[26]

The dispersion and fragmentation of classical knowledge, the scattering of those texts essential to cultural coherence and identity, forced the repackaging and compression of ancient learning into a discrete and portable canon of texts, and generated that ubiquitous figure, the wandering scholar. There was, of course, the sacred text itself and its most respected commentators: Augustine, Jerome, Ambrose, and Gregory. Ancient philosophy survived in compendiums, digests, commentaries, and paraphrases, the most important of which were Boethius's *De Consolatione Philosophiae*; Aristotle's elementary logic, which remained accessible in Porphyry (the "old logic," in contrast to the "new logic" that entered Western Europe through Arab, Jewish, and Greek channels in the eleventh century); the works of Martianus Capella; the Venerable Bede's *De Temporum Ratione*, written in 727; Cassiodorus's handbook on liberal arts; and Isidore of Seville's *Etymologies*. These remained the most accessible canons of learning available to students at the turn of the eighth century. This very compression of all ancient wisdom into a narrow range of sources fueled the search for what had been lost and gave rise to the characteristically medieval intellectual activity of the recovery, reproduction, and interpretation of available texts. This activity, in turn, created a lust for learning—a madness for books—and a characteristically medieval attitude toward the known and unknown succinctly stated by Abelard in the quotation on page 148. What one did not know was not necessarily unknown but merely elsewhere. Abelard's attitude was extensible: what the Greeks did not know might be found in the East, in Alexandria, Baghdad, or among the Coptics and Nestorians. Conceiving of the world as a scattered book of many chapters, medieval scholars reassembled it through travels and the copying, learning, and memorization of text. Those who learned and assembled this book ultimately embodied it and became themselves the objects and goals of philosophical travel. This was more than a metaphor: the value of text was enhanced by its unavailability, and the mystery of its language became progressively incomprehensible to a laity, requiring that it be interpreted by those who held the keys to the authorizing symbols contained within it.

The demand, even the rage, for learning that began in the twelfth century is difficult for moderns to understand, born as we are in a consumer-minded culture dominated by the mass media. Modern students of medieval universities characteristically ascribe the medieval kings' and communes' intense demand for scholars to the economic importance of bodies of students and masters. But the source of the demand lay in the fact that the masters held a monopoly over the unquestioned source of legal authority, the only authority other than that of force and arms. Where the written word could be pointed to, strife ended. Questions of right and justice were referred to the voice of precedent, which was in the hands of masters collected in Bologna and Paris. The authenticity, sacredness, and power of the text made those who knew the books the only authority through which public action could be legitimized.

In the Middle Ages scholars controlled the images and symbols mobilized in public action. The texts were a source of status, legitimacy, and authority for learned men. Their power was buttressed by their mobility, which was secured by various royal guarantees and privileges. The Authentic Habita granted by the Holy Roman Emperor Frederick I to all scholars within the dominions of the empire, at the request of the doctors of law at the schools of Bologna in 1158, was the first charter of academic freedom, a freedom rooted in the right of free departure and unrestricted travel. The Habita conferred security of travel "to all scholars and especially those who profess the sacred and divine laws who are pilgrims for the sake of study."[27] It also protected students from reprisals to secure the payment of debts, including protection against being seized while traveling to extract payment for the debts of a fellow countryman. Designed as an instrument to balance the localization and privatization of law with imperial guarantees of freedom from search and imprisonment, the Authentic Habita extended the protection of the law to those who traveled beyond their local jurisdictions. The Habita spoke admiringly of "those who exile themselves through love of learning, those who prefer to wear themselves out in poverty rather than enjoy riches, and those who expose their lives to every peril, so that defenseless, they must often suffer injury from the vilest of men."[28]

Essentially, the Habita granted scholars a supraterritorial status, and this status became the property of scholars as a group and of the *universitas*—an institution identical with their collective person. In 1200, after a riot in which a number of students were killed, King Philip Augustus granted a charter of liberties to the University of Paris, exempting students from the judgment of secular courts and enjoining the bourgeoisie of Paris to aid any scholar in jeopardy. In 1295 and 1297, after the flight of the masters of Paris to Rheims, Orleans, Oxford, Italy, and Spain, King Philip IV of France reiterated and consolidated many of the freedoms and privileges that had been severally granted in the preceding years—exemptions from military levies, from tolls and tributes on the goods of scholars, and from royal taxes—assuring them freedom of passage through the kingdom:

> We believe it right to have great concern for the hardships, the exertions, the sleepless nights, the drudgery, the deprivations, the tribulations and the perils which the scholars undergo to seek the precious pearl of knowledge, and to consider how they have left

their friends, their kinsmen, and their native lands, how they have
abandoned worldly goods and family fortunes to come from distant
parts to drink of the waters flowing from the fountain of life.[29]

Their very poverty was the primary source of the scholar's power, of
their ability to force communities, kings, and popes to secure their
material existence and the conditions necessary for study. Their
wealth consisted in a few books and the fees they were able to command for their exegesis of the texts. Because they owned no property
(they rented or borrowed rooms for lectures), if a university seceded
or dispersed there was no property to sequester. Surplus revenues
were almost invariably consumed in the form of drink at the end of
the term. Because of the enormous demand for the legitimizing
power monopolized by scholars, there were always cities and rulers
ready to welcome them with salaries or privileges.

Because the scholars *were* the universities, these were mobile institutions. If, as often happened, the masters left Paris or Bologna,
their students followed, and if students fled as a result of depreda-
tions they felt were unjust, their masters followed. Scholars who mi-
grated from the chief institutions of learning—Bologna for law, Paris
for theology—started up daughter and provincial universities. In Italy, the University of Vicenza was founded by scholars migrating
from Bologna in the dispersion of 1204. The new university thrived
until 1209, when the Bolognese students and masters departed for
other places. The law school established in Arezzo in 1215 by Raf-
fredus di Benevenuto was revived from its desuetude by an emigration from Bologna in 1338 but was defunct by 1373, when the
students and masters went elsewhere. The University of Padua was
founded by students dispersing from Bologna in 1220, lured to Padua
by loans, fixed rents, and other inducements. Siena won out over
Florence in the competition for scholars who left Bologna as a result
of a Papal interdict of 1321. Florence, despite the high salaries and
extensive privileges it offered, could never get professors to stay.
Finally, in 1472, Lorenzo de Medici founded the successful and pros-
perous University of Pisa.

The beacon of learning continued to be fueled by that search
for ancient texts and precious wisdom which led to the creation of
an extraterritorial Republic of Letters that declared itself in the Renaissance. Centuries earlier, Socrates had recognized a "spell" that
could draw lovers of knowledge out of their native cities and lead

them "over the wide world." The search for learning, for texts containing the wisdom of the ancients, led to the mobility foreseen by
Socrates, and this mobility underlay the power of scholars so notable
in the Middle Ages, a mobility that was neither welcome nor in the
interest of clerical or secular authorities. Increasingly, in the late
fourteenth and fifteenth centuries, universities were identified with
buildings rather than with scholarly personnel. The period of wandering scholars came to an end with humanism and the development
of residential universities—the collegiate system: "Solidly enmeshed
in their urban environments the later medieval universities could
not easily employ the threat of migration; and this marks a fundamental departure from the era when instability was the hallmark of
university life and intermittent nomadism one of the perils of the
academic profession."[30]

Church authorities had long been suspicious of wandering
scholars. In 1231 a member of the clergy found wandering (*vagus*)
was to be stripped of clerical status and to have his head shaved so
that nothing remained of his tonsure, the shaven patch denoting a
monk or cleric. At the Council of Salzburg in 1291, the clerk who
wandered "for his bellies sake" was condemned: "They go about in
public naked ... lie in bake-ovens, frequent taverns, games, harlots,
earn their bread by their vices and cling with inveterate obstinacy
to their sect, so that no hope of amendment remaineth." The Council of Salzburg in 1274 cautioned bishops against "giving the tonsure
and habit to any but were fit and proper persons, as it is so often a
cloak for wandering." The medieval Church had never really approved of wandering; and as the Church became more propertied
and territorialized, wandering for the sake of learning came to seem
less like a self-exile than an avoidance of discipline that imperiled
the soul of the wanderer. The Blessed St. Anthony had cautioned his
monks against vagrancy: "Sit in thy cell ... and thy cell shall teach
thee all things. The monk out of his cell is a fish out of water."[31] The
wandering life put scholars, especially scholars of the poorer classes,
among an underclass, a marginalized population of travelers who
were increasingly seen, in the late Middle Ages, as a cause of instability and social disorder. Wandering, as always, was a form of pollution, of social mixing, and a disarticulation of established
distinctions and categories.

The regulation of itinerancy became the concern of both the
Church and the State in the Renaissance, a period of increasing

legislation with more and more severe penalties attached to the condition of homelessness. A statute of Queen Elizabeth for the "punishment of vagabondes" included scholars among this underclass:

> It ys nowe publyshed ... that ... all ydle persones goinge about in
> any countrey of the said Realme, using Subtyle Craftye and unlaw-
> ful games of playes, and some of them saying themselves to have
> knowledge in physiomye, Palmestrye ... and all fencers, bear-
> wardes, common players in interludes and minstrels not belonging
> to any baron of this realme ... all juglers, pedlars, tynkers and
> petye chapmen ... and all scholers of the Universityes of Oxford
> or Cambridge that goe about begging ... and all shipmen pretend-
> inge losses by sea ... shall bee deemed vages, vacabounds and sturdy
> beggars intended of by this present act.[32]

With the territorialization of a feudal social order and the denser
and denser settlement of medieval society, habitual travelers—
including wandering scholars—became more suspect as a danger to
social order and discipline. The theoretical status of the scholar was
assured by his relation to sacred and authorizing texts, and yet the
social roots of scholars in a mobile underclass of bearwardes and
minstrels provided the profession with unholy associations.

The continuities between Renaissance and medieval philosophical travel are more pronounced than the discontinuities. The impulse that fueled the recovery of learning in the fifteenth and
sixteenth centuries was fundamentally no different than what fueled
the collection, copying, and exegesis of ancient texts in the twelfth
century. The authority of the ancients was no less powerful in 1400
than it had been two centuries earlier, and the basic imperatives that
had shaped philosophical travel in the Middle Ages continued to
shape it in the modern period. Having been launched by a decen-
tralization of knowledge and a reduction of the classical canon to a
few, much-copied survivals, medieval intellectual life was inexorably
shaped towards recovering ancient texts and elaborating existing
methods of reading and analysis. The dispersion of sacred items,
among which books were prominent, reoriented philosophical travel
away from the ancient centers and beginnings of Western civilization and toward that literature—scriptural and Greco-Roman—
within which that civilization was packaged and preserved. The losses
caused by the barbarian invasions often obscure the fact that it was
as literature, law, text, and the liturgies of Christianity that the clas-

sical world survived. The book, even in the conditions of scribal reproduction, proved to be the most durable, resilient, and continuous template of culture. As the ninth-century scholar and abbot of the monastery of Fulda wrote, "To Eigilus, on the Book he Wrote": "The written word alone flouts destiny / Revives the past, and gives the lie to death."[33] Necessarily, the conditions of scribal reproduction of authoritative texts and the filling in of canon shaped the conditions under which medieval literati operated and impelled them to become mobile collectors of a dispersed heritage.

This collection of texts, significantly furthered with the invention of printing, created the literary culture within which the news of the New World was received, and new information was assimilated. The amassing of a textual tradition, of an old received wisdom, was the condition for the recognition of the new, the novel, and the original which became a prominent official motive for Renaissance voyages and humanistic travel. The historian Elizabeth Eisenstein's work on printing has redefined our notions of the Renaissance by identifying it as a "communications revolution" that enhanced the fixity of text and established a cultural "critical mass" against which advances could be measured.[34] The fleshing out of a set of classical models of architecture, painting, sculpture, rhetoric, history, music, poetry, and logic by fifteenth-century humanists consolidated a republic of letters within which could be recognized variations on established themes, novelties, or departures from norms. The reorientation of philosophical travel from the centers of ancient civilization to the peripheries of the newfound world assumes this cultural achievement of generations of medieval scholars.

"They invite you to share anything they possess and show us as much love as if
their hearts went with it.... How easy it would be to convert these people—and
to make them work for us" (Christopher Columbus).
(Courtesy of the Bettmann Archive)

CHAPTER

6

THE ENCOUNTER WITH THE NEW WORLD: EUROPE'S DISCOVERY OF ITSELF

The discovery of America was important, less because it gave birth to totally new ideas, than because it forced Europeans to come face to face with ideas and problems which were already to be found within their own cultural traditions.
—J. H. Elliott, 1970

Passage supplies information not only about the world but also about the "self" of the passenger, about the lenses, premises, and assumptions through which the traveler views the other. This is true on a collective and cultural level as well as on a personal plane. Beginning with the voyages of discovery at the end of the fifteenth century, Europeans encountered a world of ethnic others who needed to be specified. This specification mobilized traditional categories and thus the Indians, for example, were at first equated with ancient pagans, as peoples close to creation, to an original nature. Degerando's recognition of the peripheries as places of human origins would have been impossible without such a mapping of classical and textual traditions upon newly found peoples.

Here the traveler's habit of comparison operated with peculiar force. The aboriginal inhabitants of the New World were seen through the lens of text and compared with the inhabitants of the ancient world, assimilating the unfamiliar to the familiar in an operation that is neither surprising nor new but characteristic of travelers. But the strange-made-familiar becoming itself the ground of comparison worked with decisive effect upon sixteenth- and seventeenth-century Europeans. Ultimately those native peoples who were initially perceived as living embodiments of ancient pagans and similarly close to the creation of the world became a basis of comparison against which Europeans perceived and defined themselves as an advanced, mature, and rational culture—a fully developed civilization.

Primitive, natural peoples could and did provide a new language of cultural self-explication, new words and concepts that were descriptive of a European culture born of medieval realities. An inherently individualistic medieval society, which coalesced out of relations of war and which evolved through the compacts, acts of association, and oaths of fealty contracted by putatively free and sovereign individuals, was not describable in the terms offered by classical languages of social orders and hierarchy. But this reality was explicable within the new, broader context, within the world of examples provided by the voyagers and the literature they produced, a literature that ultimately replaced chivalric literature in the taste of self-improving seventeenth- and eighteenth-century elites.

In the sixteenth and seventeenth centuries, postclassical European culture found its voice, a voice first recognized in projecting classical models against a newfound world, which gave Europeans important distinctions between themselves and other worlds, distant in space and increasingly regarded as distant in time—as "earlier," "prior" stages of human development. Thus the Renaissance voyages set up a dynamic of cultural refraction that modernized old Europe and produced a consciousness on the part of Europeans that they occupied a place at the center of a world, no longer merely a peripheral frontier of ancient centers. As a consequence of these voyages and of European travel generally, modern Europeans generated a new history, a natural history of man that constitutes one of the most valuable, but problematical, bequests to the industrial culture we inhabit. In this chapter, I will explore first the terms of comparison—the equation of Indians with ancients—by which the unknown was made known and then the methods by which Europeans distanced themselves from a newly found nature, using a history which narrated the terms of their difference as a progress from a state of nature.

THE INDIANS AND THE GOLDEN AGE OF PAGANISM

Paganism was the most inclusive, unambiguous category of otherness.
                                                —Michael T. Ryan, 1981

The European voyages of the sixteenth and seventeenth centuries brought to consciousness a cultural identity, one that was essentially secular rather than religious, rooted in nature rather than in books, and buttressed by observation rather than by reading. The consensus among those who have pondered the impact of the discovery of the New World upon the old is that it lay less in the importation of new ideas than in the projection of tradition within a new dimension in space. The contention of J. H. Elliott, that the importance of the discovery of America lay in the way this required the mobilization of tradition, remains unchallengeable.[1]

The Spanish, Portuguese, and Italian voyagers were not as astonished by their initial contact with unsuspected peoples as we today might expect, for these peoples were immediately categorizable. They were either the ancient Islamic enemies or some other variety of pagans, idolators, or gentiles and, as such, similar to those peoples Christianized through the acts of the apostles and the swords of crusading Christian knights. If Christianity was the most inclusive category of European identity in the fifteenth century, paganism was the "most inclusive, unambiguous category of otherness."[2] It was the undeniable paganism of newly encountered peoples that motivated the voyagers to categorize them as ancient. However respected, the ancients had been pagans, and through their similarities with the ancients a world of strangers was made known. The Portuguese explorer Vasco de Quiroga wrote in 1535: "This world over here is rightly called a New World, not because it was newly found, but because in its people and in almost everything else, it resembles the world of the first Age, the Golden Age."[3] These pagans went back to a time even earlier than of saints Peter and Paul; they were pagans of the sort that classical writers had regarded as preceding their own, the Silver Age of the poets, the iron age of historical wars. The similarity could be reinforced through the selection of what now seemed significant details:

> They go naked, they know neither weights nor measures, nor that source of all misfortunes, money: living in a Golden Age, without laws, without lying judges, without books, satisfied with their life, and in no wise solicitous for the future. Nevertheless ambition and the desire to rule trouble even them, and they fight among themselves, so that even in the Golden Age there is never a moment without war.[4]

From the beginning, the inhabitants of the New World exhibited characteristics that thwarted voyagers' attempts to place them within the traditional European categories. In the description just quoted, the Italian humanist Pietro Martire d'Anghiera (whose position at the Spanish court from 1487 allowed him direct access to information from voyagers) was conscious of the mixture of paradise and war. The nakedness of the Indians suggested innocence, as did their ignorance of money; and the absence of a state with laws, magistrates, and judges implied a prelapsarian status. And yet the element of warfare and warlikeness that was stressed by all the voyagers implied a postparadisaical state.

Columbus's first letter describing discoveries made on his first voyage stressed the pacifism of the natives of the Bahamas and Hispaniola, who had "no iron or steel or weapons, nor are they fitted to use them, not because they are not well built men and of handsome stature, but because they are marvellously timorous." Again and again, in his earliest impressions, he describes the natives as "incurably timid," "guileless and generous," pacific, unsuited for warfare. Those traits native to barbarism—wildness, aggressiveness, and warlike spirit—were found in the Caribs and in the inhabitants of Puerto Rico and the Lesser Antilles, who were reputed to be cannibals and admired by the Spaniards for their intractability and courage. This split image of the natives as pacific, thus suitable to be converted to Christianity, and as warlike, thus suitable for enslavement, obviously served the interests of the discoverers in exploiting the lands they found. The first Indians whom Columbus sent back to Spain were classified as cannibals and sold as slaves there;

he was quick to see in them a resource to defray the costs of colonization. After listing the necessary items for the colonists in Hispaniola, Columbus noted in a letter to Isabella: "Payment for these things could be made to them in slaves, from among these cannibals, a people very savage and suitable for the purpose, and well made and of very good intelligence. We believe that they, having abandoned that inhumanity, will be better than other slaves, and their inhumanity they will immediately lose when they are out of their native land."[5]

While returning to Spain after the second voyage to face an inquiry into his administration, Columbus's perception of the peoples he had found was utterly altered, in tune with the growing resistance of native inhabitants to their exploitation by the Spanish. To him, natives had shifted into the zone of savagery: "I ought to be judged as a captain who went from Spain to the Indies to conquer a people, warlike and numerous. And with customs and beliefs very different from ours, a people living in the mountains and the highlands, having no settled dwellings and apart from us."[6] He claimed that only "knights of the sword" and not "men of letters" would understand the conditions he had faced and overcome. Of course, changing those he vanquished from pacifistic Indians to aggressive savages served Columbus's self-image as knight, conqueror, and newly made lord.

Bartolomé de Las Casas, a Spanish Dominican missionary and historian, was at pains to demonstrate both the intrinsic rationality of the Indians and the fact that, though not necessarily pacifistic, their wars were essentially just and defensive wars waged against cruel conquerors. And yet the warlikeness of the Indians continued to weave a contradictory thread through images of a pacifistic and paradisaical state. In the first book to use the voyage literature as a mirror in which Europeans might see themselves and their blemishes, Sir Thomas More's *Utopia* (written 1516–17), the Utopians are not pacifists. On the contrary, they make war with a thoroughness and ruthlessness directly at odds with the ethics of chivalry, in which a European nobility validated its military functions. In his late-sixteenth-century essay "On Cannibals," Montaigne maintained that they observed only two moral teachings: "resoluteness in war and affection for their wives."[7]

The image of the New World as both Golden Age and paradise—however applicable it seemed to the richness and abundance of flora, the nakedness and absence of shame of the people, their ignorance of money, law, and the state—could not be wholly sustained in the face of the warlikeness, aggression, and "savagery" of the Indians whom the armed and expropriating newcomers confronted. Early commentators on America were able to introduce finer levels and gradations amid the varieties of Indian cultures. Garcilasso de la Vega, the child of an Inca mother and a Spanish father, received a humanistic education and ultimately emigrated from Peru to Spain. Eager to distinguish his own ancestry from the barbarism and savagery being attributed to inhabitants of the New World, he placed the most exaggerated savage traits of the Indians—the worship of devils, human sacrifices and cannibalism, living in caves and rocks, shameless nakedness, unrestrained sexuality, incest, sodomy, sorcery, and witchcraft—in an old regime, a "heathen time" before the coming of the Inca princes who made these "wild creatures ... into men, and made them capable of reason and converting to any good doctrine."[8] The Jesuit Father José de Acosta who spent seventeen years in Panama and Peru, publishing his work *The Natural and Moral History of the Indies* in 1588, distinguished three phases in the moral history of the native peoples: barbarism, community, and empire and the triumph of the state. The first inhabitants of Mexico, called the Chicimecas, were hunters, "very barbarous and savage":

> They did neither sow nor till the ground, neither lived they together; for all their exercise was to hunt, wherein they were very expert. They lived in the roughest part of the mountains beastlike, without any pollicie, and they went all naked. They had no superiors, nor did acknowledge or worship any gods, neither had any manner of ceremonies or religion.[9]

Here the state of barbarism is assumed to be presocial, resembling the Cyclopes, those antisocial peoples encountered by Odysseus: "They have no assemblies to debate in, they have no ancestral ordinances: they live in arching caves on the tops of high hills, and the head of each family heeds no other, but makes his own ordinances for his wife and children."[10] Both ancient sources and Acosta agree that the "wild man," the man within nature, is alone and solitary, without those bonds and settlements that supply a social nature. From this wild state of solitude, Acosta suggests, an evolution to the savage state occurred. In the savage state, Indians lived in commu-

nities and held the land in common, putting forth leaders as occasions of war demanded:

> For this occasion many nations of the Indies have not endured any
> kings or absolute and soveraigne Lords, but live in communalities
> creating and appointing captains and princes for certain occasions
> only, to whom they obey during the time of their charge, then after
> they return to their former estates. The greatest part of this New
> World (where there are no settled Kingdoms or established com-
> monweales, neither princes nor succeeding kings) they govern
> themselves in this manner, although there be some Lords and prin-
> cipall men raised above the common sort . . . but that in some places,
> they are yet more barbarous, scarcely acknowledging any head but
> all command and govern in common, having no other thing, but
> wit, violence, unreason and disorder, so that he as most may, most
> commands.[11]

Thus, the degree of barbarism is keyed to the level of political order, the extent to which some are raised above others to function
as "soveraigne Lords." Acosta argues that the communitarian state
that continued outside the boundaries of native empires was also a
premonetary state. "They used no gold or silver to trafficke or buy
withall, but did change and trucke one thing for another, as Homer
and Plinie report of the ancients."[12] The stage of a primitive com-
munism existing before the use of money or property, before the
development of a state, was also identified by Pietro Martire as the
condition of the native inhabitants of Cuba when they were discovered by Europeans:

> It is proven that amongst them the land belongs to everybody just
> as does the sun or the water. They know no difference between
> mine and thine, that source of all evils. It requires so little to satisfy
> them, that in that vast region there is always more land to cultivate
> than is needed. It is indeed a golden age, neither ditches, nor
> hedges, nor walls enclose their domains; they live in gardens open
> to all, without laws and without judges; their conduct is naturally
> equitable, and whoever injures his neighbor is condemned a crim-
> inal and an outlaw.[13]

This was a clear and studied contrast to European culture, a culture
rooted in property and private estates surrounded by hedges and

ditches, a culture in which justice was a profession and economic relations were increasingly commercialized.

Acosta was one of the first to propose that the origins of the state lay in the lordship and leadership necessitated by the conditions of war. Once this period was over, and war no longer waged, there was no longer a need for captains and princes, who then returned "to their former estates." Permanent kingship was an institution he attributed to the native excellence of those who exercised authority in emergencies:

> There are great and apparent conjectures, that these men for a long time had neither kings nor commonweales, but lived in troupes, as they do at this day in Florida, the Chiriguanas, those of Bresil and many other nations, which have no certaine kings, but as occasion is offered in peace or warre, they choose their Captaines as they please. But some men excelling others in force and wit, began in time to rule and domineere as Nembrot [Nimrod?] did; so increasing by little and little, they erected the kingdomes of Peru and Mexico, which our Spaniards found.[14]

Thus, in the New World, the political community seemed to be neither an outgrowth of paternity and the family, as Aristotle suggested, nor a product of the mutuality of need, as Plato argued. In this instance the state arose out of true "nobility," out of excellence in "force and wit," out of a climate of warfare that persisted in the conditions of peace.

Projected against the screen of the newfound world are not just ancient textual traditions but also a notion of the state native to the medieval period—the state as an individual estate, an individuality writ large, an institutionalization of innate virtues and nobilities of the person who exercises authority. The state has its origins in barbaric circumstances of warfare and intertribal conflict. Into the attempt to sort out the differences between native American polities and communities is injected the intrinsically medieval notion that the state arises out of society as a selection of individuals capable of defending the community against foreign and alien military threats. The historian J. H. Elliott is justified in arguing that "[b]y the end of the sixteenth century ... the experience of America had provided Europe with at least the faint outlines of a theory of social development."[15] Acosta and Garcilasso de la Vega provided the makings of a conception of a linear progress from a wild state of individu-

alism, through a stateless communitarian existence in which all
property was held in common, to the sovereign state conceived in
the image of an individual lordship—a monarchy or principality.

Among post-Renaissance philosophers, John Locke was the only
major social-contract theorist to conceive of the state of nature as
an actual historical period rather than as a logical construct or a
fiction (as Thomas Hobbes and Jean-Jacques Rousseau were both to
conceive it); he had in his library a much-thumbed and annotated
copy of the 1606 English translation of Acosta.[16] Locke's state of
nature is a layered conceptualization of a condition of natural individualism, "a state of perfect freedom to order their actions and
dispose of their persons as they think fit, within the bounds of the
law of nature, without asking leave, or depending on the will of any
other man." The state of nature was also a communitarian state in
which mankind held the earth in common, but, due to the "incon-
veniences" of that condition, the communitarian state gave way to a
polity based on contract. Locke regarded money, that feature in
which Europeans most obviously differed from primitive and natural
man, as the invention that ended the common ownership of property and introduced the possibility of inequalities in the possession
of wealth:

> [T]he same rule of property, viz., that every man should have as
> much as he could make use of, would still hold in the world without
> straitening anybody, since there is land enough in the world to
> suffice double the inhabitants, had not the invention of money, and
> the tacit agreement of men to put a value on it, introduced (by
> consent) larger possessions and a right to them.[17]

Each of the differences found in the New World could be narrated
as an "acquisition" in a sequence that led from a state of nature to
a state of political society. All those things the initial explorers found
missing in that ambiguous paradise of the New World—money, private property, kingship, sexual repression, shame—could be regarded as acquisitions that led to the moral, political, and economic
conditions in which Europeans found themselves in the sixteenth
century. Clearly, the New World neither introduced new ideas nor
created a crisis of conscience, although it may be said to have provided the materials with which Europeans clarified their conscience,
made official certain features of their culture, and focused a self-

image woven from their differences vis-à-vis an original condition of man. This condition was, for Hobbes and ambiguously for Locke, a state of war from which the sovereignty of the ruling individual arose.

DISTANCING THE OBSERVER FROM THE OBSERVED

The history of our discipline reveals that the use of time almost invariably is made for the purpose of distancing those who are observed from the time of the observer.
—Johannes Fabian, 1983

The very discovery of continents unknown to the ancients had set a clear limit to ancient knowledge, which even a dyed-in-the-wool Aristotelian, such as Acosta, gleefully overstepped. When he arrived in Peru, Acosta found the "torrid zone" so cold that he had to sit outdoors in the sun. "What could I else do then, but laugh at Aristotle's meteors and his philosophie, seeing that in that place and at that season, whenas all should be scorched with heat, according to his rules, I, and all my companions were acolde?"[18] The evidence of the senses and of experience could lighten the burden of the past. The native inhabitants of the newfound lands were regarded as inferior to their European discoverers, as primitive, simple, and natural peoples; and, similarly, the diminution of the authority of the ancients that is noticeable in the seventeenth and eighteenth centuries went along with a view of the ancients as an infantile people, as "children writ large." Europeans began to regard themselves as an advanced and advancing civilization, as an adult culture necessarily superior to ancient and classical beginnings.

The English philosopher and scientist Francis Bacon was the first to draw these conclusions and to reverse the meaning of antiquity, claiming that title for a mature and experienced European polity:

> The opinion which men cherish of antiquity is altogether idle, and scarcely accords with the term. For the old age and increasing years of the world should in reality be considered as antiquity, and this is rather the character of our own times than of the less advanced age of the world in those of the ancients. For the latter, with respect

to ourselves, are ancient and elder, with respect to the world ... younger. And as we expect a greater knowledge of human affairs and more mature judgment from an old man, than from a youth ... so we have reason to expect much greater things from our own age ... than from antiquity, since the world has grown older, and its stock has been increased and accumulated with an infinite number of experiments and observations.[19]

The implication of Bacon's reversal is clear: modern Europeans are not members of a youthful, rude outgrowth of an ancient and wondrous civilization but of an advanced stock, their experience extended by experiments and observations that have brought them far beyond their crude and barbarous beginnings. This self-conception is appropriate to a world that is a center in its own right, no longer a periphery desperately trying to retain its links with the old centers of order and beginnings or to recover lost glories and forgotten wisdom. To Bacon, the voyages added to the wealth of information that expanded the modern mind beyond any comfortable accommodation to ancient structures and orders. The enormous expansion of information accumulated through voyages, observations, and experiments required a new framework and a new order, which Bacon attempted to supply in his *Novum Organum* (1620):

We must also take into our consideration that many objects in nature fit to throw light upon philosophy have been exposed to our view and discovered by long voyages and travels, in which our times have abounded. It would be indeed dishonourable to mankind if the regions of the material globe, the earth, the seas and stars should be so prodigiously developed and illustrated in our age, and yet the boundaries of the intellectual globe should be confined to the narrow discoveries of the ancients.[20]

Seventeenth-century scientific societies attempted to regulate observation, to outline the proper subjects, and to provide a forum within which observations by individuals could be linked to advance the sciences and human knowledge in general. The science of man, as Degerando defined it, was a science of observation; and the method of observation was simple: "[I]t gathers facts to compare them, and compares them to know them better. The natural sciences are in no way more than a series of comparisons."[21]

In their observations, modern Europeans saw those people who seemed to differ most from themselves—in their nakedness, their innocence, their lack of warlike characteristics and private property—as the earliest and most primitive peoples. Being the closest to man's original state in nature, they embodied norms that elsewhere had been corrupted, contaminated, and outlived. The earliest peoples were assumed to be those who differed least from the sheer creaturehood of humanity. In a letter to King Manuel I of Portugal, reporting on the contacts made with Brazilian Indians on Pedro Alvares Cabral's voyage of 1499, Pedro Vaz de Cominha continually emphasized the beauty and health of the natives—particularly striking to men whose fleet had lost half its complement of men and seven of its thirteen vessels before reaching India:

> [T]hey are a bestial people and of very little knowledge; and for this reason they are so timid. Yet withal they are well cared for and are very clean, and in this it seems to me that they are rather like the birds or wild animals, to which the air gives better feathers and better hair than to tame ones. And their bodies are so clean and so fat and so beautiful that they could not be more so; and this causes me to presume that they have no houses or dwellings in which to gather, and the air in which they are brought up makes them so.[22]

Later, Cominha found that he had been wrong—the natives had houses. Yet his logical deduction had been based on their health, innocence, and beauty: they were in a state of nature, the earliest of men, not yet evicted from the Garden, living as the birds and animals of the forest. The differences Europeans found between themselves and the natives could thus be mediated in terms of a moral history, in which a contradictory cultural self-consciousness could be submerged, temporalized, and narrated. This history was at once a corruption and a fall from innocence and a progress, an advance beyond the simple, earliest, and most natural state of human existence. Thus, the time intervening between the natural and the civilized conditions of man, the time that mediated and explained the difference between simple and complex societies, could be regarded as a fall, as a progress, or as a mixture of both. Relations between Europeans and natives could be similarly regarded—as contacts polluting an original happiness and innocence, or as contacts raising a simple and backward people to adulthood, civility, and maturity. Europeans could be self-conscious bearers of gifts and diseases, the agents of a loss of purity, and civilizers. In the nineteenth century, these possibilities were split. As nature itself was increasingly regarded as having a history, this history was narrated in terms of evolution, a progress from primordial simplicity to evident complexity. The earlier, Christian notion of history as a fall, a barbarization, pollution, or corruption—those ideas of the effects of time that Renaissance men had invested in the Middle Ages—continue to operate within anthropology to this day. Contact between people whom God had set apart was invariably conceived as a meeting between the youth and the maturity of man. In this conceptualization of differences in space as differences in time, there is a scarcely disguised hierarchy—the notion of European superiority over others. Degerando's consciousness of the superiority of the observer to the observed is clear in his instructions to the zoologists, botanists, geographers, and other observers accompanying Baudin: "Go to them only to offer benefits. Bring them our arts, and not our corruption, the standard of our morality, and not the example of our vices, our sciences, and not our scepticism, the advantages of civilization and not its abuses."[23]

The French, on eighteenth-century voyages of exploration, seem to have enjoyed a good opinion of their motives and a clear conscience, invariably conceiving of themselves as bearers of gifts and benefits to the less perfectly civilized. Among the toasts recorded upon the departure of Baudin's expedition is one offered by an M. Millin: "To the islanders who will be able to value the good works of the intrepid mariners, who are going, at the peril of their life, to bring them civilization, useful arts, love of humanity."[24] The notion that Europeans could, if they were not so good, bring ills and corruptions upon these people—"men recently from the hand of God," according to Montaigne[25]—was the flip side of that assumption. Like explorers of many other nationalities, the French often found the natives ungrateful for the gifts bestowed upon them, and complained bitterly:

> We have loaded them with presents. The feeble and the weak, particularly children at the breast, were the marked object of our caresses. We have sown in their fields every kind of useful grain. We have left hogs, goats and sheep in their habitations, which will probably multiply, in exchange for all of which we demanded nothing. Nevertheless they threw stones at us, and robbed us of everything which it was possible for them to carry off.

This testimony by Jean François de Galaup la Perouse, a French sailor and explorer who was killed by natives on his last voyage in 1788, shows he did not believe in the innocence of the natives, but thought them "as corrupt as the circumstances in which they are placed will allow them to be."[26]

The tendency of modern Europeans to equate differences in space with differences in time, to "historize"—the essential feature of philosophical travel—continued to operate as a fundamental thesis of European natural science in the form of evolutionary theory. This temporalization of difference allowed Europeans to justify morally their exploitation and appropriation of the world's resources as tutelage, education, the bestowal of the gifts of maturity upon children. This temporal distancing of recording observer from subject observed, which was achieved through the assumption of a difference of "age," made the communicational event of contact, the mutual learning process implicit in thousands of events of intercultural communication, into a shouting across the chasm of ages rather than a meeting of peoples and the eliciting of a common motive. The covert assignment of status to peoples, implicit in the temporalizations of philosophical travel, assumed they could be understood in terms of the slot they occupied in the evolutionary order. The tutelage of "children" by an advanced, modern European culture was itself a given of nature. Violence could be read as the necessary punishment due to children for their disobedience; exploitation, as instruction in the work ethic; the command of native resources, as exemplifications of the mastery of adults over their dependents.

Anthropologists, while decrying the pollution by which Europeans with their goods and manners corrupted innocents who needed to be protected and studied before they disappeared, made exactly the same assumptions. To travel in space was to travel in time, and time was used to distance "those who are observed from the time of the observer." Time thus served to separate those who were in contact, exchanging goods, gods, clothing, and weapons, who were mutually at work in fashioning a global history. For anthropologists, the distancing of time works as it did for Renaissance historians. The ages intervening between the childhood and the maturity of man served to separate out, to make sacred, to purify those norms thought to reside in primitive society. Anthropology thus inherited the functions of Renaissance history in providing a gallery of "models of man"—distant in time but ever present and observable—that could be used in judging modernity. Ultimately, the anthropological model of primitive man replaced the ancient world as a repository of cherished norms and has come to provide a new classicism especially tailored to an industrial age.

Natives of industrial culture find this heritage problematical. On the one hand, it is useful in reducing floods of information, organizing it in some kind of linear history. By means of temporalization, the differences perceived in passage through space can be ordered in sequences with moral implications for the health, growth, and evolution of the species. Difference can be read as evidence of change from one state to another. This assumption, as I will discuss in the following chapter, was a key ingredient in fashioning a history of nature that flowered in Charles Darwin and Alfred Russel Wallace's theory of evolution, a theory that recontextualized humans and animals within a temporal, natural order and produced new conceptions of history and of time.

On the other hand, this instrument of order, as with any intellectual instrument, is blinding, as well as being, perhaps, fundamentally immoral. It hides the moments, the "presents," that bind actors to one another in the communicational practice of travelers. It necessarily lessens, by providing fixed roles for observers and observed, the agency of the "observer" as actor in the creation of a world. It led to a willed ignorance of the world that was actually being made, and that we now live in, under the rubric of child-parent relations. The temporalization of human relationships and the viewing of these relationships through the lens of history actually deny historical processes, by subverting consciousness of the present, the moment, in which history is being constantly rendered:

> The distance between the West and the Rest on which all classical anthropological theories have been predicated is by now being disputed in regard to almost every conceivable aspect (moral, aesthetic, intellectual, political). Little more than technology and sheer economic exploitation seem to be left over for the purpose of "explaining" Western Superiority.... There remains "only" the all-pervading denial of coevalness which ultimately is expressive of a cosmological myth of frightening magnitude and persistency. It takes imagination and courage to picture what would happen to the West (and to anthropology) if the temporal fortress were suddenly invaded by the Time of its other.[27]

There is no longer, on this planet, a time of the other. There is only one time and one world that generations of travelers have made. Modernity is inescapable, at least in the testimony of those who have tried to escape it in wars and travels, and is thus a reality that cannot be wished away.

Let us today abandon the evolutionary schema and dismantle the architecture connecting moments in a story that details either human progress or human corruption. Restoring context to human action in the past, through an analysis of how choices were actually made in the experience of events connecting cultures, would return to us a sense of human action as a specification of freedom rather than of necessity. And this kind of history would serve the living much more than would a notion of history as the story of how things got to be the way they are; it would end the covert subordination of the past as an explanation (read "legitimation") of our present, the story of how things should be as, in fact, they are. This stripping away of age-old intellectual baggage would aid in the construction of an event-based history of the industrial civilization in which we—comfortably or uncomfortably—reside. This is the chief task of this generation of historians, a task that may be served by a history of travel.

Darwin measuring the speed of an elephant tortoise on the Galápagos Islands
(Courtesy of the Bettmann Archive)

7

THE ALIENATED EYE: SCIENTIFIC TRAVEL

We are but nature given eyes and by a twist
of DNA, earth given to our care.

—Eleanor Wilner, 1984

For above all other senses, the eye having the most immediate and quick commerce
with the soul, gives it a more smart touch than the rest, leaving in the fancy some-
what unutterable; so that an eye-witness of things conceives them with an imagi-
nation more complete, strong and intuitive, than he can either apprehend or deliver
by way of relation.

—Henry Blount, 1634

The experience of travel has significantly shaped and contributed to modern definitions of scientific objectivity and is implicit in the development of modern consciousness: relativistic, eschewing absolutes, deifying the external perspective, the alienated, disacculturated—even voracious—eye that assumes a radical disjunction between subject and object. Indeed, I suggest that the experience of travel constitutes the sensual ground implicit and explicit in the choices and preferences that make up modern observational science, even though, clearly, the concepts and methods of this science already existed within inherited intellectual traditions and are not deducible from the experience of travel or from any other experience.

The popularity of inductive and observational science—which treats the world as observable matter rather than as a code or as a system of implicit meanings—reflects the preference for a logic open to experience, particularly the experience of travel, although experience does not create this logic. Modern science arose as Europeans were becoming self-conscious travelers inside and outside the boundaries of their culture, experiencing new peoples, plants, animals, and landscapes. As I will argue in this chapter, the methodological choices made by those attempting to integrate this experience were not arbitrary. The concepts of objectivity as disacculturation, of the assumed distance between observer and observed, of the scientific as the outside point of view, of the world as open rather than closed system—all accord with the existential and epistemological situation of the traveler described in part I.

The legitimation of curiosity as an amoral, and then heroic, motive in the Renaissance, the development of disciplines of travel, of techniques of observing and recording the world, preceded and were assumed in Francis Bacon's redefinition of science as disciplined observation and ordered experience. The Baconian theology of observation which legitimated the new science altered, in turn, the form and style of travel books which began to be conceived as a means of the objective description of the world, an inventory of its contents. In the seventeenth and eighteenth centuries, travel reports came to provide the evidential basis for new natural and social sciences.

Old forms of travel—military and commercial expeditions—were redesigned and reconceived as scientific expeditions, new, mobile structures of intellectual labor specifically designed for the accumulation of information about novel species of plants, animals, varieties of humanity. The result of the efforts of generations of mobile, recording observers was a flood of information which expanded old scientific disciplines like botany and founded new ones like geology. These disciplines were the matrix of a new history of nature that was formulated in the evolutionary theory of Charles Darwin and Alfred Russel Wallace, with whom this story concludes. In their theories we may find the latest appearance of the assumptions of philosophical travel and a return to beginnings, to the fixed problem at the root of the human experience of mobility which is at once an alienation and a search for defining origins.

THE LEGITIMATION OF CURIOSITY

*The searching mind and the restless imagination were declared sacrosanct. It was
a stupendous revolution, glorious and absurd.*
—Erich Heller, 1968

During the Renaissance traveling out of curiosity became an admired rather than a dubious motive, as the traveler was now seen as
a discoverer of the world and a manufacturer of fact. St. Augustine
(fourth century), St. Bernard (tenth century), and St. Thomas Aqui-
nas (thirteenth century) had all regarded *curiositas* as a venial sin, as
"lust of the eye," a desire "not for fleshly enjoyment but for gaining
personal experience through the flesh." The medieval notion of the
senses as avenues of sin and corruption shaped the theological attitude toward observation of the world as something inherently suspicious and leading to a love of the world and a pursuit of morally
unwarranted knowledge. Augustine had lamented the *curiositas* that
led individuals into the material world and away from the interiors
of soul and spirit in which lay all hope for salvation. Travelers go
out "to admire the mountain's peaks, giant waves in the sea, the
broad courses of rivers and the circuits of the stars—and they leave
themselves behind."[1] People in the Renaissance were possibly no
more or less curious than medievals or ancients, but in the fifteenth
century it is clear that the motive of curiosity was first legitimized,
then deified and even sacralized.

The historian Christian Zacher, in his recent work on pilgrimage
and curiosity, argues that, in the late fourteenth century, *curiositas* had
lost its morally pejorative overtones and, by the fifteenth century, was
regarded by Petrarch as a characteristic of superior minds: "Whatever
its origin, I know that in men's minds, especially in superior minds,
resides an innate longing to see new places, to keep changing one's
home."[2] By the beginning of the sixteenth century, curiosity was considered a legitimating impulse of travels; and Cardinal Raphael, cham-
berlain to the pope, granted papal permission for the publication of
Varthema's travels (1510) in distinctly postmedieval terms. Proclaim-
ing that the glory won by travelers was richly deserved as they aug-
mented geographical knowledge, he declared in his preface to
Varthema's travels that such journeys "yield no less pleasure than

profit; on which account those who have devoted themselves to such studies have always been held in the highest honor and richly rewarded."[3]

Cultural and intellectual change proceeds through the agencies of representation and communication, and nowhere is this clearer than in the role that printing played in the legitimation of curiosity as an appropriate motive of travel. Elizabeth Eisenstein argues that the impact of print in the Renaissance lay in its "fixity," its power to secure textual traditions.[4] It is print that made travel literature a popular literature, and which made it possible to integrate the observations of voyagers into a literature, into those compendiums of travel that began to appear in the Renaissance, such as those edited by Richard Hakluyt, Giambattista Ramusio, and Samuel Purchas.[5] The "feedback loop" of information through printed texts created a new category of received wisdom. Humanistic travelers were, unlike medieval scholars, able to assume the known and to focus upon what was unknown, unrepresented, or distorted in the literature. This assumption of a secure tradition is implicit in the very notion of discovery and in the redefinition of the iconographic traveler as an explorer of new worlds and unknown peoples. Lodovico di Varthema launched himself beyond the borders of Egypt and the Holy Land, claiming that these places were too familiar to be of any interest to educated readers, the imagined audience for his journal: "I, longing for novelty (as a thirsty man longs for fresh water), departed from these places as being too well known to all." His travels, in effect, were dictated by a need to go beyond what, through the agency of print, had become common knowledge: "Inasmuch as all other countries have been considerably written about by our people, I deliberated in my own mind that I would see those which had been the least frequented."[6] The significant journeys and the significant travel reports were those that added to received information. Strictly speaking, the ancients had no concept of discovery. They presumed to know the limits of the world, established by virtue of the very structure of the universe: the world extended to the edge of the ocean, which was connected to the heavens. A conqueror such as Alexander the Great was not engaged in discovery so much as in the appropriation of a known and limited world through the quasiritualistic means of circumnavigation.

Ranking curiosity among the virtues was nothing less than removing the moral restraints upon the pursuit of knowledge and promoting the seeker after knowledge of the world to the position of hero. Erich Heller, in his 1968 essay on Faust, suggests that the promotion of this figure from a villain deserving of damnation—the epitome of pride and unwarranted speculation—to Renaissance man and hero reflects an underlying "revolutionary theology of the great scientific explorers in the sixteenth and seventeenth centuries."[7]

The Theology of Observation

A primary contributor to this "revolutionary theology" of observation was Francis Bacon, who argued that it was the pursuit of knowledge of good and evil, of moral knowledge—not the pursuit of knowledge of nature, which was innocent and even prescribed by God—that had caused the Fall:

> For it was not that pure and innocent knowledge of nature, by which Adam gave names to things from their properties, that was the origin and occasion of the Fall, but that ambitious and imperious appetite for moral knowledge, distinguishing good from evil, the intent that man might revolt from God and govern himself [which] was both the cause and means of temptation.[8]

Moral knowledge, knowledge of good and evil, properly belonged to faith and religion; observation produced "amoral" knowledge and, even more, was a means by which the eye, blighted by damnation, might recover its primal innocence, restoring that coherence between humankind and nature lost with the exile from the Garden.

The theology and disciplines of observation, as defined in sixteenth-century "methods" or "regimes" of travel and by Francis Bacon, evolved against the prejudices inherent both in Christianity, which asserted the corruption of the senses, and traditional rationalism, which asserted their inadequacy. The vagaries of sense impressions, the susceptibility to illusion of those relying on experience alone, had been emphasized by ancient rationalists as reasons for preferring the certainties of mathematics to the flux of appearances. But the notions of objectivity promulgated by Bacon and the new science also emphasized the limitations, distortions, and partialities of observation. Insofar as observers understood the sources of error inherent in perception, their observations, their reports of phenomena could be trusted and corrected through the observations of others. Thus the skeptical and disciplined, rather than the credulous and casual, observer was canonized as the discoverer of truth.

Francis Bacon established a theology of observation and the basis of modern empiricisms by asserting that the senses are a natural channel between the human mind and the world, but one corrupted and occluded by what we consider culture: everyday speech, popular opinion, the worship of tradition (the ancients), individual temperament and taste, and the imagination, which leaps to conclusions on the basis of insufficient evidence. The disciplines of observation and experimentation were nothing but the stripping away of all these sources of error in order to bring back the natural correspondence between mind and nature, which is the source of progress in the sciences.

In this sense, Bacon's model of objectivity is a disacculturation, the removal of the observer from the cultural medium of perception, the conscious structuring of a sensual relationship between the self and the world. Once we ceased to set "the stamps and seals of our own images upon God's creatures and works," it would be possible to see, recognize, "and acknowledge the creator's stamps" within this creation. The corruption of the senses might be reversed if humans "would humbly and with a certain reverence, draw near and turn over the great volume of creatures, stop and meditate upon it; and, being cleansed, and free from opinions, handle them choicely and entirely." Bacon's experimental and observational science was the edge of a new theology shriving the senses of their inherited guilt, the method of induction a means of regaining an original innocence of eye and reversing the effects of the Fall. This reversal was to be achieved through observation and induction, which Bacon conceived as a form of work and action, in contrast to traditional science which he condemned as idle speculation and dispute about words and their definition: "For we consider induction to be that form of demonstration which assists the senses, closes in upon nature, and presses on, and, as it were, mixes itself with action."[9]

The Authority of the Eye

But the authority of direct observation may be something more than an ideological or a methodological postulate of seventeenth-century European science; this authority may lie in the power of the eye to create a present, a fixed moment in time. The act of observation, of witness, declares the simultaneity of the act of seeing and the thing or event witnessed, and thus creates a window in the flow of time. Conversely, a "hearing" or a "reading" of an event asserts its pastness and its completeness. Perhaps this is why universal authority is given to eyewitness accounts, the worth of which is proverbially "worth more than ten heard-says."[10]

Implicit in this concept of the eye as direct channel to the world are the superiority of direct experience to book learning and the high valuation placed upon books containing an author's experience, observations, information in contrast to those that simply stored, rearranged, or promulgated information derived from other books. This devaluation of book learning is explicit in Henry Blount's justification of his journey to Turkey in 1634:

> Wherefore I desiring somewhat to inform myself of the Turkish nation, would not sit down with a book knowledge thereof, but rather (through the hazard and endurance of travel) receive it from my own eye, not dazzled with any affection, prejudice or mist of education, which pre-occupate the mind, and delude it with partial ideas, as with a false glass, representing the object in colours and proportions untrue; for the just censure of things is to be drawn from their end whereto they are aimed, without requiring them to one's customs and ordinances.[11]

The legitimation of curiosity in the Renaissance, and Bacon's formulation of a theology of observation, redefined the character of the serious traveler. No longer the bearer of fabulous gifts, the teller of exotic or monstrous tales, the truthful traveler was recognized as one who corrected errors, who admitted the limits of the observational perspective and the partiality of personal experience. Inherent in this new image of the scientific traveler was the concept that the traveler's observations are adequate for recognizing and naming things, categorizing species, and describing observable realities, but inadequate for plumbing the depths of experience or understanding

certain mysteries better left to faith. On the one hand, the Renaissance redefined the serious traveler as a conscious and disciplined
observer of nature and humanity. On the other hand, the new canons of objectivity and methods of observation deified the traveler
who swore allegiance to them, thereby becoming endowed with a
higher purpose and a heroic cultural dimension.

THE GRAND TOUR AND THE TRAVEL REPORT

*The primary means of the investigation of social reality in pre-industrial times
was travel. The reports of travelers provided the raw materials of what was later
worked up into statistical compilations; another source was the travel correspondence so closely bound up with the art of travel.*

—Justin Stagl, 1980

Bacon's statement of the discipline of observation legitimated the
practice of Renaissance travel which had already been provided with
its method and "regime" by sixteenth-century humanists who for-
malized the Grand Tour as a means by which young gentlemen
could finish and polish an education through a course of travels. As
the historian of early modern European travel E. S. Bates observes,
from the late fifteenth to the early seventeenth centuries, the habit
among the English upper classes of "sending their sons abroad as
part of their education became successively an experiment, a custom, and finally a system."[12] And yet the Grand Tour was a wedding
of at least two prior traditions. One was the chivalric excursion undertaken by the young knight at the end of his apprenticeship, in
which we might recognize the medieval form of the Gothic *Vers Sa-
crum*, the journey expected of every Germanic youth who would establish a name for himself. Through this journey the youthful
nobleman was to become acquainted with courts and great men, as
well as to show his figure in tournaments, dancing, and entertainments. The courtly circuit, the round of tournaments, was often
combined with and sanctified by visits to places of pilgrimage—such
as St. James Compostela, Canterbury, or Rome—and was essentially
an induction into the noble class, an international class of warriors.
Wars, crusades, and pilgrimages all provided means by which a so-

cial transition from youth to adulthood could be accomplished through territorial mobility, a means by which the young knight could become recognized for who he was and make the acquaintance of those who would be useful in his career. The other source of the Grand Tour was the *peregrinatio academica*, the scholar's "journey-man's year," in which, near the conclusion of his course of study, a young scholar toured the centers of learning, particularly Paris and Bologna. In the Grand Tour, the *peregrinatio academica* and the initiatory excursion of the apprentice knight merged:

> If in the older *peregrinatio academica*, the journey of scholars, there was a kind of pilgrimage to the places of learning, so now the journey itself was seen to hold an educational and politically instructive value in the education of the cavalier. . . . The journey itself became an educational experience and could be regarded as a moving academy of the true peripatetic school.[13]

The Grand Tour, this wedding of chivalric and academic traditions, gave rise to a new profession, that of the traveling tutor or "gove-nour" who was to watch over the morals of the traveling nobleman, act as a guide, see to accommodations, introduce him to the arts, books, and learned men, and gauge his progress in the courtly and literary skills that were increasingly the legitimation of nobility. Members of this profession fashioned new methods of travel, and designed categories of observation and techniques of recording experiences, as well as writing guidebooks to Italy and France, the homes of the gentle arts and manners.

The new notion of the journey itself as an education, as a civilizing and cultivating process, implied its systematization as a curriculum. It was required that the young gentleman keep a journal to record his observations, as a kind of memorial to his investiture in the world and as a way of halting the erosions of memory by time. By the mid-sixteenth century, a number of traveling tutors had elaborated a system of observation and record keeping that distinguished the important from the irrelevant, established the proper form of description, and in general detailed the methods by which the gentleman of elegant curiosity could extract information from experience.

According to the German historian of travel Justin Stagl, in his important article on European disciplines of travel in the early modern period,[14] humanists and physicians were particularly active in

drawing up the schematics and questionnaires from which the form
of later travel reports derived. The Swiss physician and professor
Theodor Zwinger (1533–1588), Justin Hieronymus Furler (c. 1526–
1602), and the German humanist Herarius Pyrksmair, along with a
number of scholars of Basel and Italy, coined the term "Apodemik"
to describe a method of "rational travel," a technique of keeping a
travel journal, of observation and analysis. This method was based
on the widely popular "reductive-compositive" method of Peter Ramus. The Ramian method asserted that all certain knowledge began
with the "apparent" and the "evident"—with observation. Whatever
was to be known should first be described as a whole and then reduced to its parts, which would then be reduced to their parts, described, and catalogued. When this reductionistic process was
completed, the parts were to be put together once more through
their apparent likenesses and listed in "synaptic tables" into a whole,
now fully and completely known.[15]

As it was applied to travel, this method made it necessary for
the traveler to keep at least one journal, and preferably two: one in
which to record events and experiences in the sequence of their
occurrence, and the other for organizing all knowledge of a place
or region in an encyclopedic fashion. Pyrksmair's *Apodemik* method
advised travelers to divide their observations into the categories of
land and people. Descriptions of the land were to begin with a list
of place names, both ancient and modern, and then its topography:
plains, mountains, rivers, and all remarkable natural sights and natural resources. By the eighteenth century, techniques of describing
topography had been fundamentally altered by the conventions of
landscape painting. In writing about the "view" or "scene," a traveler
could demonstrate facility with language. In the eighteenth century,
the ban on subjectivity in valid travel reports was lifted, and the
travel writer was allowed and even encouraged to make use of elevated sentiments and profound raptures in the description of landscape. These developments brought about the romantic, subjective
travel report.

According to the *Apodemik* method, the traveler would observe
and describe the temperament of the people—whether sanguine,
choleric, phlegmatic, or melancholic—as well as their mores and customs, clothes and costumes, diet and manner of eating, languages,
dialects, and general way of life. Dr. Pyrksmair also insisted upon
observations of the air and its humors, since these were crucial in

shaping a people's temperament, as were the effects of latitude, longitude, and mountains, and the propinquity of oceans, seas, and lakes. The observing traveler was also to note the salubrity of the waters, the existence of hot or mineral springs, and the fertility of the fields and meadows. The technique for the description and observation of cities drew upon traditions of ancient rhetoric and the late medieval commemoration of places in civic eulogies, which required praising the city and its walls, plan, houses, monuments, industries, and affluence, as well as the fortitude and virtues of its citizens: "The eulogy, the specialized description of a town, did by its example encourage range, methodical organization and an attempt at vividness and acted as a stimulus to description at length." Descriptions of cities could be succinct and conventionalized: "Avignon has a fine bridge, a fine circuit of walls and a fine palace."[16] Or they could be elaborate. Canon Casola's description of Venice, for example, first notes the most outwardly distinguishing features of the city, its means of transport, its situation, and its canals, squares, churches, palaces, bridges, and markets. He then moves on to a description of the patricians, the status and dress of the women, and so on.[17]

This method of describing a land and people, formulated in the methods of "rational travel" of sixteenth-century humanists, was to have a long and significant life, founding the conventions of social scientific description, defining the contents of guidebooks, and decreeing the form of ethnographic reports. In the seventeenth and eighteenth centuries, the methods of travel included lists of questions that were to be filled in by travelers (*Interrogatoria*). *The Patriotic Traveller* of Leopold Graf Berchthold (1789) contained 2,443 questions in 37 categories.[18] In many cases, the new reportorial and journalistic tasks of young travelers did not expunge the old. On his educational journey (*Bildungsreise*), the young traveler was not only to record the foregoing observations, answer questions, and send home reports to those who were paying his expenses, but also to learn the practical lessons of travel, negotiate routes, deal with dangers and hardships, learn languages and manners, seek out and make the acquaintance of leading men, gain introductions to rulers and learn their maxims, copy down inscriptions, geneologies, idioms, and anecdotes, and study mechanical inventions, monsters and prodigies of nature, curiosities—in short, to take in everything worthy of note.

John and Awnsham Churchill, in giving advice to travelers in the preface of their collection of voyages (1704), recommended that every traveler keep a "table book" in which to set down observations organized under the following principal headings: climate, government, power, strength of fortifications, cities of note, religion, language, coins, trade, manufactures, wealth, bishoprics, universities, antiquities, libraries, collections of rarities, arts and artists, public structures, roads, bridges, woods, mountains, customs, habits, laws, privileges, strange adventures and surprising accidents, rarities natural and artificial, soil, plants, animals, "and whatsoever may be curious, diverting and profitable."[19] The travel books of the seventeenth and eighteenth centuries were essentially compilations of all sorts of information that encumbered the form of the journey. In these centuries travel became the primary method by which Europeans investigated, observed, and compiled a world.

The journey, from the Renaissance on, became a structured and highly elaborate method of appropriating the world as information; the most privileged official motive of travel became to see and know the world, to record it, to assemble a complete and detailed picture of it. Goethe wondered about himself and the traveler, "who, in order to enjoy something which he could perfectly well have enjoyed in peace and comfort and pleasant company, gets himself into trouble and danger because of an absurd desire to appropiate the world and everything in it in a manner peculiar to himself."[20] In this appropriation through observation and recording, generations of young, otherwise idle gentlemen like Goethe found their purpose and legitimacy. In pursuing this purpose through travel—in botanizing, in geologizing, in collecting specimens for their cabinets—they generated a flood of fact that overburdened existing taxonomies of nature and required their modernization.

The redefinition of travel as disciplined observation, as the science of induction and the art of description, effected fundamental alterations within travel literature in the seventeenth century. The truth of a text began to be measured in terms of its conformability to the terms of experience. With the new focus on "fact"—which was a product of the limited view of an observer, who could not see further than the surfaces and materiality of phenomena—"true" description of the world required the abandonment of the fabulous which had been traditionally the appeal of travel and voyage literature.

Thus the travel report was a peculiar form of literature in which all subjectivities were projected outward, into the world, as objects to be described, recorded, classified, named, and catalogued. The travel report was classically an objectification of a self; that is, the materialization of emotions, and the transformation into "objectivity" of the stranger's limitations, partialities, and ignorance. It was the mark of the nonfiction narrative, a mark of the "reality" of the narrative, that it must be bound and limited by the boundaries and limitations of experience. The omniscient point of view, of course, belonged to God and to literature. It was not appropriate to the traveler, who was limited to the experience of his senses, who experienced things in sequence, and who could not possibly cover the whole ground. There was no greater recommendation of the verisimilitude of a narrative than the narrator's admission of not knowing, or not being able to know, something, prefacing statements with "it appears to me," paying close attention to the distinction between what was observed, what was concluded from observations, and what was heard or read in other travel accounts. Too, the travel writer who would be believed must not be prolix, but must prefer simplicity to complexity, enumeration to generality, lists to composite views, and quantitative to qualitative descriptions. In the nonfiction travel text, Baconian assumptions became narrative conventions: the observer was removed from events, a mere recorder who must not confuse narrative language with Latin epigrams or flavor the report with opinions and prejudices. Fact was a given of experience rather than a collectively established statement about the world.

The believable travel report had to be written in the plain style, in "sailor's language," without literary tricks and affectations, limiting itself to observed events and evident appearances, and suppressing all subjectivity. It became the most "clearly defined convention of the eighteenth-century travel literature: a travel writer must not talk about himself."[21] The French navigator Louis Antoine de Bougainville, in his narrative of his voyage around the world in 1766–69, conscientiously repudiates the literary style, claiming that his journal was written by a "seaman" and "chiefly ... for seamen," a presumption that could not but flatter his audience. Characteristically, he represents his plain style not as a literary achievement but as a result of the erosions his passage had worked on him, of the experiences that had changed him from a *littérateur* to a backwoodsman and voyager:

> I am now far from the sanctuary of science and learning; the ram-
> bling and savage life I have led for these twelve years past, has had
> too great an effect upon my ideas and style. One does not become
> a good writer in the woods of Canada or on the seas.... I am a
> voyager and a seaman; that is a liar and stupid fellow, in the eyes
> of that class of indolent, haughty writers, who in their closets, rea-
> son *ad infinitum* on the world and its inhabitants and with an air of
> superiority confine nature within the limits of their own inven-
> tion.[22]

Here Bougainville cites that familiar process native to travel, the sim-
plication of life, as the transformation of the highly educated child of
the Enlightenment into a "common man." It is clear that the artless-
ness, simplicity, and amateurishness of the sailor's language were
themselves a kind of art, a convention and style that became obligatory for those who would be believed and have their experience of
the world used in the fashioning of representations of it.

This redefinition of philosophical language as the language of
common sense, of simply worded observations, unquestionably expanded the company of the learned to include many who lacked formal education. William Dampier, a seaman, merchant, privateer, and
inveterate wanderer all his life, who had neither Greek nor Latin,
learned what he knew from travel and became a correspondent with
the gentlemen of the Royal Society, keeping his journals with this
audience in mind. In his introduction to the *Voyages* (1906), he writes
that his audience consists of "[t]he judicious [who] are not taken in
with ... Trifles; their end in Reading, is Information; and they easily
distinguish the reality and fiction."[23] And yet the astronomer Edmond
Halley was much vexed with Dampier for failing to record the variations of the needle on all of his voyages across the Pacific, and pleased
with the careful observations of the privateer captain Woodes-Rogers,
from which Halley compiled the tables that demonstrated the truth
of his hypothesis about comets.[24]

This redefinition of philosophy as science and the reduction of
science to the disciplines of observation permitted unlettered and
uneducated men to be absorbed into an information structure that
gave them a dignity and standing irrespective of established social
rankings. The distinction between a sailor and a philosopher was between one who kept a journal, made observations, and was skilled
with instruments and one who did none of these things. Captain James
Cook climbed to international celebrity status from the lower social

depths. In his published journals he disclaimed, as was obligatory by his time, any pretensions to literary style: "I have given the best account of things in my power. I have neither had an education, nor have I acquired abilities for writing. I have been almost constantly at sea from my youth and have dragged myself through all the Stations, from a Prentice Boy to a Commander."[25] Here, as elsewhere, simplicity, the very absence of education, was what guaranteed truth; in Baconian terms, it meant that the purity of the senses had not been polluted by words, opinions, or predilections. In his essay "On Cannibals," Montaigne argues that the value of his unnamed informant's report was enhanced by his having actually lived among the Brazilian Indians and by the fact that he "was a simple, plain fellow, which is a nature likely to give true testimony." Montaigne observed that intelligent and well-educated people might notice more things but would also be more likely to leap to conclusions and to change details in order to make their observations accord with their theories. To provide valid observations, "it needs a man either very truthful or so ignorant that he has no material wherewithal to construct and give verisimilitude to false conceptions, and one who is wedded to nothing."[26]

This Baconian philosophy was translated for seamen in the Royal Society's "Directions for Seamen Bound on Far Voyages"(1665–66). These instructions, issued in the first numbers of the Society's *Philosophical Transactions*, which subsequently became a clearinghouse for information and reports from a worldwide network of curious and botanizing gentlemen, assured seamen and navigators of their importance to a science whose purpose was "to study Nature rather than Books, and from the Observations made of the phenomena and Effects she presents, to compose such a History of Her, as may hereafter serve to build a Solid and Useful Philosophy."[27] The Society's instructions focused entirely upon quantitative measurements, in accordance with Bacon's recommendation that "all natural bodies and qualities be as far as possible, reduced to number, weight, measures and precise definition; for we are planning actual results and not mere theory."[28] Voyagers, navigators, and travelers of all sorts were enjoined to record the movement of the compass needle from true north along with the longitude and latitude of the observation; to observe the inclination of the dipping needle; to note the ebbs and flows of the tides with their times and heights; to sketch plans of coasts, recording promontories, rocks, and shoals, with bearings and soundings. The observant mariner should also note the character of the ocean's bottom; changes of wind and weather at all hours (especially hurricanes, water-spouts, and the latitudes and longitudes where the trade winds begin, change and cease); unusual meteors; lightnings and thunders; and the salinity of the sea at various depths, temperatures, and places.

The instructions of the Royal Society reflect the process of the refinement and mechanization of observation. The Churchills advised travelers to go nowhere without the minimal measuring instruments—a watch, a small and a large telescope, a compass, and the best maps—"to make curious remark of their exactness and note down where they are faulty."[29] Alexander von Humboldt and Aimé Bonpland, on their expedition to South America in 1799, were particularly well furnished travelers and totally accommodated observers. They carried a variety of chronometers, achromatic telescopes, a *lunette d'épreuve* with micrometer, a variety of sextants, an artificial horizon, quadrants, a graphometer, various dipping needles, magnetometers, pendulums, barometers, hygrometers, electrometers, cyanometers, microscopes, surveying and assaying equipment, Leyden phials, galvanic apparatus—and duplicates of all of these instruments. In the reports of scientific travelers of the eighteenth century, the most elevated sentiments were commonly combined with the most exact measurements: "We could not withdraw our eyes on the summit of the peak, from beholding the color of the azure vault of the sky. Its intensity at the zenith appeared to correspond to 41 degrees of the cyanometer."[30]

THE EXPEDITION

Many a time the naturalist, when almost within reach of a summit on which he eagerly longs to stand, may doubt of whether he still has strength enough to reach it, or whether he can surmount the precipices which guard its approaches. But the keen air which he breathes makes a balm to flow in his veins that restores him, and the expectation of the great panorama which it will display to him renews his strength and courage. He gains the top.... Standing as it were above the globe, he seems to discover the forces that move it, at last he recognizes the principal agents that affect its revolutions.

—Horace-Bénédict de Saussure, 1790

There is something not wholly rational about the intense hunger for data, measurements, facts, and observations that fueled the proliferation of travel and travel reports from the sixteenth century forward. Erich Heller attributes the rage for data to the Renaissance legitimation of curiosity and the removal of knowledge from the domain of morality. This liberation made men unsure of what *ought* to be known and led to "a preposterous superstition: everything that can be known is worth knowing—including the manifestly worthless."[31] Bacon's religion of the fact privileged any datum so long as it was verified, and the pages of *Philosophical Transactions* provided a means of verifying a world of facts, even to the point of absurdity: "where the wild Penny-Royal or Kittany grows, no Rattle-Snakes are observed to come."[32]

Thousands of individual acts of collection and observation, of appropriating the world as knowledge, occurred within the frame of a historical period in which Europe encompassed a world and its trade. The collection of information, the advance of learning, and the filling in of all the blanks in the book of nature made official and legitimate more forceful appropriations of the world and the building of European empires. In Napoleon's triumphant parade into Paris after the Italian campaign of 1798, the procession of the booty—looted art works, trophies of war—was headed by the botanical specimens that Baudin had collected on his first voyage to the West Indies. But the distinction between a military appropriation of the world through war and intellectual appropriations through observations was not really as firm and clear to practitioners of the new science as it is to us. Bacon had spoken of the collection of fact as an active, even aggressive activity, a putting of "nature on the rack," a forceful interrogation. By the methods of induction, through the arts and sciences, he sought a recovery of both human innocence and man's "empire over creation," apparently not imagining these to be contradictory aspirations.

Appropriating the world as information became the chief dignifying motive for travels. It also gave rise to that institution unique to the eighteenth century, the scientific expedition, which essentially fit contemporary intellectual purposes and functions to older mobile social forms, the merchant and military expeditions of previous centuries.

Charles de Brosses, author of *Histoire des navigations aux Terre Australis* (1756), was the first to recommend that scientists be in-

cluded as members of voyages of discovery. In response to his recommendation, Bougainville took two scientists with him on his
voyage of 1767–68—a botanist, Commerçon; and an astronomer,
Verran (whose servant was discovered, by the Tahitians, to be a
woman disguised as a man). Cook, on his first circumnavigation on
the *Endeavour* in 1768, was accompanied by three gentlemen of the
Royal Society: Charles Green, an astronomer who was to observe the
transit of Venus, the principal scientific objective of the voyage; Joseph Banks, a naturalist of large fortune and later a president of the
Royal Society; and Dr. Daniel Solander, a natural philosopher. With
Banks was Sydney Parkinson, a draughtsman and artist; Alexander
Buchan, another artist specializing in landscape and figure drawing;
and Herman Spüring, an assistant naturalist. The ostensible purpose
of this voyage was to collect information—to map coasts, to search
for the "southern continent" originally reported by Quiroa, and to
collect specimens. The secretary of the Royal Society, John Ellis, in
a letter to Carl von Linné (Linnaeus), the Swedish naturalist and
formulator of the sexual system of classification, described the expedition as scientific in its fundamental purpose:

> No people ever went to sea better fitted out for the purpose of
> Natural History. They have got a fine library of Natural History;
> they have all sorts of machines for catching and preserving insects;
> all kinds of nets, trawls, drags and hooks for coral fishing: they have
> even a curious contrivance of a telescope, by which, put into the
> water, you can see the bottom at a great depth, when it is clear. . . .
> In short, Solander assured me that this expedition would cost Mr.
> Banks ten thousand pounds.[33]

Mr. Banks could, with a clear conscience, spend a sum which was the
combined yearly income of a thousand middle-class families, on this
new form of the Grand Tour, a circumnavigation of the globe; he
was contributing to the grand effort to amass and order all possible
facts that could be gathered from observation and experiment, for
the furtherance of invention and the well-being of mankind.

In the next centuries, the scientific expedition became the chief
vehicle for amassing information about the world, a wealth of detail that required a transformation of Baconian "Natural History"
into a Darwinian "History of Nature." It is not surprising that
trusted intellectual instruments—particularly those supplied by the

tradition of philosophical travel—were used in the ordering of
this informational wealth. Many questions remain about this
transformation of the expedition as an ancient social organization
of travelers into the scientific expeditions: How was observation par-
ticularized into the academic disciplines, the divisions of intellectual
labor that give us our present structure of knowledge? What rules
and compacts pertained in this new form of travel inspired by intellectual purpose and scientific passion? But these are questions
apart from our present purpose—to suggest how the flood of information and observation gathered by traveling naturalists transformed cultural patterns, those taxonomies and ordering devices
used in the assimilation of newfound worlds to tradition.

The New Botany

The most significant impact of travel into and out of Europe after
1500 lay not in any *crise de conscience* afflicting the age but in the slow
transformation of structures of knowledge by means of which the
flood of information and observation gathered by traveling naturalists was assimilated into pre-existing patterns of meaning. Observations of newfound peoples could be ordered through the
temporalizations native to Western traditions of philosophical travel,
and regarded as primitive or early species of humanity. But the flood
of reports of new species of plants and animals was more difficult
to order within traditional taxonomies designed for the identification of European species. The first impressions of the voyagers to
the New World were of an enormous profusion and prodigality of
nature. As Columbus reported of Hispaniola:

> There are six or eight kinds of palm, which are a wonder to behold
> on account of their beautiful variety, but so are other trees and
> fruits and plants. In it there are marvellous pine groves, and there
> are very large tracts of cultivatable lands, and there is honey, and
> there are birds of many kinds and fruits of great diversity. In the
> interior there are mines of metals and the population is without
> number. Espanola is a marvel.[34]

Such descriptions of the new Eden, whetting the appetites of colonists, also delineated the problems facing gentlemen voyagers and

amateur naturalists, who were generally more curious and hungry for information than were the officials and governors of the new provinces. Initial impressions of similarity faded with a deeper sense of difference, as the newly discovered was often found to be anomalous within existing categories. As Sir James Edward Smith, first president of the Linnean Society, observed: "The whole tribe of plants, which at first sight seemed familiar to [the Botanist's] acquaintance, as occupying links in nature's chain, on which he is accustomed to depend, prove, on nearer examination total strangers, with other configurations, other oeconomy, and other qualities."[35] The overwhelming variety of new and nameless plant and animal species could only with difficulty and much intellectual effort be likened to known and categorized species, a challenge taken up by the naturalists among the voyagers to the New World. A Dr. Wallace, a Scottish physician and colonist of New Caledonia in Central America (Darién), aboard the ship *St. Andrew* in 1700 noted "a hundred more Birds we have got no name to" in his communication to the Royal Society, and acknowledged his bewilderment at the profusion of exotic varieties:

> This place affords legions of monstrous Plants, enough to confound all the methods of Botany ever hitherto thought upon. However, I found a shift to make some specimens, and that is all I can do. I say some specimens, because if I should gather all 'twould be enough to load the "St. Andrew." For some of their leaves are three ells [11 feet] in length, and are very broad, besides these monsters reducible to no tribe, there are here a great many of the European Kindred (but still something odd about them).[36]

The first problem facing amateur botanists was simply to identify these species, a problem that intensified their already strong sense of the inadequacy of the ancient systems of botanical classification inherited from the ancient Greeks. Aristotle, Theophrastus, and Dioscorides had identified many species that did not grow everywhere in Europe, and neglected to describe many other species familiar to sixteenth-century Europeans. Sixteenth-century German and Italian botanists, operating within a science already in a state of crisis, were now confronted with hundreds and thousands of anomalies.

But the development of botany, and a new history of nature generally, did not bring about a break with received traditions or a revolution in the sense of a repudiation of past sources of order; rather, the old, and in particular the Aristotelian, approach to classification was generalized, extended, and rendered dynamic by the accommodations required in its assimilation of the new. Here the "past" is a resource, a crucial resource, not a burden. This is particularly clear in the efforts of Andrea Cesalpino, the sixteenth-century Italian herbalist, geographer, and natural scientist who used a rigidly Aristotelian approach to the classification of the deluge of new data. He, like many naturalists, was wedded to the ancient notion of the fundamental order of nature as a hierarchy of forms ranging from the simplest to the most complex. Specimens were to be grouped together according to their likenesses and separated according to their differences. The naturalist was to proceed from the higher to the lower, from the general to the specific, by a process of *determinatio*, which was conceived as the addition of identifying peculiarities; and from the lower to the higher by the process of *abstractio*, removing or abstracting differentiating marks. Cesalpino's *De Plantis* (1571) established the principle of classifying plants on the basis of analogies between their parts and the functions of animal organs—reproduction, nutrition, and locomotion—a system that ultimately led to Linné's system of the sexual classification of plants.

The profusion of specimens and data entering into European taxonomies required an extension and refinement of traditional ordering concepts. In the process, new realities were construed in terms of inherited and traditional constructs, and those constructs were expanded and elaborated as a result. The ancient idea of a hierarchy of nature, of a "chain of being," underwent a subtle but significant transformation as new links were installed among the old. The very notion of there being links and connections among species, along which change and transformations might occur, predisposed botanists to read into the variety of species a history or development or evolution. The assumption of an evolution, of a generative link among species, was implicit in Linné's system of classification, a system of five categories nested within one another: class, order, genus, species, and variety. Linné believed that there had been a progress from a small number of primeval or "mother" species to a large number of species through a process of fertilization and cross-fertilization. When cross-fertilized, the mother species produced varieties that, when they bred true, themselves became species. Implicit in this categorization was the story of differentiation and variation

from uniform, "created" species to a larger number of variegated
and differentiated, "evolved" species.

The Promise of Geology

The transformation of the botanical sciences in the seventeenth
and eighteenth centuries—essentially the production of more elaborate and functional systems of classification—provided the necessary tools in the establishment of a geological record, a new
chronology upon which a genuine history of nature could be constructed. The new, finer taxonomies allowed botanists to notice
that fossil animals were similar, and perhaps related, to living
species. Those fossils that were once merely curiosities, used as
evidence of the historicity of the Flood, became the clues that permitted an exact dating of geological strata and the setting-aside of
biblical chronology. The geologist G. L. Giraud-Soulavie (1725–
1813) worked out the stratographical record in the succession of
layers of calcareous rocks in the mountains of the Vivarais in
southeast France. He divided them into five layers, or ages, the
oldest filled with fossils of extinct animals (such as Amonites, Bel-
emnites, and Gryphytes), some of which appeared in the layer
above, along with fossils more clearly related to living species. By
establishing the proportion of fossils within a given stratum related to living species, that layer could be dated:

> Such is the general picture ... presented by our old hills of the
> Vivarais. ... The progress of time, and, above all, of increased ob-
> servation will augment the number of epochs that I have given, and
> fill up the blanks; but they will not change the relative places which
> I have assigned to these epochs. ... The difference between the shells
> in the rocks rests on the difference in their relative antiquity, and
> not on mere local causes. If an earthquake were to submerge the
> Amonite-bearing rocks of the Vivarais beneath the Mediterranean,
> the sea returning to its old site would not bring back its old shells.
> The course of time has destroyed the species, and they are no lon-
> ger found in the most recent rocks.[37]

Using fossils to identify and date distinct strata was made possible
by the adoption of common generic and specific names for both
living and extinct animals and plants. Botany was the most crucial

tool in creating a geological history that set aside biblical chronology. Giraud-Soulavie and C. L. D. Cuvier (1769–1832) worked out the strata of the Seine Basin; William Smith worked out the order of strata in Britain and France and fixed the subdivisions within the Jurassic (oolitic) strata—an order valid throughout Europe.

These intellectual achievements were partly built on the activities of travel. The new generation of botanists, geologists, and scribes of nature were invariably travelers, and their insights were structured by their journeys. William Smith was one of the beneficiaries of the expansion of the realms of philosophy to the unlettered, a man who worked for his living as a surveyor or engineer and who had been fascinated with rocks since childhood. Through his travels across Britain, he was able to establish the foundations of the geological record that would become the matrix of evolutionary theory. As superintendent of construction for the Somerset Coal Canal, he noted that "each stratum contained organized fossils peculiar to itself, and might in cases otherwise doubtful, be recognized and discriminated from others like it, but in a different part of the series, by an examination of them." Here the basic tenet of philosophical travel could be applied with clarifying effect: differences in strata could be read as an order of time. The crystallization of this notion into a map of time was achieved, significantly enough, on a journey Smith took in 1794 north to Newcastle and back through Shropshire and Wales to Bath. Swift passage in an open carriage presented in rapid succession the strata of the gently undulating central plains, repeatedly offering their general and invariable order: "No journey, purposely contrived . . . could have better answered my purpose. To sit forward on the chaise was a favor readily granted; my eager eyes were never idle for a moment; and post-haste travelling only put me on new resources. General views under existing circumstances were the best that could have been taken."[38]

Geology became a science that recruited travelers and justified new species of travel. Roy Porter, in his history of geology (1977), argues that the popularity of geological study in the Revolutionary and Romantic periods owed much to the fact that it could not be undertaken without travel: "One stimulus was travelling. The surging popularity of scientific travelling as the recreation of a Grand Tour merged insensibly."[39] Many geologists, natural historians, and polymaths of the generation were raised on voyage literature, which the Earl of Shaftesbury recommended in 1710 as "the chief materials to furnish out a library. . . . These are in our present day what books of chivalry were in those of our forefathers."[40] Indeed, voyage literature provided the principal food group in the literary diet of the young Alexander von Humboldt, who was inspired from his earliest youth by an ardent desire to travel. This literature focused him on the "vague and undefined" and provided an escape from the "narrow circle of sedentary life."[41]

Not only did rambling and geologizing provide an erudite recreation for young gentlemen, it increasingly channeled the purpose of observation away from appearances and to those forces that generated appearances. The search for links below the surface of the visible world distinguished the founders of modern geology from their fact- and observation-collecting intellectual progenitors. Humboldt set out on his five-year expedition to South America searching for "the connection of facts, which have long been observed. . . . The discovery of an unknown genus seemed to me far less interesting than an observation on the geographical relations of the vegetable world, on the migration of the social plants."[42] Humboldt's generation assumed an essentially ecological approach to nature, looking for the connections among phenomena, for the relationship between living and inanimate nature.

Like those of many of his contemporaries, Humboldt's journeys were governed by what Baconian science lacked; he searched for the forces that generated distinct facts and phenomena. Pursuing that chimera, the "natural order" of created being, he wished to arrange the facts and observations he accumulated not in "the order in which they successively presented themselves but according to the relation they have to each other amidst the overwhelming majesty of nature." To Humboldt the purpose of the journey was to allow the observer "to raise himself to general ideas on the cause of the phenomena and their general connection."[43] Geology not only promised a nexus, a connective between isolated faxts, but invested new significance in topography which had been of little interest to prior discoverers. Vast tracts of wilderness were now pregnant with meaning. Humboldt criticized the "exploring mentality" of his predecessors, who had been content with mapping previously unknown coastlines and shoals, and contrasted these superficial journeys with his own more difficult passage into the heart of a great continent. Geologizing was an adventure into the unknown, and it was in these terms that Horace-Bénédict de Saussure, the eighteenth-century geologist and mountain climber who first mapped the Alps, celebrated his vocation:

> We must quit the beaten tracks and climb to the lofty summits, whence the eye can take in at one sweep a multiplicity of objects. Such excursions are toilsome, I admit; we must relinquish carriages, and even horses, endure great fatigue, and expose ourselves some-times to considerable danger.[44]

Geological travel was a new version of philosophical travel which blended ancient and modern themes. The old themes of the dangers and vicissitudes of travel, of the athleticism of the journey, are blended with the new emphasis upon observation and the notion that revealed objects represent the forces at work in the globe, forces that are the true object of the heroic endeavors of the geologizing traveler. The journey up and through the wilderness is a journey of enlightenment in no allegorical sense, for it ultimately reveals the agents of revolutions that make the landscape intelligible as the effect of a historical dynamic.

The Dynamics of Time

The rivers and rocks, the seas and the continents, have been changed in all their parts; but the laws which direct those changes, and the rules to which they are subject, have remained invariably the same.
—Samuel Playfair, 1820

The science of geology is inseparable from the revolutionary era that supplied its controversies and solutions. Particularly fruitful of the ideas that founded scientific geology, and produced a new history of nature, was the controversy between the Neptunists and the Vulcanists over the nature of the processes that had produced the infrastructure of the world. In brief, the Neptunists followed the German geologist Abraham Werner in believing that the primary cause of strata was the slow precipitation of rocks from a primeval sea. The Vulcanists followed James Hutton, a Scottish geologist, who asserted the primacy of violent upheavals, earthquakes, and volcanoes.

Hutton succeeded in formulating the law that was to become the foundation of a new history of nature and a new vision of time, the law of the "permanent agency of the same causes in nature." According to Hutton, all the forces of nature that are observable in the present—erosion, glaciation, sedimentation, uplift, subsidence, and volcanic action—were at work in the past and shaped the history of the world that we see.[45] This law, which historians of human history may well envy, linked the visible natural forces to the invisible abysses of time, the present to the past, by asserting that the complexities and variations that travelers might see across the face of the earth could be understood in terms of the interaction of a few simple processes that produced them. In essence, the forces of change were the only things that did not change. It is this interior dynamic, shaping all of history and giving rise to the observable, that became the object of the travels of Charles Darwin and Alfred Russel Wallace. In the processes of change one might find the story of origins.

Hutton's law had immediate and profound repercussions in the study of natural history. In the first place, it deranged the implicit terms of cosmogony—the study of beginnings, ends, and purposes in nature—by refuting the notion that beginnings are an act of creation and ends an act of destruction. The law thus erased the terms which bracketed human history as a moral progress or a corruption. Creation and destruction were not separable acts but ongoing processes simultaneously at work always and everywhere, as frozen water splits rocks from its matrix, flowing water strips hills and builds up plains, laying down sediments that form new rocks to be uplifted and again carved by erosion into mountains.

The simultaneity of destruction and creation, a lesson inevitably learned by a generation that had witnessed the great political revolutions at the end of the eighteenth century, was perhaps the most disturbing and creative apprehension bequeathed to Charles Darwin's generation and to subsequent generations of philosophical, now scientific, travelers. The power and simplicity of Hutton's formulation of the mutuality of destruction and creation, and its persuasiveness, lay in the fact that these processes were observable in both human history and nonhuman nature. As Alexander von Humboldt, a contemporary of Hutton, observed:

> There is something that leaves a melancholy impression on the mind seeing a crater in the center of a fertile and well-cultivated country. The history of the globe instructs us, that volcanoes destroy what they have been a long series of ages in creating. Islands, which the

action of submarine fires have raised above the waters, are decked by degrees in rich and smiling verdure; but these new abodes are often laid waste by the renewed action of the same power, which caused them to emerge from the bottom of the ocean.[46]

The time necessary for the construction of mountains, plains, successive layers of strata, was now understood to have been millions, rather than thousands, of years. The accuracy of biblical chronologies was irrevocably discredited. Not only did Hutton assert the essential complementarity of the forces of creation and destruction, he denied that these forces had a beginning, an end, or a purpose: "In the economy of the world . . . I can find no traces of a beginning, no prospect of an end."[47] A radical statement for the age, this assertion forever submerged the basic terms of cosmogony into theology. There was no longer a place for teleology in the study of nature.

This denial was the essence of Hutton's heresy, and it shattered the Christian notion of time as a moral journey narrating the story of salvation and damnation. Orthodox contemporaries accused Hutton of reviving the pagan doctrine of "eternal succession"—the cyclical recurrence of events—and denying the act of creation which begins history and nature. Charles Lyell, a Huttonian who in 1830 was the first to write a history of the new science of geology, was profoundly disturbed by this dissolution of traditional parameters of time and compared Hutton's revolution in geology to Newton's in physics:

> Such views of the immensity of past time, like those unfolded by Newtonian philosophy in regard to space, were too vast to awaken ideas of sublimity unmixed with a painful sense of our incapacity to conceive a plan of such infinite extent. Worlds are seen beyond worlds immeasurably distant from each other, and beyond them all, innumerable other systems are faintly traced on the confines of the invisible universe.[48]

Yet Hutton's law was not easily dismissible as a philosophical assertion, a mere idea. It was demonstrable and observable; it was, in fact, the focus and form of observations. In geology, theory was idle speculation unless it could be shown in rocks; and Hutton was able to indicate places in the rocks of the Scottish mountains that revealed the proximity of violent volcanic action and gradual processes of sedimentation and uplift. Samuel Playfair, Hutton's Boswell, was particularly impressed with a journey Hutton organized to Seccar Point on the Scottish coast. There the hills plunged vertically into the sea, and their strata did not conform to vertically positioned underlying rocks:

> Dr. Hutton was rightly pleased with appearances that set in so clear a light the different formations of the parts which composed the exterior crust of the earth, and where all the circumstances were combined that could render the observation satisfactory and precise.... The palpable evidence presented to us of one of the most extraordinary and important facts in the natural history of the earth, gave a reality and a substance to those theoretical speculations which, however probable, had never till now been directly authenticated by the testimony of the senses.[49]

It was left to the following generation, that of Charles Darwin and Alfred Russel Wallace, to propose an adequate solution to the problem that concerned Alexander von Humboldt—the unexplained relationship between animate and inanimate nature. In the solution, Darwin and Wallace utilized the basic assumptions of philosophical travel combined with the Huttonian notion that the globe and all the life it contained had been shaped by uniform agencies observably at work in the present. Hutton proposed that the great variety of natural life that had overwhelmed European travelers in the seventeenth century might be ordered in terms of the forces that had produced this variety, forces everywhere and always at work, though few in number. This was the key that Darwin and Wallace would use to unlock the mystery of the change and variation of species.

A HISTORY OF NATURE: DARWIN AND WALLACE

It is certainly a wonderful and unexpected fact, that an accurate knowledge of the distribution of birds and insects should enable us to map out lands and continents which disappeared beneath the ocean long before the earliest traditions of the human race.
                                                —Alfred Russel Wallace, 1869

Darwin and Wallace were both consummate practitioners of the traditions of philosophical travel and heirs of more recent traditions of natural history. They succeeded in focusing the essential ideas of geology—the simultaneity of creation and destruction, the notion that beginnings could be found in the processes of change, the sense of a vast dimension of time implicit in the observed—upon the problem of species character. With their work, natural history becomes a genuine history of nature, a story of an evolution which was caused by the relations between creatures and the environment to which they were adapted.

Both Darwin and Wallace were travelers, observers, and collectors of nature. Indeed, Darwin regarded his civility, even his genius, as residing in his observational powers, "superior to the common run of men," and sharpened on his four-and-a-half–year journey aboard the *Beagle*. The voyage produced, he observed:

> the habit of energetic industry and of concentrated attention to whatever I was engaged in, which I then acquired. Everything about which I thought or read was made to bear on what I had seen and was likely to see; and this habit of mind was continued during the five years of the voyage. I feel sure that it was this training which has enabled me to do whatever I have done in science.

The disciplines of the scientific journey had transformed and civilized him, changing him from an obsessive sportsman and shooter of game birds into an observer and collector of nature. Like Wallace, he ultimately handed over to his servants the task of collecting specimens. Carrying the first volume of Lyell's *Principles of Geology* with him on the voyage and receiving the second volume in Montevideo in 1832, Darwin responded to the challenge of the landscape in Huttonian terms: "On first examining a new district nothing can appear more hopeless than the chaos of rocks; but by recording the stratification and nature of the rocks and fossils at many points, always reasoning and predicting what will be found elsewhere, light soon begins to dawn on a district, and the structure of the whole becomes more or less intelligible."[50]

As all geologists were taught to do, Darwin read landscape as a template of time and was often moved to wonder by the eons implicit in geological formations. The plains of Patagonia awakened in him emotions similar to those evoked in Playfair by the strata at Seccar Point: "All was stillness and desolation. Yet in passing over these scenes, without one bright object near, an ill-defined but strong sense of pleasure is vividly excited. One asked how many ages the plain had thus existed and how many more it was doomed thus to continue." It was on his voyage that Darwin began to focus upon the problem that was to be resolved in his theory of natural selection—how to relate the causes that had shaped the structures of the earth to the variations in species and the differences among allied species. He suspected that a solution might be found in the observation within diverse environments of allied species, or of varied families of a single species. A common bird like the Antarctic species *Chionis alba* might hold the solution to this puzzle: "This small family of birds is one of those which, from its varied relations to other families, although at present offering only difficulties to the systematic naturalist, ultimately may assist in revealing the grand scheme, common to the present and the past ages, on which organized beings have been created."[51]

On the journey, variations within a species and between different families of a species appeared clearly related to variations in the environments inhabited by those families. Wide variations in the beak structures of the families of finches in the volcanic Galápagos Islands—to become one of Darwin's prime examples of adaptation—were clearly related to the diversity of environments and food supply. The germ of the idea of evolution, that variations are "selected" and preserved within particular environmental niches, was present in Darwin's observations of the most obviously adaptable of species, humans. He observed of the people of cold and rain-swept Tierra del Fuego: "There is no reason to believe that the Fuegians decrease in number; therefore we must suppose that they enjoy a sufficient share of happiness, of whatever kind it may be, to render life worth having. Nature, by making habit omnipotent, and its effects hereditary, has fitted the Fuegian to the climate and the productions of his miserable country."[52] Darwin drew his theory of evolution from the process of mortality that was so abundantly evident in nature, renaming it "natural selection." His own obsession with death, an obsession he dates from the experience of his mother's early death, was transformed during his voyage into a law of progress, a law governing the preservation of variations and the formation of species character.

On another journey, in October 1838, Darwin arranged the pieces of the puzzle into a central idea: individual variations within the offspring of any thriving and increasing species are conserved and perpetuated through reproduction insofar as they serve to adapt that species to "many and highly diversified places in the economy of nature."[53] The progress of adaptation and selection that fitted the species more perfectly to its niche is a force as continuous and uniform as erosion, vulcanism, or glaciation. Thus the origin of species lies not in any single act of creation but in ongoing relations of a species with the environment to which it has "adapted." In the endless mortality of nature, a mortality that does not fall equally upon all members of a population, lies the creative principle of change and variation. A difference—in the structure of the beaks of birds, in reproductive strategies, in coloration, in habit—was conserved by place and perpetuated through generations insofar as they continued to fit an individual to a place. Darwin proposed this theory in a paper entitled "On the Tendency of Varieties to Depart Indefinitely from the Original Type," which appeared, along with Wallace's contribution, in the *Journal of the Proceedings of the Linnean Society* in 1858 and was fully argued in his *Origin of Species* the following year.[54]

Wallace's proposal was more traditionally attuned to the existing tendencies of geological and philosophical travel. He claimed that differences between plant and animal species of the same genus within separate but contiguous environments indicated the history of those environments, as they offer evidence of the natural forces of geology over long periods of time. Here was a subtler and more thorough prosecution of the cardinal rule of philosophical travel—that differences found in space may be read as differences in time. Wallace, on his extensive journeys through the Malay archipelago, had been puzzled by the differences in the distribution of different plants and animals. Malaysian species predominated on some islands while species native to Australia predominated on others. In his notebooks, he observed that the distribution of species might help "in determining past changes in the surface which have left no geological record."[55]

The main object of Wallace's journeys was to collect specimens of natural history, and, in all, over a period of six years, he collected 125,660, many of which were new. In the process, he was alerted to the distributions of these species and their territory, range, and variations. The habit ingrained by the history of geological and philosophical travel led him to argue from the visible to the invisible.

Difference, he said, is an indication of change, and "the change which organic forms have undergone is a measure of time."[56] Much of the brilliance of Wallace's argument was submerged by the boldness of Darwin's theory of natural selection, a theory that struck many contemporaries as bringing a cloudy picture into sudden, sharp focus.

And yet it was Wallace who brought the traditions of philosophical travel to the highest pitch of resolution. If plants and animals on separate islands were similar, this was *prima facie* evidence that at some point in geological history, those islands had been joined or had at least been closer to each other. If, on the other hand, separate islands within the same area had radically different distributions of species, this was evidence that they had never been connected or had long been separate. Through observation, the naturalist could reconstruct past events that had never been witnessed by human eyes or recorded by human hand. The present could be used as a tool to reconstruct a past:

> The history of extinct animals teaches us that their distribution in time and space are strikingly similar. The rule is that just as the productions of adjacent areas usually resemble each other closely, so do the productions of successive periods in the same area; and as the productions of remote areas generally differ widely, so do the productions of the same area at remote epochs. We are therefore led irresistibly to the conclusion, that change of species, still more of generic and family form, is a matter of time. . . . The amount of individuality in the productions of a district, will be . . . a measure of the time that district has been isolated from those around it.[57]

Simply put, similarity is an indication of spatial or temporal proximity, while radical difference—the individuality of a family or a species—is an indication of temporal or spatial distance. Here difference and similarity have become tools of historical reconstruction and analysis, keys to the recovery of events that shaped nature.

Wallace did not limit his use of these tools of analysis to nonhuman nature; and he, like Darwin, was continually impressed with the continuities operating in human and natural history. But Wallace insisted upon significant qualifications before applying the rule of resemblance and difference to human time. He observed that the distribution of Papuan and Malaysian peoples, with their significant physiognomic and temperamental differences, roughly accorded with the distribution of Australian and Malaysian zoological and botanical productions through the archipelago. Papuan peoples dominated those islands that had, in some remote time, been attached to Australia, while Malay ethnic groups populated the volcanic islands extending south and east from Java.

But, because of the mobility of the human species, it was impossible to read this distribution of peoples in the same way one would read the distribution of other animals. Human history, the history of travel, and the contacts between peoples had effected differences in physiognomies, languages, customs, technologies, and art that had little to do with nature. Ethnographic travelers to these islands "are exceedingly apt to be deceived in places where two races have long intermingled, by looking on intermediate forms and mixed habits as evidence of a natural transition from one race to another, instead of an artificial mixture of two distinct peoples."[58] Darwin had been struck by the vast difference between the primitives he found in Tierra del Fuego and civilized beings: "I could not have believed how wide was the difference between savage and civilized man: it is greater than between a wild and domesticated animal, inasmuch as in man there is a greater power of improvement."[59]

Wallace was less inclined to regard civilized and industrialized peoples as an improvement upon primitive ones. "There is in fact almost as much difference between the various races of savage as civilized peoples, and we may safely affirm that the better specimens of the former are much superior to the lower examples of the latter class." He noted that there were many more examples of human degradation among civilized peoples than among savages. The lesson of human history Wallace learned on the peripheries of civilization illustrated a *devolution*—the failure of modern civilization to "train and develop more thoroughly the sympathetic feelings and moral faculties of our nature, and to allow them a larger share of influence in our legislation, our commerce, and our social organization."[60]

Wallace anticipated the moral imperatives implicit in the new anthropology that was growing directly out of natural history and was closely identified with evolutionary theory. He insisted upon the superiority of uncivilized beings and preindustrial society. This superiority lay not in the propinquity of the uncivilized to the beginnings of time, as it had for state-of-nature theorists of the sixteenth and seventeenth centuries. Rather, it lay in the integrality of preindustrial societies, in their clearly evident adaptations to the environment, in the moral health of their social arrangements. The industrial world offered only contrasts to those uncivilized peoples who retained a system of solidarist social norms, who apparently felt none of the anomie and rootlessness native to the modern condition. The focus of ethnographical travel in the twentieth century has been upon these features of native cultures, endangered by contacts with industrial civilization.

The Return to Beginnings

Four hundred years of scientific travel and disciplined observation produced a history of nature that was clearly a product of tradition and marked by the traveler's motives and tendencies. The search for beginnings ultimately led to the idea that origins are to be found in processes of change observably at work in the present, processes of selection and adaptation which root a species in place, in a specific ecological niche. The theory of evolution is a form of what anthropologist Clifford Geertz has called "local knowledge" that insists on those connections between individual and place as definitive of the character of that individual, or species, or culture.[61] Evolutionary theory posits a primal coherence—a fit between individual and environment—as a source of change and the conservation of variations. It is a theory that accords with the condition of the wanderer, who posits a "home," a state of coherence, from a condition of flux, transience, and uncertainty; the first garden—that first, biblical place of origins—was, after all, a myth told in the tents of nomads. A theory of the rootedness of biological productions in local conditions is peculiarly a theory of the uprooted, a product of the alienated, disacculturated, inductive eye.

But this is a theory that rests upon a massive base of evidence collected by generations of wandering naturalists, cultists in the religion of observation, collection, and description. We have not wholly comprehended the motives evident in the collections of museums of natural history, in arboreta, hothouses, private collections of specimens, the legions of books, reports, and observations that schooled a taste for the rare, the tropical, and the exotic in generations of Europeans. Wallace's first vivid memory of travel was of riding on the roof of a coach on the way to London to view the "Zulus and Aztecs" on exhibit there. He understood that the image of the exotic and rare that drew him to Malaysia was a product of the work of generations of collectors, transporters, arrangers, and namers of specimens. "In our hothouses and at our flower-shows we gather together the finest flowering plants from the most distant regions of the earth, and exhibit them in a proximity to each other which never occurs in nature."[62] He would never find that proximity in nature, where each species inhabits a different region or ecological niche, for this exhibit was a product of uprooting, decontextualization, and recontextualization.

We may understand the activity that assembled a new vision of nature in its own terms and legitimations as an admirable and altruistic effort to collect all forms of knowledge, fact, and observation that suddenly inspired Europeans from the Renaissance forward to advance the sciences and improve the human condition. Or, this massive cultural effort to assemble a world, to appropriate it as specimen, observation, knowledge, may be regarded as a fig-leaf of European empire and power. It is even possible to go back further and find what the medievals termed the "lust of the eye," operating in the ostensibly innocent and renewing activity of collection and observation. The passion for collection was clearly a passion for appropriation, for incorporating a world, and on more than one occasion Wallace recognized something libidinous in his activity. He was particularly overcome by scientific passion when he captured a new species of *Ornithoptera*, which he named *Ornithoptera Croesus* for its spectacular coloration: "On taking it out of my net and opening the glorious wings, my heart began to beat violently, the blood rushed to my head, and I felt much more like fainting than I have done in apprehension of immediate death."[63]

Paradise Revisited

Wallace's understanding of his own activity was clearly inspired by the modern science of geology with its perception of the simultaneity of the processes of creation and destruction. Darwin had recognized the beginning of species being in ends, in death, in mortality, which selected and perpetuated nature's variations. Geology also equipped the observations of collectors like Darwin and Wallace with eons of time measured in millions of years in which observable processes are continuously at work. Wallace became conscious of the

paradoxical nature of his activity and of the contradictions inherent
in his tradition as he held in his hand the corpse of a King Bird of
Paradise, one of the first Europeans to do so:

> I thought of the long ages of the past, during which the successive
> generations of this little creature had run their course—year by
> year being born, and living and dying amid these dark and gloomy
> woods with no intelligent eye to gaze upon their lovliness; to all
> appearances such a wanton waste of beauty. Such ideas excite a
> feeling of melancholy. It seems sad that on the one hand such ex-
> quisite creatures should live out their lives and exhibit their charms
> only in these wild, inhospitable regions, doomed for ages yet to
> come to hopeless barbarism; while on the other hand, should civi-
> lized man ever reach these distant lands, and bring moral, intellec-
> tual and physical light into the recesses of these virgin forests, we
> may be sure that he will so disturb the nicely-balanced relations of
> organic and inorganic nature as to cause the disappearance, and
> finally the extinction, of these very beings whose wonderful struc-
> ture and beauty he alone is fitted to appreciate and enjoy. This
> consideration must surely tell us that all living things were *not* made
> for man. Many of them have no relation to him. The cycle of their
> existence has gone on independently of his, and is disturbed or
> broken by every advance in man's intellectual development.[64]

Wallace's reaction echoes an observation by Blaise Pascal, the
seventeenth-century French philosopher, who said that nature made
her truths independent of one another, and that it is human art that
makes them dependent. The observing traveler, while in passage,
thus connects all that is discrete and rooted, selecting and removing
examples of rarity and beauty and placing them within an artificial
world of knowledge, a world in which the relations of things to one
another are precisely stated and fixed.

At this moment Wallace suspects that the naturalist's activities
are not amoral and innocent, as Bacon would have it. Those acts of
observation, collection, and description, which were to restore a lost
coherence between human beings and nature, are here repetitions
of an original sin, in which knowing is intimately related to death
and decontextualization. His knowledge of this magnificent bird was
not passive and inductive but active, a cause of its death and con-
version into a specimen of an order, family, genus, species. The in-
trusion into nature by the naturalist, by conscious, educated, civil
man—precisely the one who knows best how to appreciate this rar-

ity—is literally the destruction of the creature and of its relationship to the setting to which it was adapted and naturally selected. Wallace, like Darwin, saw the creative force of nature at work in the processes of mortality, and here the naturalist—and the civilization he represents—is an agent of that mortality.

It is the traveler and exile who posit a garden, a holy state of coherence, from a condition of detachment, passage, and estrangement. In the seventeenth century, the alienations of travel became a discipline and a dignity; the separations of the traveler from context became the essence of his objectivity, the source of the alienated and intelligent eye. But this man's return to paradise invariably brings its destruction, just as Wallace, holding the King Bird of Paradise in his hand, knew that his very knowledge of it caused its death. The departure from context leads to knowledge, but this knowledge is clearly rooted in loss, out of which arises an image of what is lost.

III

TRAVEL AND IDENTITY

"Knights who are at the wars eat their bread in sorrow; they have one good day after many bad; and they are vowed to all manner of labor; they are forever swallowing their fear; they expose themselves to every peril; they give up their bodies to the adventure of life in death" (Gutierre Diaz de Gomez, 1414). *(Photo courtesy of Giraudon/Art Resource)*

8

THE SPERMATIC JOURNEY

If I now feel that I have come to a turning point in my life, this is not because of what I have won but because of what I have lost. Within me, I feel a deep intense strength that will enable me to live as I intended.

—Albert Camus, 1963

It is appropriate to open this section, on travel and identity, with a consideration of travel as a "gendering activity," a source of behaviors and representations definitive of masculinity in many cultures and periods. Here I assume that identity in general is a social reality that derives from nothing more substantial than the recognitions, categorizations, and identifications in which people habitually engage, and nowhere more frequently than in the activity of travel. Gender is a category of identity—but one rooted in other realities, in the experience of biological reproduction, in social relations, in acts of recognition and representation. In this chapter, I address the question of the extent to which the cultural patterning of travel—the mobility of the male and the sessility of the female—reflects underlying sexual and reproductive determinants that supply the "constraints and incentives that canalize our choices."[1] In chapter 9, I examine the effects of mobility upon social relations, the ways in which territorial passage creates social structures of a particular kind; while in the final chapter, I turn to those experiences of recognition and representation of identity frequent in travel that become a source of pleasure and possibility for the "shape-changing" traveler.

The gender-specific nature of civilized travel may be seen in the very character of the transformations of passage. These transformations derive from an experience of loss, separation, distancing, and reconnections of always diminishing depth. These have been positively and negatively evaluated in history while remaining identifiably the same, a purgation and diminution of the traveler. Here it would seem that the voice of the subject is most intransigent and speaks most clearly against the grain of our predilections, which are to see travel as a positive force constructive of identities and human relations. In parts I and II, I have described the virtue European travelers made of the constraints, limits, and purgations of travel. In the sixteenth and seventeenth centuries, the estrangements of departure were celebrated as the liberation and purification of the senses. The stripping away of the subjectivity rooted in common language and custom provided the epistemological conditions for a true and scientific description of the world of nature. The subjectivity generated in passage is what is left over after the social being of the traveler is stripped away, a pure observer; and this residue is elevated into a cultural ideal by the New Science: natural, asocial man, the free autonomous individual whose truth is inseparable from his alienations. Modernity in its European forms has been interpreted here as the coming to consciousness of the mind of the traveler, and this consciousness focuses upon the essential conundrum at the heart of the transformations of travel: objectivity is a consequence of a loss of self.

This notion of travel as the source of loss which is a gain is not solely Western; it is found in other cultural traditions, where travelers are perceived to be purged of extraneous associations that interfere with their connectivity to nature. Bashō, the great seventeenth-century Japanese pioneer of haiku and an aesthetic traveler of the first rank, used travel no differently than did European naturalists, though the outcome of the purifications of his journey was poetry rather than science:

> Go to the pine if you want to learn about the pine, or to the bamboo if you want to learn about the bamboo, and in doing so, you must

leave your subjective preoccupation with yourself. Otherwise you im-
pose yourself upon the object and do not learn. Your poetry issues of
its own accord when you and the object have become one—when you
have plunged deep enough into the object to see something like a
hidden glimmering there.[2]

In the West, the search for this "glimmering," the "in-itselfness" of
objects, becomes a method and a discipline that assume the loss of
defining context. This self-conscious discipline of observation, which
requires the stripping away of an enculturated self, succeeds in
erecting a new edifice of knowledge parallel and supplemental to
classical traditions. Out of this edifice is born a new idea of history
as an amoral sequence of transformations that give figure, character,
and line to the species, adapting it to a variety of circumstances,
climates, and topographies. Travel has long been valued, in both
West and East, because it annihilates the ego of the traveler, reduces
patriotism, acquaints travelers with a common nature, fate, and identity that persist beneath the diversity of cultural types and careers.

In the West, travel produces a science; in the East, an aesthetic
and an asceticism—and yet at bottom these are significantly the same.
The erosions of the journey free the wanderer from human attachments to dwell for a season of passage in pure materiality and to
delight in the resonances that may be heard when human tongues
are silent or incomprehensible. This agreement that cuts across cultural categories suggests a commonality that tells us something about
the nature of the force of mobility—which is corrosive, reductive,
and simplifying—as well as something about the material upon which
this force has traditionally operated—man. The representative traveler, throughout much of history, has worn a masculine persona. In
this may lie a source of the commonality of themes, the agreement
on the essential nature of the transformations of travel I have noted.

TRAVEL AS MAN'S FATE

*Potency is a masculine triumph over men's natural alienation from the processes
of reproduction.... [It] is the name men have given to their historically wrought
success in mediating experienced contradictions in their reproductive consciousness.*

—Mary O'Brien, 1981

In a vast portion of human history, men have been the travelers; and travel literature is—with a few significant, and often modern, exceptions—a male literature reflecting a masculine point of view. This comes as no surprise to those who have digested the insistence of modern feminists that men have generated and monopolized representational realities in which the voice of women is silent, undercut, or assumed. In the history of patriarchal civilizations—and, as yet, there are no other kinds—humanity has worn the mask of masculinity, and travel has been a performance of this persona.

The masculinization of motion and the feminization of sessility are clearly products of cultural patterning, many examples of which occur throughout the travel literature. In patriarchal cultures, the mobility of men—especially of young, unattached men—is overdetermined and powerfully charged by the reigning images of masculinity, whether of the wandering knight or of the wandering holy man, the shaman or the actor. This image of the stranger and traveler had enormous influence on patriarchal societies, an influence attested to in the life of Samuel Jemsel the Karaite, who began his travels in 1641:

> I was possessed by a violent and insatiable desire to visit the places of God ... as I had learnt that eminent men such as Rabbi Isaac and Rabbi Solomon Levi had also been inflamed with the desire of accomplishing the holy journey. I, being urged on like them by a sort of divine instinct, did not lose sight of the execution of my project: I would not have suffered myself to be turned aside from it by any reason whatsoever. This desire to set out which had formed itself in my mind was so violent that it was impossible for me to remain in my own home, or to go about my accustomed business.[3]

Man's search for eminence, for recognition, for a consummation and certainty of self has long been channeled through the agency of travel, from the time Telemachus set forth in search of his absent father, Odysseus, in order to confirm his paternity—a doubtful matter in the best of circumstances. At the beginning of his journey, Telemachus was honest when, asked by Athena (disguised as visiting Mentes) whether he was Odysseus' son, he answered, "Friend, I will speak as frankly as you desire. My mother says that I am his son, though I myself have no knowledge of it—what man can be sure of his parentage?"[4] In his journey Helen recognizes in him the image of his father and confirms his identity. In travel men have sought to appropriate not just a world but a self-image, a projected masculine persona which assumes the form of father, god, stranger, hero, holy man, knight.

Travel is a gendering activity in much of human history, one that represents the identity of the person doing it over and above any instrumental purpose the journey may serve. But gendering— the creation of the masculine and the feminine—is a dialectical process that proceeds through the creation of opposites out of differences. There is no free and mobile male without the unfree and sessile female, no knight without the lady, no father without the mother. The dialectics of gendering may go unobserved in travel literature, dominated as it is by male activities, while the journeys of women are secret, necessitated, or accomplished through the agency of men. But the mutualities of gendering are apparent in the travels of Telemachus, urged upon him by the impossible situation created by Penelope's refusal to choose another husband from among the suitors who are consuming his patrimony. The representative travels of the son may begin in the unrepresented travels of the mother, or in the conditions of sessility that define the maternal condition. The travels of Olaf the Peacock reveal something about the source of the masculine image appropriated in heroic travels, suggesting something of the narcissism inherent in this species of travel.

Olaf's travels from Iceland through Norway to Ireland and back in the tenth century are prescribed to him by his mother, Melkorka, the daughter of an Irish king taken as a concubine by Vikings and sold to Hoskuld of Iceland for three marks of silver. Melkorka, in her transportation, is deprived of her native tongue and pretends dumbness until she is overheard speaking Irish to her newborn child, through whom her lost identity and status are made known and recovered. When Olaf comes of age, Melkorka marries to supply her son with trade goods (wool, tweed, sheepskins, cheese, tallow, falcons, and sulphur—the chief products of Icelandic export). She also supplies him with tokens—a teething ring, a belt, and a knife—with which to stimulate the recognition of his Irish relatives. Olaf succeeds in this project, winning reputation, a fine suit of clothes (whence his name of "Peacock"), powerful protectors and patrons abroad, much property and wealth. On his return home, he is recognized not as a son of Melkorka the concubine but as a great man and the son of a princess: "Olaf's voyage brought him great renown, and now his true lineage was made known. . . . This was soon known throughout the country, as was the honour that had been bestowed on him by the great men he had visited."[5]

Olaf's is a journey to origins, one that makes visible a prior female journey in which a self was stripped away, to be restored by the son. The implicit dynamic here suggests that the male heroic journey may be a consequence of the repression of the mobility of women projected onto their sons, as mothers teach their male children the gains to be made outside the boundaries of the familiar which enclose and confine them.

There are many ways in which the representational mobility of men and the sessilities, or passive and unrepresented mobility, of women condition and assume each other within patriarchal gender systems. But to what extent does this cultural patterning of mobility reflect underlying sexual and reproductive determinants that channel one's liberty? Mobility clearly governs mutual recognitions and identifications in a society, out of which structures of identity are crystallized and gender differences specified. In this sense, society is rooted in fixed images of identity that contain within them a specification of relations to a variety of others, relations that themselves contain the potentials of power. But why is it men rather than women who have traveled to confirm and appropriate the most expanded image of themselves—in fame, honor, name, and recognitions? Why is it the male rather than the female persona that requires confirmation in tests of manhood, demonstrations of prowess, assertions of dominance? The history of travel offers a wealth of examples of men who have been willing to risk the very condition of identity (life) in the affirmation of an identity superior to bare existence and biological necessity, trading life for glory, death for fame. This would seem to be an irrational choice and one requiring explanation.

Mysterious, too, is the notion of the essence of the male identity demonstrated in travels and wars as "freedom," repetitively performed in departures and separations. The history of travel in the West has been an evolution from travel as a human destiny into a human freedom. But, since travel is a male-dominated activity for much of human history we must ask whether this, too—this conception of freedom—is not fundamentally a projection of masculine experience generalized into a "human nature" now appropriable by all.

If this conception of freedom as autonomy is inherently masculine, what does it tell us about men, their mobility, modes of definition, potency? In what way does travel, as a gendering activity, confront men with their essence—freedom? Within the traditions of Western civilization, and of heroic journeys in particular, travel is clearly an assertion of the power of male narcissism. These travels narrate the foundations of lineages, states, civilities, reputations as a product of male potencies. Closely examined, they reveal the truth asserted by the psychologist and midwife Mary O'Brien, that potency is the masculine triumph over "men's natural alienation from the processes of reproduction" and that patriarchal civilities are institutionalizations of "experienced contradictions" in male reproductive consciousness.[6]

Men's participation in biological reproduction is only for the briefest moment of ejaculation, idealized as the apotheosis of masculinity but in actuality experienced as a wasting, a diminution and loss of substance, even as a death. After this event, men are biologically superfluous unless they create their own necessity, as they do in wars and travels, in the acquisition and defense of women from men much like themselves. The connectivities of civility established in travels are a compensation for a rooted absence of connection to the species: "The fact is that men make principles of continuity because they are separated from genetic continuity with the alienation of the male seed." Paternity and patriarchy are laboriously established and maintained fictions which serve the purposes of human association, identification, and linkage; but these are also complex and obsessive denials of the fundamental estrangement rooted in the male gender, a compensation for men's intrinsic alienation: "In a very real sense, nature is unjust to men. She includes them and excludes them at the same moment."[7] Though they seem to have been well compensated for this injustice with undying fame, bricks stamped with their names, kula shells, medals, monuments and texts, these are only the concretized illusions of an immortality and power intimately associated with death, alienation, and dismembering.

TRAVEL AS FICTIONAL DEATH

Man becomes himself only after having solved a series of desperately difficult and even dangerous situations; that is, after having undergone "tortures" and "death," followed by an awakening to another life, qualitatively different because regenerated.

—Mircea Eliade, 1958

It is perhaps thus, as a version of the reproductive experience of men, that travel is conceivable as a "fictional death," a stripping and wasting away of self which reveals the irreducible core of that self. Men become what they are, and perpetuate themselves, through what they lose, as Camus observed, rather than through what they gain.[8]

The alienated relationship of men to the biological future of the species frees them to construct other continuities out of deeds, books, cities, names, and reputations, and urges them to the fashioning of a second, artificial, male "nature"—a civilization. The detachment of men from their seed at the moment of generation thus charts male travels and the relations between men are thus engendered: "Relations between men have an objectively causal base; they are relations of those who are forced to be free."[9] It is only that men make a virtue of their estrangement and call it freedom, making the journey and the risk of death, not biological reproduction, the chosen field for the generation and perpetuation of their identities.

All of the classical myths instituting civilization represent male sexuality as the generative, world-creating sexuality. The heroic journey is essentially a spermatic journey in which the male seed is broadcast, rooted in localized wombs, generating lineages and connectivities. The travels of Heracles and Odysseus are scarcely disguised "marriage journeys" which established spatio-temporal links between separate peoples. On his journeys—begun as a penance for the killing of his wife and children in a fit of madness—Heracles founded the ruling dynasties of Lydia, the Spartans, the Argives and Scythians. He was classically the originator of patrilines, sleeping with a serpent woman (an image of autochthony) in Scythia, fathering three children upon her, the youngest of whom, Scythes, gave his name to his people. Heracles also fathered three children with Omphale, queen of Lydia, others with her serving women, and was absorbed within the female sphere, wearing necklaces, bracelets, a woman's turban and taking up spinning and weaving. He slept with Thespius' fifty daughters—some say in a single night—impregnating them all. Among all the children he sired there were—with the doubtful exception of Macaria—no daughters, as these are useless in the founding of a patrilineage.

We might read these myths in the way that the anthropologist Bronislaw Malinowski recommends, as straightforward "charters" of civilized institutions, were it not for the puzzling frequency of dismemberment in them. The civilizing journey of Osiris was a founding journey which made the world known and recognizable, but his arrival home was dismaying. He was killed by his brother Typhon, his body cut into twenty-six pieces and scattered. Osiris' wife and sister, Isis, found the pieces and gave one to each of the twenty-six districts of Egypt, where from henceforth it was worshiped as the guarantee of the fertility of the soil. Only his privates could not be found; and Isis made a clay model of these and installed it in the capital as an object of unifying worship, thereby instituting phallicism as the focus of public ceremony. This myth asserts male sexuality as fertile, creative, and disintegrative; female sexuality as in-gathering and integrative. Dionysus, the "stranger god," was torn apart and reconstituted shortly after his birth. In his journeys he installed his cult which invariably involved—symbolically or actually—the dismemberment of male children. Pentheus of Thebes was killed by a band of maenads led by his mother who, according to Aeschylus, removed his right arm at the shoulder or, according to another version, tore off his head. Dionysus caused the Argive women to devour their male infants raw, in repetition of his own repeated dismemberment and reconstitution.

Mircea Eliade notes that symbolic dismemberment is a distinctive feature of shamanistic initiations and curing rituals, which follow a standard pattern: "dismemberment of the body, reduction to a skeleton, renewal of the internal organs ... mystic ascents and ... descents into the world underground." Eliade interprets the meaning of dismemberment, the disarticulation and reconstitution of the body in shamanistic rituals, as an expression of the "desire for absolute freedom—that is, the desire to break the bonds that keep him [the shaman] tied to the earth, and to free himself from

his limitations."[10] The event of dismemberment is commonly a feature not simply of the arrivals of founding gods and of shamanistic
rituals but of travels and arrivals in general and may be seen as a
source of the peculiar, even obsessive interest many European travelers evince in cannibalism, an interest usually projected upon uncivilized peoples and acted out by them. The normally skeptical
Captain Cook was quite pleased when he received incontrovertible
proof of cannibalism among the Maori of New Zealand. He found a
freshly gnawed human forearm which the natives insisted they had
eaten: "And to shew us that they had eat the flesh they bit and naw'd
the bone and draw'd it thro' their mouth in such a manner as plainly
shew'd that the flesh to them was a dainty bit."[11] Chandra Mukerji,
in her fascinating study of road lore among hitchhikers, reports that
a common story told by men on the road was of a farming couple,
somewhere in a remote rural area, killing and dismembering hitchhikers.[12]

Here the act of mapping, structuring, ordering, civilizing a
world—the act most demonstrative of male potency—centers upon
the dismantling of the male body, upon an act of disintegration.
These myths of, concern about, and performance of dismemberment
are statements of a contradiction and an attenuation of the illogi-
cality of reality. In founding a world, boundarying space, connecting
separate peoples, the spermatic founder is deconstructed, disinte-
grated, and scattered, to be reconstituted as territory, ingested by
communities. The killing, dismemberment, and consumption of the
god-stranger must be understood as a genuine rendering of the
generative act as it is experienced by the male. These myths state
simply: in becoming a constitutive "member" of the species, man is
dismembered.

The spermatic journey is a drama of disarticulation and a
template of male experience. But there is another meaning to the
age-old notion of travel as a suffering, a loss, a travail: it is at
the same time the gain of a world and the articulation of space, the
projection of the male ego outward and into the future. In these
generative acts, which diminish as they objectify, the actors, founding gods, and heroes create continuities and structures, making landscape sacred, starting cults and clans, diffusing the arts, knowledge,
mathematics, music, the alphabet. In creating a larger necessity and
a "man's world," men are acting not from their strength but from
their weakness, their biological deficiency, the fact that they cannot

spin a future out of their own bodies, but only out of their minds and efforts and deaths.

The dismemberment of the world-constituting god might be interpreted as an acting out of the essential contradiction that men, in contributing their chromosomes to the embryo of the future, die as men and are reduced. In forging links to others through their travels and exchanges, men provide what is missing from their relations to biological continuities. In fashioning a mythic time out of the deeds of gods and a historic time out of their own deeds, men overlay and subordinate biological time with a time of their own creation, creating that "second," civilized, nonbiological nature in which their suffering and alienation are recognized and honored as an independent, autonomous existence.

THE KNIGHT ERRANT

It seems that man alone is a figure of profound, tragic and noble philosophical significance, while woman alone is a welfare problem.
—Mary O'Brien, 1981

Every culture worthy of the name has its notion of the person, the "I," the ideal and representative self. This conception, when broadcast through the available means of communication, provides the materials from which members of a culture assemble an identity. The normative person of postclassical European culture is unique in that this is not an image of a member of a community—as the "free man" of ancient society was—but a figure defined in terms of an absence of relationships, in terms of "freedom," separateness, and autonomy. This figure—the independent, separate, self-sufficient man—begins as a self-image of a medieval warrior class generalized in the figure of the noble and knightly character. As I suggested in chapter 1, this is a figure born in a multitude of departures and passages as well as an inherited feature of Germanic culture, as Tacitus suggests in his account of the *comitatus* in his *Germania* (c. 100 A.D.) The Icelandic family sagas presuppose and celebrate a faith best stated by Gouka-Thorer, a "vagabond-man" enlisted by Olaf Haraldson in 1031 for his attempt to recover the throne of Norway, who, when offered baptism, refused: "I and my comrades have no faith but in ourselves, our strength, and the luck of victory; and with this faith we slip through sufficiently well." The image of the self-sufficient, self-defending man is invoked even in the swearing of allegiance to a liege-lord, as when Arnljot Gellene offered his services to Harald: "My faith has been this, to rely upon my power and strength, and which faith has hitherto given me satisfaction: but now I intend rather to put my faith, sire, in thee."[13]

This image of the person was generalized throughout the continent of Europe through the predations of Norse and Germanic warriors from the eighth century on and entered England when the land was conquered first by the Danes in 1016 and then by the Normans in 1066. With the latter conquest came trial by battle and, in the course of some generations, the characterization of the peasantry as "unfree." There began that process of the spread of the ideal to wider parts of the population and its concurrent demilitarization. The generalization of the knightly image of the person was achieved primarily through the agency of the common law, initially the law of barons and knights in the king's court but, from the time of Henry II, the law of all free men. By the thirteenth century, the legal historian Frederic William Maitland observes, "the lay Englishman, free but not noble, who is of full age and who has forfeited none of his rights by crime or sin is the law's typical person."[14]

The image of the warrior provided subsequent generations of Europeans with their conception of nobility: "Basically, such men were free—that is, they were men not included in the normal social categories."[15] Though subsequently demilitarized and appropriated by various species of commoner, this conception of the free person as a separate and distinct political entity retained its integrity and was formally written into the constitutions that founded modern democratic institutions. The liberty guaranteed by the *Declaration of the Rights of Man and the Citizen* was, according to Marx, a liberty founded not "upon the relations between man and man, but rather upon the separation of man from man. It is the right of such separation. The right of the circumscribed individual, withdrawn into himself."[16] Isaiah Berlin similarly noted that this separation, the distinctiveness of the individual unit, is the essence of Western conceptions of freedom: "The essence of the notion of liberty, both in the 'positive' and the 'negative' sense, is the holding off of something or someone—of others who trespass on my field or assert their authority over me."[17]

In the nineteenth century, this conception of the individual was regarded as a negation of social relations, a synonym for political and social fragmentation. But Émile Durkheim corrected this error and recalled the earliest appearances of the "free man," when he regarded the conception of the autonomous individual as a "faith," a religion, and the cornerstone of social morality: "In reality the religion of the individual is a social institution like all known religions. It is society which assigns us this ideal as the sole common end which is today capable of providing a focus for men's wills."[18]

The conception of the autonomous individual is not and never has been a description of social reality in which people are obviously and always reliant upon each other. Rather it is, and was from the beginning, a description of a point of view upon society, a point of view originally native to one outside social categories, that decreed a particular way of conceiving of social relations. The conception of the individual provides a morality that is socially transcendent, from which all relations must be evaluated as a product of the choices, wills, purposes, and contracts of those engaged in them. Rousseau understood this when he recommended *Robinson Crusoe* as the first book his ideal pupil, Émile, would read. The condition of Crusoe, the solitary and separate individual, "is not that of social man, and probably it is not to be that of Émile, but he should use it in the evaluation of all other conditions. The surest way for him to rise above prejudices and to bring his own judgments into line with the true relations of things is to put himself at the point of view of the solitary man."[19]

This conception of the normative person was originally associated with travel, and the experience of travel remained its primary verification. The right to "free departure" and the right to bear arms were de facto definitions of free status, and immobility was synonymous with unfreedom: "The right to bear arms, to follow the war-leader in expeditions undertaken each Spring, and so to share in the profits of war, all constituted the basic criteria of liberty."[20] The image of the autonomous and separate individual remained, in its subsequent generalization and demilitarization, intimately associated with mobility. The historian Alan MacFarlane argues that by the thirteenth century England could be considered an individualistic society: "The majority of ordinary people in England from at least the thirteenth century were rampant individualists, highly mobile both geographically and socially."[21] Thomas Hobbes, in his definition of freedom, was not proposing anything new or radical but rather enunciating assumptions implicit in medieval social realities: "Liberty, that we may define it, is nothing else but an absence of the lets and hindrances of motion. . . . And every man hath more or less liberty, as he hath more or less space in which he employes himself. . . . And here also the more ways a man can move himself, the more liberty he hath. And herein consists civil liberty."[22]

This conception of freedom, I have argued, assumes a certain kind of experience—the experience of the journey. It is deeply embedded in the alienations that define the relations of men to the species, relations performed in travels. But whatever the sources of this image of the person, and whatever its experiential confirmations, it has been historically generalized into an image of human nature and, as such, has lost its gender and cultural specificity. What was man's fate has become, in industrial culture, woman's option. It is in this context that the image of woman alone, separate, and free acquires a "tragic" significance it never had for men, for it is a matter of choice rather than of those biological constraints and incentives, those "necessities," that canalize choices. It is perhaps in this sense that man's has become a truly human nature.

A nomad camp *(Photo by George Rodger, Magnum Photos)*

9

TRAVELING SOCIETIES: AGENTS OF HISTORY

You share with me this mortal suffering; there is no difference between us. If we defend each other from now on, we can return home safe and sound. If, when you meet troubles, you overcome them together, when you get a meal you divide it to eat, when there is sickness you support each other, we can manage without losing a single man.

—Ch'oe Pu, 1488

The social death of the solitary wanderer, the unaccommodated traveler, provides an imperative to association within a traveling group. The young Ibn Battuta perceived this imperative when, as a young man of twenty-two just setting out on his travels, he entered Tunis and saw the members of his caravan greeted: "But not a soul greeted me and no one there was known to me. I was so affected by my loneliness that I could not restrain my tears and wept bitterly, until one of the pilgrims realized the cause of my distress and, coming up to me, greeted me kindly."[1] A fellow traveler went so far as to provide him with a wife.

All travelers who know the bleakness of the solitary journey will also understand the joy with which Lodovico di Varthema took up with a Persian merchant, one Cognizionor, who accepted Varthema as a friend of the road and companion: "He answers me 'God be praised! For I shall have a companion who will explore the world with me.' We remained fifteen days in the same city of Scherazo, and ... Cognizionor said: 'do not leave me, for we will explore a good part of the world,' and thus we set ourselves together en route to go towards Sambragante."[2] Cognizionor also became Varthema's father-in-law, giving him his daughter in marriage. Journeys necessitate the ability both to form attachments and to break them. The traveler, in having to learn how to make contingent, transient, terminable relationships—which are not necessarily superficial—"soon ... becomes accustomed to making friendships quickly, enjoying someone intensely, and then breaking off with little sorrow."[3] The vulnerability of the solitary traveler, and the resulting fear, makes the traveler porous, needy, and alert to the possibilities of association.

Nonterritorialized human relations are grounded in the conditions of motion, in chance encounters, in common dangers and common alienations from place, in common strangership. Mobility constructs sociabilities that may dissolve on arrival or be territorialized and structured in topography. Traveling societies are peculiar, not easily identifiable associations; they do not coincide with our image of a rooted, centered, bounded society. Often without roots in history, they are formed for special occasions and purposes and dissolved when those purposes are realized. They are mobile molecules within permanent structures—language groups, nations, regions—that themselves have no specific place, structures that are peculiarly unbounded and uncentered. In their traditional form, as nomadic societies, they are held together by kinship—but a kinship that is segmented and often fictional, focused upon a mythical ancestor, hero, or god. In their modern form of expeditions, such societies are no longer held together by the fictions of kinship but by oaths and destinations. The bonds actually cementing these groups are intrinsic to the experience of the journey and persist only as long as the journey does. Inherently fissionable and fusionable, these organizations constantly expand and contract with changing conditions.

The history of expeditionary travel has yet to be written and can only be essayed here, though this is a core subject of the history of travel. Such a history would detail the roots of ancient expeditions in the nomadic people and its transformation in the *comitatus*, the oath-bound associations of leaders and followers that brought down the western Roman Empire. It would describe the demilitarization of the expedition in the seventeenth century and the new meaning given to the military term *company* with the formation of trading companies and associations of merchant adventurers wedded to the more rational passion of money making. It would necessarily investigate the evolution of the scientific expedition with its concomitant intellectual, political, and cultural purposes. Clearly, this is a rich, rewarding, and significant topic which cannot be fully explored in the scope of this chapter; I can only suggest the primary economic, social, and political features of mobile societies and something of their evolution from nomadic peoples to military expeditions.

Nomadic societies are conglomerations of economically and biologically autonomous units which may subsist independently of, and even in hostility to, one another. This self-sufficiency of the mobile unit has been described variously as "disunity" by ancient observers and as "individualism" by modern witnesses. Exemplifying a segmentary rather than a hierarchical or categorical structure, such societies are involved in a continuous dynamic of fission and fusion. The cohesion within them is maintained by opposition to various categories of others, by often fictional ancestors, by the conditions of the journey, by continual negotiations between leaders and followers. Internally, such units are "democratic," governed by the consent of all mature males who enjoy an equality with one another, though this equality and democracy is qualified in the course of historical time by the coercive power acquired by the leaders of military expeditions. Relations between the segmentary units are maintained through markets, long-distance communication, segmentary lineage structures and genealogical histories, political oppositions, relations of treaty and war.

Such societies occupy a great number of economic niches, as pastoralists, hunter-gatherers, raiders, itinerant laborers, traders, professionals in transport and commerce. The wealth of such societies is often fluid, movable, and invested in social relations rather than in fixed property. Politically these societies are characterized by a polarity between leaders and followers, varying in different circumstances to embrace democracy, dictatorship, or aristocracy (when a body of nomadic warriors subjects an agricultural population to its control). All of these characteristics are functional and can be traced to the primary factor conditioning and shaping these societies: their mobility. I will explore each of these features in turn.

The importance of such societies and the need to understand them should be obvious: they are the primary agents of history, the means by which cultures "expand," by which empires are constructed and conquered, by which history—most often the story of wars and migrations—is made. These societies, I will argue, are a source of the "state," of those forms of polity and association that provide the basis of our chronology—as the nomadic people was territorialized in the ancient *polis*, as the band of followers bound by oath to a leader gave its form to feudal Europe, and as the merchant company shaped the modern world. The roots of our present, the society of travelers in which we live and move, lie deep in the history of traveling societies.

NOMADIC SOCIETIES: TRAVELING LIGHT

This is one of the charms of the desert, that removing as it does nearly all the accessories of life, we see the thin thread of necessities on which our human existence is suspended.

—Freya Stark, 1963

The nomadic condition was the original human condition; the idea of a permanent and localizable home, a historical acquisition. It was to this condition that Thucydides, the first critical historian, writing in the fifth century B.C., traced the origins of the Greeks. In nomadism, too, he found the source of the inferiority of ancient Greeks to his own contemporaries:

> It appears ... that the country now called Hellas had no settled population in ancient times; instead there was a series of migrations, as various tribes, being under the constant pressure of invaders who were stronger than they were, were always prepared to abandon their own territory. There was no commerce, and no safe communication either by land or sea; the use they made of their land was limited to the production of necessities; they had no surplus left over for capital, and no regular system of agriculture, since they lacked the protection of fortifications and at any moment an invader might appear and take their land away from them. Thus, in the belief that the day-to-day necessities of life could be secured just as well in one place as in another, they showed no reluctance

in moving from their homes, and therefore built no cities of any size or strength, nor acquired any important resources.[4]

Nomads were thus characterized by their poverty, by their existence on the margins: without capital or walls behind which wealth could be accumulated, without bonds to a particular place, without commerce or secure means of communication between groups, without agriculture, and, consequently, without the totemic substances of Western civilization—bread and wine.

In the nomadic condition, ancient observers saw what they no longer were. The mobile peoples who surrounded the core of civilization and constantly encroached on the frontiers of civility "could only be defined through an accumulation of negatives: nomads eat no bread, do not plough, do not sow, do not live in houses ... they have no statues, no temples, no altars."[5] Neither had these unstable and wandering peoples any conception of "honor" or "shame": "As for these barbarians, certain of them go about entirely naked and have the women and children in common like their flocks and herds, and since they recognize only the physical perception of pleasure and pain they take no thought of things which are disgraceful and those which are honourable."[6] Without the constant presence of the observing, judging eyes of fellow citizens, these peoples—though often warlike—had no military virtue or efficiency. Brasidas, the most successful Spartan general during the Peloponnesian war (431–404 B.C.), observed of the fierce and nomadic Illyrians that "they fight in no sort of order, they have no sense of shame about giving up a position under pressure. To run forwards and to run backwards are equally honourable in their eyes, and so their courage can never really be tested."[7] Two thousand years later, Charles Doughty saw exactly the same military qualities in nomadic tribes of Arabia: "the bird-witted beduins who, in their herding life have no thought of martial exercises, may hardly gather together ... but like screaming hawks they fight dispersedly, tilting hither and thither, every man with less regard of the common than of his private interest."[8]

But the poverty of nomadism, which stood in such obvious contrasts to the luxury of civilized life, could also be regarded as a virtue, an asceticism—as it was valued by Tnephacthus, a prince of Egypt who, when he campaigned in Arabia, was often obliged to go without food for days and otherwise live on simple fare: "He, enjoying the experience exceedingly, denounced luxury and pronounced a curse on the king who had first taught the people their extravagant way of living."[9] Tnephacthus was perhaps the first denizen of civilization, but not the last, to find therapeutic and purifying the "test of nomadism, that most deeply biting of all social disciplines," according to T. E. Lawrence (Lawrence of Arabia).[10] The Arab geographer Ibn Khaldun (1332–1406) also regarded the simplicity of nomadic existence as a source of virtue: "The desert people are closer to being good than settled peoples because they are closer to the first state and are more removed from all the evil habits that have infected the hearts of settlers."[11]

Indeed, modern students of nomadic societies interpret their characteristics positively. The anthropologist Frederik Barth insists that pastoral peoples should *not* be regarded as impoverished. It is only that their wealth takes a different form than that accumulated in goods, houses, lands, and gardens: the herd is their capital. Moreover, it is mobile and automatically increasing capital; for a herd expands geometrically as a population without the heavy labor required of the agriculturalist, who must turn land into surpluses of food by the sweat of his brow or, more likely, by the sweat of the brows of his servants, slaves, and dependents. Since the leader of a pastoral group must, of necessity, invest this capital in social rather than material relations, the herd is given as bride-price; assigned to sons, sons-in-law, or followers; or coined into reputation through the feasting of guests.[12] The economist Pierre Bonté argues even more radically that pastoralism is the historical source of capitalism, pastoral societies being intrinsic to "an historical process by which the dominance of capitalist production has become established."[13]

There is really no quarrel between the ancients, who saw nomadic and pastoral peoples as poor, and modern observers, who see them, often, as rich in mobile and convertible forms of wealth. The travel required of hunting and gathering, or pastoral, peoples dictated a minimal and transportable material culture, which left behind no architecture, statues, temples, or other permanent evidence. "Simplicity and meagerness, therefore, are the salient characteristics of the material culture of such peoples."[14] Captain Cook understood the distinction that often escaped ancient witnesses of nomadic life:

> From what I have said of the Natives of New Holland [Australia] they may appear to some to be the most wretched people upon Earth, but in reality they are far happier than we Europeans; being

wholly unacquainted not only with superfluous but necessary con-
veniences so much sought after in Europe, they are happy in not
knowing the use of them. They live in a tranquility which is not
disturbed by the inequality of Condition: The Earth and Sea of
their own accord furnishes them with all things necessary for life,
they covet not magnificent Homes, Household stuff and etc., they
live in a warm and fine Climate and enjoy a very wholesome Air,
so that they have little need of clothing and this they seem to be
fully sensible of, for many to whom we gave cloth and etc. to left it
carelessly upon the Sea beach and in the woods as a thing they had
no manner of use for. In short they seem to set no Value upon
anything we gave them, nor would they part with any thing of their
own for any one article we could offer them; this in my opinion
argues that they think themselves provided with all the necessarys
of Life and that they have no superfluities.[15]

Nomadic peoples have long offered a therapeutic reality to the natives of wealthy and established civilizations, as well as an opportunity to strip away the superfluous and think back to one's original
needs. The "poverty" of nomads, their "hidden" and circulating
wealth, is also evidence of the corrosive force of mobility long recognized by heroic travelers. Clearly, they travel most easily and ef-
ficiently who travel light. Elisha Kent Kane, an American naval doctor
who led expeditions to the Arctic in search of Sir John Franklin in
1853, 1854, and 1855, noted this reductionism as an improvement:

> We afterwards learned to modify and reduce our traveling gear,
> and found that in direct proportion to its simplicity and our ap-
> parent privation of articles of supposed necessity were our actual
> comfort and practical efficiency. Step by step, as long as our arctic
> service continued, we went on reducing our sledging outfit, until at
> last we came to the Esquimaux ultimatum of simplicity—raw meat
> and a fur bag.[16]

The unfetteredness of the mobile life, its absence of accommodations, and the simplicity of material circumstance constituted much
of what travelers termed the freedom of nomadism, a freedom the
ancients regarded variously as rootlessness, instability, or absence of
attachment to any particular spot.

It is the fact of motion that dictates the poverty of nomadic
societies in immovables, in the more impressive and lasting representations of wealth and potency. The "poverty of ritual" noted in

nomadic societies is also, apparently, the product of a mobility that dematerializes gods, cutting down on the size and number of idols nomads may worship. Often the conduit of the world's religions, nomadic peoples are themselves, strangely enough, often irreligious or lax practitioners of established faiths. The Basseri, nomads of South Persia, are, like the nomads in Arabia and North Africa, often lax Muslims, praying individually and irregularly. Barth finds this poverty of ritual an expression not only of the absence of the stable accoutrements of religion but also of the extent to which the Basseri "vest their central values in, and express them through, the very activities most central to their ecologic adaptation. This is perhaps possible for them only because of the peculiar nature of that adaptation—because of the picturesque and dramatic character of the activities which makes of their migrations an engrossing and satisfying experience."[17]

Here mobility is a substitute for ritual or, more exactly, absorbs the necessity for rituals of transformation by providing a continuous experience of change through yearly migration. Mobility satisfies needs that, in settled society, would be met by ceremony, performance, worship. The migratory track and range also map and "mythicize" territory, establish sacred sites, places of gathering. As T. G. H. Strehlow notes of the landscape mapped by Australian aboriginal hunter-gatherers: "The Simpson desert was criss-crossed from South to North and from East to West by the myths of the traveling totemic ancestors and ancestresses; and these mythical travel routes provided lawful points of social contact between the totemic clans and the local groups joined by them."[18] The migration invests landscape with a magic and potency that is consumed and perpetuated on a regular basis. This dynamic of motion creates "country," articulated as specific magical sites and the paths between them. "Ceremonial centers" are often crystallized out of patterns of migration: both Mecca and Jerusalem took their origins as sites of periodic feasts and gatherings of nomadic peoples.

The essential condition of mobility also dictates the adaptability and openness to innovation long thought characteristic of traveling societies. T. E. Lawrence attributed this adaptability to the very "poverty" of the nomadic condition: "[T]hey show themselves singularly receptive, very open to useful innovations. Their few vested interests make it simple for them to change their ways."[19] Nomads are often involved in pastoral pursuits, but adapt to many economic circumstances: as hunter-gatherers, as itinerant laborers, as predators and raiders, as traders and workers in transport, and, currently, as tour guides.

Nomadic societies are also inherently "consuming" societies in which leisure, rather than labor, is a primary value. All observers of such societies have been impressed by how little work hunter-gatherers and pastoralists do. In Arnhem Land, Australia, aborigines work fewer than four hours a day to satisfy subsistence needs. The anthropologists Richard B. Lee and Irven De Vore, in a study of the !Kung bushmen, conclude that men and women work an average of 2.5 man-days a week to feed themselves.[20] Among hunters, it is labor rather than the availability of game that dictates migrations: the camp moves not when the food supply is exhausted but when the effort expended in gathering food is felt to be too great in proportion to the returns—that is, when food gathering begins to require more than a comfortable amount of labor.[21] Similarly, pastoral societies move not when grazing is exhausted but when it takes more than an acceptable amount of time to bring the herds to and from the grazing grounds. In herding societies, where most of the work with the herds is done by children and young adults and household tasks fall most heavily upon the women, the men lead lives of relative leisure; and Bedouin men spend much of their time in talking, drinking coffee, and smoking, or in the semi-sport of raiding.

As in our own postindustrial society of travelers, the leisure characteristic of the life of adult males in traveling societies is an invisible form of wealth and the chief reason for the sociability many have found among nomadic peoples. As Charles Doughty observed: "These orientals study little else, as they sit idle at their coffee in their male societies: they learn in this school of infinite human observation to speak to the heart of one another."[22] Nomadic societies live from the bounty of nature, the fecundity of the herds, and those surpluses extracted from settlements rather than through labor. Since herds, wild animals, and natural food sources increase without the direct intercession of human labor, and since migration is the chief adaptation that maximizes the availability of food supplies, it is mobility, consumption, communication, and leisure—not labor or work—that create meaning and identity for nomadic peoples as for ourselves.

The self-sufficiency and autonomy of the primary reproductive unit is the distinctive feature of mobile social structures, which have been called "segmentary social systems." The autonomy of the traveling group was the chief reason, according to Strabo, that barbarian peoples were so easy for civilized armies to conquer: "Now the wanderings of the Greeks to the barbarian nations might be regarded as caused by the fact that the latter had become split up into petty divisions and sovereignties which, on the strength of their self-sufficiency, had no intercourse with one another; and hence, as a result, they were powerless against the invaders from abroad."[23] Barth, with other observers of contemporary nomadic societies, cites the separability of the primary household from others as the most striking feature of social structures predicated upon mobility: "The independence and self-sufficiency of the nomad household, whereby it can survive in economic relation with an external market but in complete isolation from all fellow nomads, is a very striking and fundamental feature of Basseri organization."[24]

Essentially, mobile societies consist of small households of kin and clients that exist independently from—sometimes even in hostility toward—other, similar households, camps, and bands. These autonomous groups link up through markets, common feasts, gods, lineage, alliances, hospitality. Because of this feature, the words *individuality* and *independence* are often used to define the essence of traveling societies: "Independence is a primary feature of pastoral life, expressing itself both institutionally and in terms of personality attributes."[25] As the anthropologist P. H. Gulliver observes of the Turkana nomads of Northern Uganda: "A group of two or three families may sometimes move and keep together for a time, but such associations are always transitory, for the essence of Turkana nomadism lies in the individual freedom of each family under its own head."[26]

Fusion, Fission, and Pilgrimage

The independence of the familial productive unit leads to a dynamic many have noted in traveling societies, their rhythm of fusion-fission, of coming together and splitting apart: "Sometimes, as in the dry season, the food-gathering unit might be no greater than the nuclear family; at other times it could include the whole community or even, when the ceremonial season was advanced, parts of several communities."[27] Joseph Birdsell and G. H. Strehlow have suggested that this pattern among Australian hunter-gatherers is dictated by food supply.[28] When food is scarce, during the dry season, larger aggregations will divide into their primary units as families extend themselves across their range and domain; while in times of plenty, these units will come together in momentary aggregations, festivals, and feasts.

Religious ceremonies, feasts, and celebrations are often the outward occasion for a season of fusion. The primal character of the pilgrimage as a coming together of normally separate groups to celebrate a common bond links the primitive mobile condition of mankind to religious pilgrimage and, ultimately, to tourism. The ritual journey is, historically, a means for the actualization of the largest external structure that unites separate, mobile, autonomous social segments in that larger unity represented in common gods, common worship, and common traditions. Travel, of course, is the primary means by which this unity is realized, just as it is the means by which disaggregation occurs.

Long before Christ and Mohammed reconsecrated them as places of Christian and Muslim pilgrimage, Jerusalem and Mecca had been places at which related tribes gathered during seasons of plenty for common feasts. Pilgrimage originates in feast and festival—the joyous celebration and meeting of ordinarily autonomous nomadic groups—and affirms a unity of law, kinship, religion, and clan, the largest external structure that binds and unifies natively independent units. The Hebrew pilgrimage (*hagh*), like the preMuslim Arabic pilgrimage (*haj*), denotes both a journey and the festival celebrations at a shrine and explicitly refers to the original and seasonal nomadic journey. All the males of linguistically related Hebrew tribes were enjoined by common law and traditions of worship to gather at the temple in Jerusalem three times a year, at Passover, Weeks, and Booths (Tabernacle). Before Passover became, by tradition, the commemoration of the journey of the people of Moses out of Egypt, it had been a commemoration of the nomadic condition and involved a three-day trip into the desert, followed by a feast. The feast of the Tabernacle, or tents, required the construction of an improvised altar out of unhewn stones and, according to the historian of religion William Popper, was "a dramatic revival of the ancient desert life and wanderings."[29] The Muslim *haj* still concludes with a journey from Medina to Mina, where pilgrims' heads are shaved and they are released from the ascetic state of *Ihram*. Then, in a recapitulation of the earliest, pre-Muslim traditions surrounding the pilgrimage to Mecca, the pilgrim *must* engage in three days of feast; fasting is positively forbidden.

The festive origins of the pilgrimage in those moments of fusion when the segments of nomadic societies came together remained a strong undercurrent even in the medieval Christian pilgrimage; it was a "survival" strongly denounced by clerics, who insisted upon the solemnity and seriousness of pilgrimage. A few years after the death of the Venerable Bede in 735, an English missionary in Germany wrote to Cuthbert, the archbishop of Durham, that there was a great need "to check the practice of pilgrimages, for many, both men and women, go abroad for the purpose of living licentiously, without the restraint they would find at home, or are tempted by the vices of the cities in France and Lombardy to fall from the paths of virtue."[30] In Sir Thomas More's *Dialogue on the Adoration of Images*, the interlocutor notes that the majority of the pilgrims who come to Canterbury "cometh for no devotion at all, but only for good company to babble thitherward, and drinke dranke there, and then dance and reel homeward."[31] In *The Canterbury Tales*, Chaucer's pilgrims are thus not violators but celebrants of the original character of pilgrimage when they use the pilgrimage as an occasion for a holiday, for a riotous gathering sanctified by all that is holy and unifying; and Chaucer is historically accurate in his portrayal of pilgrims:

> *Every man in his wise made harty chere*
> *Telling his fellows of sports and of cheer*
> *And of mirthes that fallen by the waye*
> *As custom is of pilgrims, and hath for many a daye.*[32]

Pilgrimage is a survival of the fusion process characteristic of eminently fissionable traveling societies, but the "normal" condition of segmentary societies is disunity. Moments of unity are rare, but supremely important, and it is in their unified forms that the hosts of nomads—Mongols, Arabs, Huns—have left their most indelible marks on the pages of history.

Fusion of the autonomous units of nomadic societies is also achieved through political means, but less through a rigid political structure than through a flexible body of rules governing alliances and oppositions. Frederik Barth and others call the political structure characteristic of nomadic societies an "oppositional" political structure, in which groups fuse and unite according to the level of opposition they face. Consolidation of the nomadic unit into confederations, leagues, and alliance systems is thus a product not of internal but of external forces, of war. As the anthropologist Marshall Sahlins suggests, "the lineage segment cannot stand alone but can only stand 'against.' "[33] The level of cohesions achieved among nomadic units is thus a function of the strength and number of opponents, a rule that is perfectly expressed in the Bedouin proverb:

> *I against my brother.*
> *I and my brother against my cousin.*
> *I, my brother and our cousin against the neighbors.*
> *All of us against the foreigner.*[34]

The rules governing alliances and enmities within oppositional political structures are few and simple: the friend of my enemy is my enemy; the enemy of my enemy is my friend; the enemy of my friend is my enemy; the friend of my friend is also my friend. This system of rules governs a pattern of political consolidation and fragmentation which may produce those conquering hosts who swept across Eurasia and North Africa from the seventh through the thirteenth centuries, as well as that fragmentation and disunity that made the barbarian nations an attractive target for the expansion of the ancient Greeks and Romans:

> The level of political consolidation contracts and expands: primary segments that unite to attack or repel an enemy at one time may fragment into feuding factions at another, quarreling over land and personal injuries. Moreover, the degree to which political consolidation proceeds typically depends on the circumstances external to the tribe itself. The existence of well-organized predatory neighbors, the opportunity to prey on a nearby society, will give impetus to confederation.[35]

Acephalous (literally "without a head"), segmentary social systems, oppositional political systems, the pattern of fusion-fission that characterizes mobile societies cannot be regarded as products of any one stage of historical development—as features of preindustrial existence, as purely traditional. These are found too often in modern circumstances, in the persistence of "cold war," in patterns of modern sociability, in the structures of tourism. It would be a mistake to see modern nomadic societies—pastoral peoples, gypsies, motorcycle clubs, tour groups—as survivals of an early, or premodern, institution. Originally, as today, these social and political structures were a consequence of mobility. The independence of the mobile unit—whether an individual or a collectivity—derives from the ability to detach itself from a locale and to move across territory while retaining integrity. The segment is produced by passage, by the unity and cohesion required by passage, as illustrated in expeditions and caravans: "Even the later independent caravan . . . remained a kind of small, wandering state, threading its way between numberless smaller or larger settlements of peoples of a more or less predatory kind."[36] The survival of this mobile unit also depends upon its ability to negotiate relations with sedentary social units, to "arrive," and to establish relations of exchange. Only by seeing this structure as the product of mobilities may we explain why it appears in so many continents and periods in essentially the same form. This is an example not of the diffusion of a system or idea across space but of the consistent effects of a unitary force, the force of mobility, upon human relations.

The Origins of Patriarchy

Segmentary lineage systems—systems that trace temporal relations back through "brothers" and "uncles" to a common ancestor—are characteristic of nomadic and mobile peoples. This system rests upon the fiction of a patriarch, most often a "grandfather," through whom linkages between separate, autonomous lineage "segments" may be traced. An unnamed Turkana informant succinctly explained this system to the ethnologist P. H. Gulliver: "We are one family and different from other people. Kopegamoi is like our grandfather, for he was a big man long ago; we remember. I do not know the name of my father's father. That is how we say it is."[37]

Patriarchy is perhaps one of the strongest ideas of wandering peoples, an idea that would necessarily occur to strangers of the same language group in meeting, who would try to establish some ground of the familiar, overcommunicating about what they had in common, suppressing their differences. Their common link may turn out to be a brother, a well-remembered man of long ago who left the pasture of his people and wandered to some other land, founding a race of "Cain" or "Abraham," "Seth" or "Israel." Almost invariably the segmentary lineage is found among mobile and dispersed peoples, often in conjunction with patriarchy and endogamy.

Segmental lineages are normally endogamous—sometimes along both the male and the female lines, in which case the possibilities of a common ancestor will be doubled. The evidence suggests that endogamous, patriarchal, segmental lineages, such as one finds among nomadic tribes and our biblical progenitors, are a chief means of countering the tendencies toward fission inherent in the self-sufficiency of the nomadic unit; and that the fiction of a common ancestor is a way to counteract territorial displacements, departures, and dispersals. When Jacob, the grandson of Abraham, retraced his grandfather's journey in order to find a wife among his cousins, his grandmother's and grandfather's people, he was doubling his identities and affirming bonds that held a people together despite wide geographical dispersals, constant migrations. This rule of endogamy within the patriline was powerful enough to justify Lot's incest with his daughters, so that the patriline, with the cohesion and common identity it structured, would not die out.

The common ancestor, the "big man" who lived long ago and is remembered in story and song, is a functional fiction for nomadic units detaching from one locale, journeying through the lands of hostile or indifferent others, forming attachments in another locale. A common identity would be particularly valuable for a composite people like the Israelites, formed originally out of nomadic tribes from the pasturelands of Mesopotamia, who found themselves returning to the land we still deem most holy. Their sense of being "of one family and different" than the peoples among whom they continuously dwelled—Amorites, Hittites, Phoenecians, Philistines, Samaritans, then Greeks and Latins—was affirmed in the recitation of lineages which became an oral literature, then written law. Names and personifications were attached to collective identities whose history was recited as the history of remembered, migrant heroes linked generationally: "[T]he patriarchs are neither merely individuals nor the personifications of tribes, they are the fathers who take part in the life of the tribe. The legends center around them, intermixed with fairy tales and minor features, which the sons involuntarily stamp with their character, and all the great events happening to the tribe are ascribed to them."[38]

Patriarchy is a purely representational reality ("That is how we say it is") that is functional for mobile social groups. It mitigates detachments and departures, provides a common identity to the traveling group, and often eases arrivals for strangers among whom a related segment, and ally, may often be found. Perhaps this explains the power and persistence shown by the fiction of the patriarch over three millennia, a period of history that has been a story of migration, travel, returns, by which distinctive human groups have niched themselves in a variety of topographies.

ARMED STRANGERS: MILITARY EXPEDITIONS AND THE SEEDS OF THE STATE

He who was a Roman or a Frank has in this land been made into a Galilean or a Palestinian. He who was of Rheims or Chartres has now become a citizen of Tyre or Antioch. We have already forgotten the places of our birth; already these are unknown to many of us or not mentioned anymore.... Words of different languages have become common property known to each nationality and mutual faith unites those who are ignorant of their descent.

—Fulcher of Chartres, 1120

I and my companions are only doing what our predecessors did, which is not against the King; for we hold him who commands us as our lord, and no other.... We have made a new king whom we obey, and as Vassals of another lord, we may well make war against those we have sworn to fight, which is our business and not yours.

—Lope de Aguirre, 1561

Mobility constructs sociabilities that may dissolve on arrival, or be territorialized and structured in topography. In the Crusades, mobility formed a new society out of disparate individuals and territorialized that society in a locale. Fulcher of Chartres was impressed with the variegated character of the expedition to Jerusalem of 1096: "And whoever heard of such a mixture of languages in one army?

There were present Franks, Flemings, Frisians, Gauls ... Lotharingians, Alemanni, Bavarians, Normans, English, Scots, Aquitanians, Italians, Dacians, Apulians, Iberians, Bretons, Greeks and Armenians. If any Briton or Teuton wished to question me I could neither reply nor understand."[39] Initially united only by oaths to a common god and to one another, these fragments of nations became one society on the journey, united through battles, common suffering, common sins. With the conquest of Jerusalem, this traveling society became territorialized, began collecting rents from the subject population, learned new and common words, forgot their places of birth.

The force of mobility is a source of both solidarity *and* detachment, a cement *and* a solvent of human association. The military expeditions of the ancients, the bands of warriors that inundated the western Roman world and fundamentally altered it, those clusters of lords and followers who made the Crusades, who mapped, explored, and settled the wider world in the sixteenth and seventeenth centuries, are important not only for what they did, as historical agents, but also for showing us how social groups are formed and maintained on bases other than territory, lineage, and language—the primary infrastructure most often assumed in our discussions of society and history. The solidarity such groups maintain is formed out of common direction, a uniformity of condition, the common identity of strangers, and common opposition to settled groups—all of which serve to create, perpetuate, and regulate mobile societies. Such groups are, for the most part and for obvious reasons, self-governing.

Alfred Russel Wallace found a society among the traders and merchants in the Aru Islands, who taught him how little regulation was necessary in such societies, which appeared to be "without government":

> This motley, ignorant, bloodthirsty, thievish population live here without the shadow of a government, with no police, no courts, and no lawyers; yet they do not cut each other's throats; do not plunder each other day and night; do not fall into the anarchy such a state of things might be supposed to lead to. It is very extraordinary! It puts strange thoughts in one's head about the mountain-load of government under which people exist in Europe, and suggests that we may be overgoverned.[40]

It was a common interest in trade and profit that united these "discordant elements into a well-behaved community" and created a "public opinion" that suppressed all lawlessness.

Oath-Bound Associations

The factor of mobility, too, makes mobile societies almost invariably democratic, relying on the ongoing active consent of their members. The threat of detachment is never empty: each unit of the traveling society may vote with its feet. If only for this reason, traveling societies, even in their original form as the nomadic segment, are essentially voluntary associations, continually validated or invalidated through communication and counsel: "A camp community of nomads can only persist through continuous reaffirmation by all its members. Every day the members of the camp must agree in their decision on the vital question of whether to move or to stay camped, and if they move, by which route and how far they should move."[41] The importance of counsel and talk in these societies has long been noted; without discussion, the traveling group obviously cannot move, determine its direction, negotiate the dangers of passage.

The unity of the mobile group can never be assumed, as it may be among walled and bounded human associations. All societies, but mobile societies in particular, are born from and perpetuated in communication which projects possible futures and elicits common motives. Indeed, in the Greek world, the need for counsel remained a bond between territorialized political communities and those bands of armed men sent abroad on expeditions. When the oligarchic coup of 411 B.C. severed Athens from its navy and hoplites stationed in Samos, leaving them without a city, the soldiers were encouraged to think of themselves as an independent political entity: "It was no loss to lose a people who no longer had any money to send them . . . and were also incapable of giving them good advice—which is the thing that justifies the control of the armies by the state."[42]

Ancient expeditions, which resembled mobile cities in their autonomy and self-sufficiency, evolved into oath-bound associations of men, such as those that descended upon Mediterranean societies with increasing frequency beginning in the fifth century. The details of this evolution from nomadic societies held together by the fiction

of paternity and structures of lineage, to the *polis* continually reproduced in mobile expeditions, to the armed expedition of men bound
by their oath to a leader or leaders, has yet to be examined and
would prove most interesting to the history of travel.

In the history of expeditions, the importance increasingly falls
upon the oath as the bond between individuals, such as the oath of
association sworn by Jewish pilgrims who went on the *sibbab*, the
voyage to the Holy Land, which involved an exchange of blood: "One
man thrusts a needle into his finger and invites the intended companion of his journey to swallow the blood of the wounded finger.
He and that other person become, as it were, the same blood and
flesh."[43] The covenantal oath, rather than lineage, became the cement of those traveling societies who made the Crusades, extended
the boundaries of Christendom, and colonized the world from the
fifteenth century on. These were expeditions of oath-bound associations of men who, by their voluntary assignment, gave themselves
the law they were sworn to obey for so long as they belonged to
the expedition. The documents attesting to such oath binding, the
covenants and articles sworn by traveling groups, are the first real
constitutions, if by *constitution* we mean a document that actually
founds an association, not a description of precedents and existing
arrangements.

The expedition that took Lisbon from the Moors in 1147 was
one such oath-bound association, made up largely of "lesser folk
who were dependent on no great leader except omnipotent
God"[44]—men recruited from the channel ports and islands, Flan-
ders, Boulogne, Norfolk, and Suffolk, enrolled under their individual captains. As custom dictated, they drew up a charter that
recognized the ancient law—"A life for a life, a tooth for a tooth,"
the most primal form of reciprocity. The articles of agreement
founding this society forbade all displays of wealth, the keeping of
servants, and the public presence of women. It decreed weekly services by clergy and appointed a priest for each ship. Two judges and
a representative for each thousand men formed the council that governed the expedition and made the decisions as to sailings, landings,
provisioning, the order of battle, and the conduct of the campaign.

Such legal instruments served to homogenize status by decreeing
a common law for individuals from disparate nations and creating an
"artificial," but real, equality among members of the group. Long a

distinctive feature of traveling societies, this equality was the reason
Fynes Moryson recommended travel, especially in Germany, to young
English lords too accustomed to the ministrations of servants:

> [A]nd since wee use to despise the company of meane people at
> bed or board, there wee may learne to serve ourselves.... There
> wee may learne to admit the company of meane men, where may
> at times poore fellowes, yea, very coachmen, shall be thrust to be
> our bedfellowes, and that when they are drunke; and like men will
> often set by us at the Table, and in some places ... they drink always
> round, so as we shall be sure to pledge like men, and drink to them
> in the same cup.[45]

T. E. Lawrence noted this rough and familiar equality in the desert
life in which "man lives candidly with man. It is a society in perpetual movement and an equality of voice and opportunity for every
male."[46] The egalitarianism of human relations on the road, where
there is no history to muddy social recognitions or to prejudge the
outcome of social encounters, and where character and humanity
are always revealed afresh, has long recommended travel to those
whose status has come to define them too closely.

Leaders and Followers

As for the political structure of such societies, the leaders scout the
trails and arrange accommodations, while others follow; but these
two entities—leader and followers—are mutually dependent. The
leader does not exist who has no followers; and the follower, as one
who comes behind, may depart at the first break on the horizon, at
will. As has been mentioned, these societies are often described as
democratic because all authority comes from the consent of the
group, focused through leaders who govern by their charisma, skill,
and personal character. Lévi-Strauss noted of the Nambikwara, a
seminomadic tribe of Brazilian Indians who are hunter-gatherers
during the dry season and gardeners during the rainy season:

> Personal prestige and the ability to inspire confidence are the basis
> of power in Nambikwara society. Both are indispensable for the
> man who has to act as guide during the hazardous nomadic period
> of the dry season. For six or seven months, the chief is entirely

responsible for the leadership of his group. It is he who organizes
the departure, chooses the routes, decides on the camping places
and the duration of each camp. ... power derives from consent and
it depends on consent to maintain its legitimacy.[47]

The qualities that elicit consent—and that are prized in a leader of
mobile groups—are generosity and the ability to seize the initiative,
to guide, to find food sources, and to calculate and time journeys.
In effect, leadership depends not upon office, lineage, social standing, or position, but upon performance; and the leader may be
reabsorbed into the followership as a result of a poor performance
just as he emerged from it on the promise of a good one. Clearchos,
the Spartan captain of a significant contingent of the mercenary
army that marched with Cyros into Mesopotamia in 401 B.C., on the
expedition described by Xenophon, was almost thus demoted when
his men refused to obey him and began to stone him. Clearchos
saved himself and his position as leader by bursting into tears and
frankly confessing the realities of political power in a mobile society: "Since you will not obey me, I will go with you and suffer whatever I must suffer. For I consider that you are my country and my
friends and comrades; and with you, I think I shall be honoured
wherever I may be, but without you, I think I am not able either to
help a friend or hurt an enemy. Where you go there I will go also:
that is my resolve."[48] Understanding that his authority, his ability to
command, was generated by the consent of his followers, Clearchos
knew that without them his power was illusory, his dignity as a leader
empty.

Power here is clearly a consequence of the relations between
leaders and followers mediated through consultation and counsel,
the importance of which we can see in all traveling expeditions, in
the *Iliad*, the *Odyssey*, the Crusades, the expeditions of Drake and
Magellan, or privateering ventures of the seventeenth and eighteenth centuries. The leader personifies, crystallizes, or obviates the
necessity for a consensus among his followers. According to Marshall Sahlins, the leader of a hunting-gathering society rules through
personal loyalties created by "generosity, fearful acquiescence
through magic, inclination to accept his opinions through demonstrations of wisdom, oratorical skill and the like. Leadership here is
a charismatic, interpersonal relationship."[49] This remains true for
military expeditions.

Most effective leaders of expeditions have understood the roots of their authority to be in the followers; and much of the art of leadership consists of the techniques, manipulations, and dodges required to conceal, mitigate, or obfuscate this underlying reality— which nevertheless is clear when the followers refuse to obey or exercise their option of departure. This occurred to Sir James Lancaster in 1592, on one of the expeditions leading to the founding of the British East India Company. Lancaster, an adroit leader of men and master of the syntax of negotiation, was forced by his crew to return to England after lying in the Nicobar Islands for months awaiting the Portuguese treasure fleet. The wastage aboard the flagship had been enormous, and only 33 men were left out of an original complement of 198, "[w]hereupon our men took the occasion to come home, our captain at that time lying very sick, more like to die than live." When the captain recovered from his fever and laid a northerly course, "[o]ur men made ansere that they would take their direct course for England, and would stay there no longer. Nowe seeing they could not bee perswaded by any meanes possible, the captaine was constrained to give his consent to returne, leaving all hope of so great possibilities."[50] In December 1592, Lancaster bowed to the will of his followers and set a course for the Cape of Good Hope; but the trust binding leader and followers had been broken. The men appointed a committee to check the captain's headings and oversee every change of course. When, in spite of these precautions, they somehow arrived in the Caribbean (Lancaster had designs on Pernambuco, in Brazil), the men mutinied, marooned Lancaster on Mana Island, and joined the growing body of free companions who made their living raiding Spanish ships in the Caribbean.

The best analysis of the fluidity that seems to characterize political relations between leaders and followers in traveling societies is Frederik Barth's description of a Norwegian herring fleet. The fishing boat, the independent and autonomous unit that makes up the fleet, is engaged in the same pattern of search, hunting, or stalking a prey found in the earliest hunting-gathering societies. The fishing vessels tend to cluster together, and the crews concentrate on discovering "the movement of the other vessels, and most time is spent chasing other vessels to ... unplanned and fruitless rendezvous."[51] The patterns of clustering and fission are shaped by the reputations of the captains, their past performances, and their luck. A captain with a good reputation and a record of good catches will often strike out on his own, other vessels following, but only with the support of his crew. Good skippers have crews who respect their judgment, giving them greater independence of movement than captains with lesser reputations. The latter will tend to follow rather than lead; for a bad catch matters less if other boats fail, too, and generally the measure of success or failure is relative to the success or failure of other vessels.

This pattern appears in other forms of hunting and gathering, in raiding and trading. When Gunnar Hamundarson (the most famous warrior of tenth-century Iceland and hero of *Njal's Saga*) and his brother Kolskegg decided to go raiding with Earl Hakkon Sigurdson of Norway, the king lent them two ships: "They had no difficulty manning them because Gunnar had a fine reputation."[52] The chiefs with the highest reputations commanded the best followers and fiercest fighters, among whom certain distinctions were recognized. When Harald Harfager (Fairhair) manned a dragon-ship for raiding in 867, his distribution of his troops represented an estimation of their qualities:

> The forecastle men were picked men for they had the King's banner. From the stem to mid-hold was called *rousn*, or the fore-defense; and there were the berserks. Such men only were received into King Harald's household as were remarkable for strength, courage and all kinds of dexterity; and they alone got place in his ships, for he had a good choice of house-troops from the best men in every district.[53]

Clearly, Harald's crew consisted of potential leaders in their own right, along with wild men, berserkers, whose chief virtue was their sustained ferocity. Implicit in the political structure of leader-follower is a potential "class" distinction between those capable and those incapable or undesirous of leadership. The former, leaders and candidates for leadership, may become an "officer class" or aristocracy. The expedition of Greek mercenaries recorded by Xenophon was clearly democratic in the sense that the ranks affirmed or disaffirmed their leaders, but these leaders, captains, and officers were drawn from a class of men whom Xenophon reminded of their obligations: "Perhaps it is fair to expect you to be a bit better than they [the ranks] are. You are captains, you see, or you are in com-

mand of troops and companies, and while there was peace, you had
more wealth and honour; then now when war has come, we must
ask you to be better than the mob, and labour for their behalf, if
necessary."[54]

The Legacy of the Expedition

The political options present in the leader-follower duality (democracy, aristocracy, even—in exceptional circumstances—dictatorship)
have been institutionalized in various historical forms of the state.
Both the ancient *polis* and medieval lordship were institutionalizations of traveling societies, realizing in different ways the possibilities inherent in the leader-follower duality. The ancient *polis* was a
realization of the power of the following; the medieval lordship, a
formalization of the position of the leader. The *polis* still shows its
roots in the nomadic segment in the assumption that the "people"
retain a collective integrity independent of any leadership, while the
medieval band of lord and followers retains no such assumption,
and the relations of the followers to each other is mediated through
the relation of each to a leader.

The free, independent *polis* is clearly rooted in the nomadic following. The very "independence" of the city from other similar entities was all that the Greeks meant by "freedom." The ancient Greeks
believed that a city retained its integrity even when uprooted from
its home ground, so long as relations of equality among its citizens
persisted. The destruction of the walls, temples, and buildings of
Athens in the second Persian invasion of 480 B.C. was not the destruction of Athens, as the statesman-general Themistocles indig-
nantly pointed out when he was trying to get his allies to confront
the armies of Xerxes north of the isthmus of Corinth. To one who
objected that a man without a city had no right to urge those still
with one to abandon it, he retorted, "[I]t is quite true, you wretch,
that we have given up our houses and our city walls, because we did
not choose to become enslaved for the sake of things that have no
life or soul." The soul of the city was its people and the relations
they bore to each other, and this was eminently transportable. Themistocles threatened that if the Greeks did not support them, Athens
would move to Sicily, and that the "Greeks will soon hear the news

that the Athenians have found themselves as free a city and as fine a country as the one they have sacrificed."[55]

Similarly, if every citizen of an ancient *polis* was by definition a soldier, every soldier of an expedition was by definition a citizen; and an army was thought of as a city in embryo, a body of citizens that might, in the right conditions, territorialize itself. In advising the Athenians to send forth the greatest possible force against Syracuse, in Sicily, in 417 B.C. the general and statesman Nicias used this implicit formula: "We must act on the assumption that we are going off to found a city among foreigners and among enemies." The relief force that the Corinthians sent to Epidamnus in 432 B.C. was advertised as a new colony. Participants in the expeditions were assumed to be citizens of a new political body as well as shareholders in a political joint stock company: "Those who went out there were to have absolutely equal rights, and those who were not prepared to sail at once, but still wanted to have a share in the colony, could buy this share . . . for the sum of fifty Corinthian drachmae."[56] This stock offer assumed a distinction between those who traveled and those who did not—the former being considered citizens of a new political entity, the latter thought to be merely investors in a commercial adventure until they joined the "colony" as citizens. In the ancient world, the highest status and most indelible reputation an individual could achieve was as a founder of a city. This ambition inspired Xenophon to visualize a city of his own founding when he saw the army, unified by a hard march through hostile territory, camped on the shores of the Black Sea (the Euxine): "He saw all these on the Euxine, where so great a force could never have been collected without vast expense, and he thought it would be fine to found a city there, and to add territory and power to Hellas."[57] But the men refused, wishing to return home with the loot and captives acquired on the march.

The assumption that the soldier was a citizen, and that the army was a city in potential, supplied the expansive dynamics of the Greco-Roman world, the means by which Mediterranean civilization reproduced itself upon an expanding frontier: "[The] double-beat systolic and diastolic of a city occasionally contracting into an army, of an army expanding into a city, is to be accounted for by the original identity, still clearly perceived, of the soldier and the citizen."[58] But this identity is rooted in the solidarity and independence of the nomadic segment, the obvious power of the following, which may, in appropriate circumstances, fission off from its matrix and live a life of its own, or join with other segments in a confederacy, an alliance, an army. Ancient expeditions, rooted in a *polis* which is itself a territorialization of the nomadic segment, give evidence for the thesis originally proposed by Franz Oppenheimer in 1914 that the "state," in at least one of its forms, emerges from the organization of the nomad camp, from "the subjection of a peasant folk by a tribe of herdsmen or by sea nomads."[59]

The ancient assumption that the essence of the mobile society lay in the followership contrasts with the medieval assumption that the essence of the mobile segment lay in the leadership—in the lord, the free and sovereign individual. The armed following—the *comitatus*, a group of free armed men who contracted themselves individually to obey a leader for specific military purposes and for a specific period—was a crucial ingredient in the construction of the new political and social structure of feudalism. The relationship between leader and follower was the primary cement of this new power structure: "That the noble order of the Frankish kingdom became the germ-cell of the West was an event of world-historical significance. The armed retinue, whose nature derived from the period of migrations, was the basis of this noble power."[60]

The bond between lord and follower, as in mobile societies generally, was a personal and private one based upon mutual respect and common interest. This relationship "was freely entered upon, based on fidelity and obligating the follower to give counsel and military aid, the lord to give protection and largesse." The language symbolizing the relationship of follower to lord reflected its source in mobile societies. *Gesinde*, which originally meant "road companion," ultimately came to refer to the armed, free follower of a lord. *Reise*, which in modern German means simply "journey," originally referred to the obligation of the follower to accompany his liege-lord on seasonal campaigns. This relationship forged in passage supplied the language for many other social bonds. In Norse law, for example, a woman joined in marriage "as the companion joined to her husband by the ties of the follower."[61]

But here the focus of the leadership-followership duality is clearly upon the persona of the leader, the lord, and there was little or no assumption—such as one finds in ancient expeditions—that the followership constituted a membership independent of the leader, bound by ties of equality and mutual aid. Indeed, as free and independent individuals contracted to a leader, each follower might himself become a lord by attracting a following, accumulating property and reputation. Leadership of an expedition carried the implications of "kingship." When Olaf Haraldson, son of King Harald Fairhair, went on his first Viking expedition in 1007, at the age of twelve, to raid the Baltic, Finland, Gottland, and Sweden, he immediately assumed the title and position of king. As the chronicler Snorri Sturluson explains, "It was the custom that those commanders of troops who were of kingly descent, on going on a Viking cruise, received the title of king immediately, although they had no land or kingdom."[62]

The segmental character and inherent fissionability of all traveling societies was here translated into the autonomy of the individual retainer, who preserved his freedom insofar as he kept the right of free departure, and who might become a lord if he could attract a following. The status of lord remained the primary reward of leadership of expeditions well into the Renaissance, and was the chief motive of generations of crusaders to the holy land, colonists and conquistadors to the new world. Leadership of an expedition of free men continued to be ennobling, a promotion to a lordship. When the wealthy Cuban farmer Hernán Cortéz received the appointment to lead the expedition against Mexico, he immediately improved his "estate," mortgaging his lands to provide himself with a retinue suitable for a new lord.[63] Christopher Columbus, originally the son of a Genoese weaver, became a lord and "Admiral of the Ocean Sea" through his voyages. When he returned to Spain in chains after his second voyage, charged with malfeasance, he demanded that he be judged by his peers, "by knights of the sword and by men of action," and regarded himself as defending "the lordship which my king and queen had given into my keeping."[64] All of this suggests that the "autonomy" of the nomadic unit here refers to the individual rather than the group, and that each individual is a potential "lord" just as, in the ancient world, each armed body was a potential *polis*, an independent political community.

The test of the independence of the follower was, as always, his right of departure, which became, in the Middle Ages, a "right to rebellion," the ability to detach oneself from prior allegiances and effect new ones. In the eighth-century *Old Saxon Genesis*, by an anonymous author, Lucifer is portrayed in the idiom of the time as a rebellious armed retainer who would himself become lord:

It pleases me little, to have a lord.
I can with my own hands as many wonders work,
I have power enough to erect
A statelier throne, one higher yet in heaven.
Why must I serve for his grace, give to him allegiance?
I can be God like him. Strong companions stand by me.
In a fight they will not fail. Strong-minded heroes
They have chosen me lord, famous warriors.
From such one has good counsel
Takes good counsel from such folk-supporters.
They are my ready friends, they are brave in their minds intention.
I can be their lord, rule this kingdom.
It does not seem right to me, that I
Should have at all to implore God for any gifts.
No longer will I be his follower.[65]

The lordship Lucifer seeks is identical with the leadership of a band
of armed followers who owe their leader the obligation of "counsel"
and guidance as well as military support.

The subtraction of obedience from an old lord and its addition
to a new one was repetitively committed by the turbulent and restless
conquerors of the New World. But the formula for such detachments
came from the old world and the tradition of the *comitatus*, evoking
the right of departure which belonged to every free follower. When
Lope de Aguirre instigated the murder of Pedro dé Ursua, the leader
of an expedition into the Amazon basin in 1560–61, in search of El
Dorado, he justified his act in accepted terms:

I say that I denaturalize myself from the Kingdoms of Spain where
I was born; and if I have any rights there in consequence of my
parents being Spaniards, and Vassals of the king ... I give up all
my rights and I deny that he is my king and lord; and I repeat that
I know him not, neither do I wish to know him, nor obey him as
such; but rather, being in possession of my own liberty, I elect from
this time forth my prince, king and natural lord, Don Fernando de
Guzman.[66]

Aguirre killed this new king, too, and justified his violence as only a
repetition of the behavior of his predecessors, "for we hold him who
commands us as our lord, and no other." In any case, such acts were

in the nature of his business and "were the natural consequences brought on by wars, and war could not be called by that name if such acts did not take place." There was nothing dishonorable in such acts of treason, he noted that "war was so honourable a career that the angels in heaven had theirs."[67]

Traveling societies, in both their tribal and expeditionary forms, erode neat distinctions between state and pre-state, tribal and advanced, prehistorical and historical societies. For these are small, independent proto-states—traveling cities and bodies of potential overlords—with clear and obvious roots in tribal, nomadic organization. These groups have acted as primary agents of history, in projecting power, establishing frontiers, and removing from settled societies anomalous and unsettling elements, like those men who were sent into the Amazon with Pedro dé Ursua and Lope de Aguirre to "relieve the Provinces of Peru of much corrupt blood, by sending forth many idle people, who might otherwise cause some fresh insurrection."[68] The persistence of certain features of these societies— the segmentary social structure, the oppositional stance to the world, the political structure of leaders and followers—may be explained by the persistence of the force, mobility, that shapes these forms of human relations. Necessitating the autonomy and separability of the mobile unit, it dictates the manners, adaptations, and relations within individual traveling groups and shapes the relations of these groups with other, sedentary societies. In this form of society, we may also find the origins of states, in their different historical appearances, which are only adaptations and territorializations of the different possibilities inherent in the duality of leaders-followers. Mobility requires this unique and identifiable authority structure, inherently democratic and consensual, but which often invests the responsibility and power of the followers in leaders who are expected to "go first," to negotiate the passage, and to fix the terms of arrival.

(Top) Boswell as he would see himself, and (bottom) as seen by the painter Sir Joshua Reynolds. *(Courtesy of the Bettmann Archive)*

10

TRAVEL AND THE TRANSFORMATIONS OF SOCIAL BEING

No man has of himself the notion that other people have of him, especially those who know him little.

—James Boswell, 1766

Travel has long been a means of changing selves, a method of altering social status, of acquiring fame, fortune, and honor— even a profession of shape changing, for acting has long been an itinerant profession. The transformation of social being in travel, becoming someone else through territorial passage, is a cliché of the literature, and so common in experience that territorial mobility supplies our chief metaphor of social transformation: that is, *social mobility*, denoting alterations of status as movement from one social place to another. Here I will consider both the ground of this metaphor and the way in which movement from one place to another alters social status.

The social transformations of travel are closely connected to the origins of identity, the ways in which a person's selves are defined and made visible. We may find the origins of the self in the process by which it is changed. Closely examined, the social transformations of travel strongly suggest that social being in general derives from nothing more than the mutual identifications, categorizations, and recognitions in which people normally engage, particularly during arrival. Social being and its chief categories—race, gender, and class—proceed from observations and identifications by others. If the intellectual transformations of travel are a product of the way in which mobility makes the traveler more purely an observer, the social transformations of passage are a consequence of the traveler's being observed by a shifting audience of witnesses actively engaged in the clarification of his or her promise and danger. An identity may thus literally be left behind with the circle in which it is rooted.

THE SHAPE-CHANGING TRAVELER

Man is man through other men; God alone ... is God through himself.
—Kabyle (Algerian) proverb

The transformations of social being in travel suggest that there is no self without an other; and that, at bottom, identity is done with mirrors. With a change, a twist, a distortion of those reflections, an identity is transformed: thus appears the shape-changing traveler, the stranger who might be a god or anything else. From the recognitions and observations by others are created categories of persona, simplifications, rigidities, masks, and veils which constitute the essence and reality of social being. Marcel Mauss, in his highly suggestive but sketchy essay on the concept of the person in Western cultures, notes that the word *persona* originally meant "mask" and referred both to the masks of a tragic actor and to the castings made of the dead and set up on busts in the atriums of Roman patricians' houses. To have a mask, or a persona, was literally to have a name and to be somebody. The history of the concept of the person in the West has yet to be written, though Mauss draws its trajectory, "from a mere masquerade to the mask, from a role to a person, to a name, to an individual, from the cast to a being with a metaphysical and ethical value, from a moral consciousness to a sacred being, and from the latter to a fundamental form of thought and action."[1]

I have to admit to feeling a certain vertigo in contemplating this subject, for—although we are forbidden to believe that something can come out of nothing—social being, identity, and the structures of related identities (social structure) seem an unquestionable reality that grows out of nothing. Social realities and social power, that is, seem to be generated purely through the relations of individuals to each other and in the reflections set up by those relations.

Playing the Lord and Courtier: James Boswell

James Boswell, the Scottish lawyer and the famed biographer of Samuel Johnson, was a traveler who enjoyed more than most the fluidity of identity, the possibilities of social shape changing inherent in travel. On his Grand Tour in 1764–66, he played the lord and courtier in the minor courts of the Germanies and the philosopher in Geneva, where he courted Rousseau. Although he had planned to journey into Italy "not as milord Anglais, but merely as a scholar and a man of elegant curiosity,"[2] he found, when he arrived, that the role of lover was more rewarding. In Corsica, he was at no pains to dispel the popular impression that he was a secret British envoy to Pasquale di Paoli, the liberator of Corsica, because he enjoyed too much those "small elegancies" of which, he admitted, much of his happiness consisted: receiving his morning hot chocolate on a silver server engraved with the arms of Corsica and being attended by the local nobility, or by an armed escort when he rode out into the hills:

> One day when I rode out, I was mounted on Paoli's own horse with rich furniture of crimson velvet, with broad gold lace, and guards marching along with me. I allowed myself to indulge a momentary pride in this parade, as I was curious to experience what could be the pleasure of state and distinction with which mankind are so strongly intoxicated. When I returned to the Continent after all this greatness, I used to joke with my acquaintances and tell them that I could not bear to live with them for they did not treat me with proper respect.[3]

Back in England, appearing at a masquerade in the costume of a Corsican bandit and freedom fighter, his sash stuffed with daggers and horse pistols, Boswell was the hit of the London season. Admitting his love of distinction and greatness, he thoroughly enjoyed the intricate game of achieving status in high society and was an expert at social shape changing. He traveled from Berlin to Brunswick as one Herr Sheridan, a French merchant at Berlin, in a common postwagon in the company of commoners "and other blackguards," but changed, in Koenigslutter, to a private carriage for the last stage, "in order to enter Brunswick as a gentleman." At the inn, he was "quite the Laird of Auchinleck, serious and calm."[4] (Auchinleck, in southwest Scotland, was Boswell's family home.)

Boswell appeared to be enamored not so much of the script or persona he was playing at any moment as of the role changing itself, the shifts of status, the alterations of personality. It was moving from one identity to another that released his most irrepressible celebrations of himself, and he enjoyed travel because it allowed and furthered this passion. At times his love of change worried him, as upon his departure from Berlin (where he was refused an audience with Frederick the Great and as a consequence fell "quite out of conceit with monarchy"): "I recalled all my scenes of pleasure at Berlin, where I was cured of the black Hypochondria. Yet I was glad to go. So much do I love change. I dread that this love may increase. But my warm regard for the old Auchinleck shall ever fix me." His primal role as Laird of Auchinleck provided Boswell with the vision of a potential audience to ratify all the recognitions and honors acquired in his travels. When the Princess of Brunswick consented to a dance with him, he thanked her: "Madame, I return your Royal Highness a thousand thanks for the honour you have done me. This will serve me to talk of to my tenants as long as I live."[5]

What made Boswell something more than a garden-variety sycophant was the astonishing self-consciousness of his acting, his enjoyment of his effect upon people and of theirs upon him: "Can I help it if I find mankind take an affection for me at once?" He enjoyed the impressions he made upon the court of Brunswick, his most successful venue in Germany: "I could see a certain joy in the faces of the courtiers when strangers are announced. No wonder. It furnishes them with new ideas, and indeed, I could observe their Highnesses also pleased." Boswell was intensely aware of the medium of recognitions in which he acted, its powers and pleasures. He understood that he was a lunar personality, deriving light from the nearest and brightest star: "It is certain that I am not a great man, but I have an enthusiastic love of great men, and I derive a kind of glory from it." His genius lay in his acute understanding of the source of his identity in audiences, often largely composed of charmed and enlivened older men. He dwelled affectionately upon his image as mirrored in the admiring eyes of others. In the court of Brunswick, Boswell was pleased when he was mistaken for the duke as he escorted the duchess to her loge in the opera.

> My mind was clear and firm and fertile. It contained in itself both male and female powers: brilliant fancies were begotten, and brilliant fancies were brought forth. I saw my error in suffering so much from the contemplation of others. I can never be like them, therefore let me not vainly attempt it in imagination; therefore let me not envy the gallant and the happy, nor be shocked by the nauseous and wretched, I must be Mr. Boswell of Auchinleck, and no other. Let me make him as perfect as possible. I think were I such a one I should be happy indeed; were I such another I would be wretched indeed without considering that were I really these people, I could not have the same ideas of their situation as I now have, for no man has of himself the notion that other people have of him, especially those who know him little . . . I reflected upon my moments of despair when I did not value myself at sixpence. Because forsooth, I was but an individual, and an individual is nothing in a multitude of beings. Whereas I am all to myself. I have but one existence. If it is a mad one I cannot help it.[6]

Ironically, Boswell began to consider the question of his true, inner self in the context of theater, a subject of intense interest in the Enlightenment and the setting for discussions of genuine or natural identity—individuality. The eighteenth-century concept of the authentic self originated as a new role fashioned by such distinguished actors as Jean-Jacques Rousseau, who, like Boswell, was acutely aware of the power of the reflection of the other, of society, to shape, distort, and alter human passions, and thus human nature.

In recognizing the fluidity of identity, Boswell is a valuable witness, because he is a self-aware and self-observing participant in the process that generates the parts of the social mechanism—parts in the senses both of scripts literally written into the very fabric of culture, and of components of a mechanism that generates social power, the power originating in the mutual reflections of human relations. A traveling shape changer who played the lord, the desperado, the young spark and dandy, and the worshiper of great older men who had made their mark in the world, Boswell knew what he had to offer; he listed his best qualities as "liveliness, warmth of soul, a candid soul," and the capability of being "glad at the end of a quarrel." Indeed, he would even write scripts of imagined quarrels and reconciliations with his elderly and indulgent patrons. The climax of one such went as follows:

> BOSWELL *(almost weeping)*: I rejoice at being ill at present, as it gives us this opportunity. Even when I was most angry, I could not help, now and then, having returns of fondness for you as strong as ever.
>
> LORD EGLINTON: Like what one feels for a mistress, was it not?
>
> BOSWELL: Just so, my lord.

Boswell was, in today's jargon, entirely dependent upon these men for his sense of self-worth: "Wherever I come I find myself loved. . . . Is it possible for me not to be flattered when in a day or two I can make strangers of all kinds regard me? Sure I am this could not be done without external merit, as to my internal worth, I am not always certain."[7]

It is this sort of reality that makes successful travelers into actors, and comic acting an itinerant profession. Moderns are somewhat accustomed to despising actors such as Boswell, who have no "real" identity, that internal and invisible consciousness of sameness and continuity which is assumed to characterize the contemporary persona. But the notion of an inner, natural self, distinct from society and its attributions, is a peculiarly modern idea, a product of the eighteenth century and romanticism; and Boswell should not be condemned for exemplifying a more ancient conception of the self as an outward and visible thing constructed of the reflections of others.

The Curious Traveler: Pietro Della Valle

An earlier traveler who came to enjoy shape changing while away from home was Pietro Della Valle, a nobleman, who left his native Rome in 1611 after his parents died and his betrothed called off the wedding. The first European to enter the second pyramid in Egypt, he sent two mummies back to Rome. The woman he had married while traveling—the daughter of an Assyrian merchant—died on the road. He carried her embalmed body with him through Arabia, Persia, India, and finally to Rome, where it was installed in the family vaults. These activities may not have seemed odd to a Roman, but they did to the Portuguese colonials, predictably despised by Della Valle, and to the Indians, whom he valued as an audience, and who remarked upon the pendant he wore in his left ear as a remedy for his weak eyesight.

Della Valle's detachment had its painful side, and he admitted that, "had any of my nearest relations been living, as they are not, perhaps I should not have gone from home."[8] In India he was pleased to find in the persona of the yogi a mask to legitimate his bereavements, for the yogi was a "vagabond and despiser of the world" whose role gave dramatic and positive form to what was otherwise merely an absence. Travel was clearly a distraction for Della Valle, and he enjoyed the changes of face, mask, and persona made inevitable by passage through the world:

> Having passed through the Syrian, and afterwards the Persian, I am again invested with our European garb. In Turkie and Persia you would not have known me, but could not mistake me in India, where I have almost resumed my first shape. This is the third transformation which my beard hath undergone, having here met with an odd barber, who hath advanced my moustachios according to the Portugal mode, and in the middle of my chin, shaven after the Persian mode, he hath left the European tuft.[9]

Della Valle became a composite of his journeys, which ultimately purged him of bonds to his native place and people: "[A]fter so many Travels and so many sufferings both of Body and Mind, I am so changed that I can scarce acknowledge my self an Italian any longer."[10] Although he loved costumes and masquerades he decried the same fondness in the Portuguese as a sign of "the tendency which they have towards disorder, and their unwillingness to conform themselves to others." But he nevertheless participated in masquerades and clearly enjoyed the figure he cut when he appeared at a party in Goa dressed as an Arabian gentleman of the desert, "which was accounted very brave and gallant."[11]

Della Valle gratefully accepted the role often involuntarily assumed by the foreigner who must communicate primarily with gestures and a few words—as entertainer and comic actor, whose style is different and thus slightly erotic. As an oddity free from local constraints, Della Valle was delighted to grant the request of an Indian prince (whom he called a "royalet," noting that to enhance their own status, European monarchs promoted native chiefs and officials to the status of kings and even emperors) to be allowed to watch him eat. Della Valle called for his eating equipment from his inn, but explained that he could not give a full performance:

> The king and all the rest admir'd these exquisite, and to them, unusual, modes; crying out with wonder, *Deuru, Deuru*, that I was a Deuru, that is a great man, a God, as they speak. I told the king that for eating according to my custom there was needed much preparation of a table ... but I was now travelling through strange countries and treated myself "alla soldatesca" ... leading the life of a Gioghi [yogi], and consequently had not with me such things as were necessary. The king answer'd that it sufficed him to see this much, since thereby he easily imagined how all my other things would be, and that, in brief, he had never seen any European like me, and that it was a great contentment to him to see me.[12]

Perhaps the most saving, purgative, and valuable role that Della Valle played abroad was that of the curious, altruistic traveler, an iconic performance in the sixteenth century as a result of the Renaissance voyages. An ambassador described him as a Roman who "travell'd over so great a part of the world out of curiosity" and "writ down what he saw," but his companions did not share his curiosity, "as indeed the Portuguese are not at all curious."[13] When questioned about his extensive journeying by a local queen who asked whether it was from discontent, "either of love, or the death of some dear persons," he insisted that he traveled "only out of desire to see divers countries and customs, and to learn many things which are learnt by travelling the World; men who had seen and convers'd with many several nations being much esteem'd in our parts." This ennobling motive distinguished him from mere merchants, as he was careful to point out to a king who asked him whether he had brought articles to trade: "I answer'd him that in my country the nobles of my rank never practis'd merchandise, but only used arms, or Books, and that I addicted myself to the latter and meddled not with the former." The positive function of his role as curious and altruistic observer lent him not only dignity but the ability to create power and fame for the foreigners he visited; he recorded the story of a woman about to undergo suttee (cremating herself on her husband's funeral pyre), grateful to Della Valle for "the Fame which I should carry of her to my own country."[14]

THE UPWARDLY MOBILE TRAVELER

It would not take me long to learn the language, perhaps—but then I had to learn the ways, to know the people, to make myself known and acknowledged by them. . . . I invoked the day when, breaking the fetters that held me bound, I should make myself recognized for what I was worth by the new people.
                    —Silvio Villa, in Everett Stonequist, *The Marginal Man*, 1930

Finding selfhood in the recognitions of others has been a saving grace for generations of travelers. An immigrant to the United States who had been imprisoned for theft and forgery in Russia celebrated the death of one social being and the birth of another in these terms: "America accepted me as I was. America gave me a chance to stand on my own feet. I was taken in with my shameful past, as if I were equal to the best. And I have repaid America with the respect that only death itself can take from my heart."[15] It was clear to him that his journey had compartmentalized a social history, cleared his name of pejorative recognitions, and allowed him a new audience of recognitions in which to weave a social fate. It was equally obvious to an Italian immigrant, Silvio Villa, that his ultimate arrival in the "land of promises" depended upon the recognitions and identifications of the natives, that is, earlier arrivals.[16]

Travel transforms collective as well as individual identities. A traveling group is a society insofar as it establishes the rank and status of its members, and its collective social persona may differ while traveling from what it was at the point of origin. Generations of emigrants from the shores of Europe achieved an elevation of social status while heading for the colonies, mere passage transforming them from peasants and churls into "white men" and members of a noble race.

The Creation of Race

François Pyrard noted the transformations of dignity in Portuguese officials, sailors, and soldiers after passage around the Cape of Good Hope: "[A]ll these soldiers and seamen, after they have passed the Cape, gave them titles of nobility, otherwise they would be greatly blamed and despised by the other Portuguese resident in the Indies, for they bear to one another the greatest respect, even the highest to the lowest, and do greatly esteem one another."[17] At the Cape the soldiers in passage to India threw the symbols of their former status, their spoons, into the sea and abandoned "all their former manners and customs." Pyrard noted that the titled nobility on these voyages went along with this assumption of the dignity of "gentlemen" by the soldiers and sailors, "seeing that it is understood among themselves but not by the Indians."[18] This is not the only instance in which, freed of their pasts, voyagers have ennobled one another, demanding the respect due to gentlemen.

Any new, agreed-upon status in passage must be ratified by an audience upon arrival, for there can be no change in social being unless it is recognized by a third person. Although the Portuguese sailors and soldiers changed their status in passage, their new honors had meaning only in relationship to people who did not share them. Departure may wipe out a social past, passage may permit an elevation in status, but these new arrangements must be ratified before a social audience ignorant of contravening information. The Portuguese made every effort to secure recognition of their new status from native populations. As Pyrard noted:

> And although these enrolled soldiers have no titles or dignities, yet they do not omit to assume honor among themselves, calling themselves all "gentlemen" though they be of low condition.... These titles which are used among themselves, are only to make the Indians believe that they are all of goodly and illustrious parentage, having no race of Vile Churls among them Wherefore they will not that any Portuguese or other [European] should do any Vile or dishonourable work, nor should beg his livelihood, they will rather maintain him to the best of their power. Insomuch that the greatest of them treat the lowliest with honour, and they infinitely prize the title "portuguese of Portugal" calling such a one *homo blanco*, or "white man." All the poor Indians they despise, as though they would trample them under their feet. So these Indians were all amazed when we told them that these fellows were sons of porters, cobblers, drawers of water and other vile craftsmen.[19]

Before an audience of newly discovered and pacified ethnic others, Europeans could and did represent themselves as a noble race, having no "Vile Churls" among them. Their actions may often have told differently, however, as the Portuguese were not above the use of violence and terror to establish their status.

But here originates a new persona, in its original meaning of mask: the persona of "white man" and the mask of race. This new dignity could compensate for the loss of home and the wastings of travel. In Venezuela a poor shoemaker, of Castilian descent, gave Alexander von Humboldt some pearls and enjoined the naturalist to note down on his tablets "that a poor shoemaker of Aroya, but a white man ... had been enabled to give us what, on the other side of the sea, was sought for as a very precious thing."[20] In the voyages and colonizing expeditions of Europeans, the differences between Spanish, English, Dutch were homogenized into a general and abstract category—white—just as the myriad peoples they encountered were fitted to another mask, equally abstract—black or brown. Differences were transformed into an antithesis which was repetitively performed, and racism—a seventeenth-century European invention—became a world-organizing principle. It was in the exchanges between these antitheses, these new "races," that new, imperial powers were born, a global market was created, an industrial economy— the first global economy—was engendered.

Prestige Trade

The transformations of social status effected in departures, passages, and arrivals are superficial in that they derive from appearances and from a conscious, mutual reflection on appearances. Pietro Della Valle was amused at the superficiality of the techniques used by Portuguese "nobodies" who would become *hidalgos*—literally, people with "known" names—simply by dressing well and calling one another by terms of honor. In Goa, Della Valle noted, new status was legitimated through costume: "[S]ilk clothes are the general wear of almost everybody; which I take notice of because to see a merchant and a mechanick in a dress fit for an *Amorato* [dandy] is a very extravagant thing, yet amongst them very ordinary, the sole dignity of being Portugals sufficing them (as they say) to value themselves as much as kings and more."[21] But because status derives from appearances, it may be manipulated through the alteration of appearances and in performance. Because prestige and status arise from something so impalpable as the perceptions of others, these values demand concrete form and are often represented by the objects that elicit recognitions—clothes; jewelry; objects of social, rather than use, value.

In the concrete form of "status objects," prestige may be traded and social value may be organized in an economy. The trade in prestige in the Trobriand Islands is a good example of this phenomenon. Though much studied by anthropologists from Malinowski forward as an example of non-Western or noncapitalist trade in gifts and status, the kula trade is neither primitive nor preindustrial, having reached its fullest development only in the first decades of the twentieth century, one hundred years after the first European contacts. This is trade in shell necklaces and arm bands in which status, fame, and recognitions are embedded. It is properly speaking a "luxury" trade: "[T]he kula is not done under stress of any need, since its main aim is to exchange articles which are of no practical use."[22] Despite their considerable aesthetic properties, the "value" inherent in these objects is a product of the exchange between trading partners, and the necklaces and arm bands symbolize the long-distance and lasting relationship between individuals, whose names become attached to the objects. Thus, the shell is more properly compared to a trophy, a famous painting, a car once owned by a celebrity, an eponymous jewel, than to an object, a thing, or a commodity. The "name," or fame and reputation, of one involved in the kula trade rises or falls in relation to the circulation of these items:

> These names are produced by exchanging the valuables. But when one gives away a valuable it is said that one's name "goes down," and one's partner's "goes up." Only when the article is given again to a third person does the first person's name go up, the desired result of the Kula action. It is by virtue of this structure and its repetition that one's name "goes around" . . . it becomes "known" (literally, "seen").[23]

Fame means the circulation of one's name beyond the circle of face-to-face relationships, but a successful transaction depends upon the encounter between long-term partners, overseas "friends," and upon the manipulation of appearances. In the kula trade, success depends upon the ability of a trader to extract valuables from his trading partner, and "beauty magic" is often used to seduce one's partner into "throwing" valuables at his overseas friend and guest: "My head is bright, my face flashes. I have acquired a beautiful shape like that of a chief. I have acquired a shape that is good. I am the only one; my renown stands alone."[24] The seduction of the trading partner, who often figures as female in spells and beauty magic, is the aim of this manipulation of appearances, and the idiom of sexuality is often explicit in the formulas members of an expedition use to encourage one another before going ashore to trade: "Let us copulate with them so hard that blood flows from our pulled-back foreskins."[25]

A popular mythical hero of Kiriwanan kula lore, Tokosikuna, begins his career as an ugly cripple whom none of the women find acceptable. But he travels to the legendary island of Kokopawa and there acquires a magic flute. The flute utterly transforms those who play it, and it turns Tokosikuna into a straight, beautiful, smooth-skinned, and much younger man; he returns home and marries all the women. This makes the other men angry, and they try to kill Tokosikuna many times during trading voyages; but his wit, strength, and beauty enable him to avoid all their machinations, get the best kula valuables, and retire to the Amphlett Islands, where he lives out his life as a respected, beautiful, charismatic, and wealthy chieftain who can bedeck his wives with valuables.

This myth is a travel brochure promoting the prestige trade and representing its most desirable outcome. The transformation of appearances is the beginning of the social transformations and elevations of status in prestige trade, as is explicit in one of the spells chanted by recent arrivals as they comb their hair, oil their bodies, and paint their lips with the extract of the betel nut: "Here we are ugly; we eat bad fish, bad food; our faces remain ugly. We want to sail to Dobu; we keep taboos, we don't eat bad food. We go to Saraboayna; we wash, we charm the leaves of the silasalia; we charm the coconut. . . . We arrive in Dobu beautiful looking. Our partner looks at us, sees our faces are beautiful; he throws Vayg'u [kula valuables] at us."[26] Here mobility is clearly a medium for the deployment of a fantasy self which might acquire reality only in the eyes of others and concrete form in gifts, shells, and valuables. Travel has for long been the medium of peculiarly male fantasies of transformation and self-realization, but women have long provided a most significant audience, legitimating, officializing, or undercutting such claims to masculine social stature.

THE SUBVERSIONS OF TRAVEL

He that cannot dissemble, cannot live. But he that so dissembles as he is accounted
a dissembler, indeed hath not the skill to dissemble, but is noted with that infamy,
so as another shall be believed upon his word, than he upon his oath.
                                                            —Fynes Moryson, 1610

Travel is clearly subversive of the assumption implicit in all social
structures that an individual has one, real, consistent persona and
character. Travel has long been thought of as morally dangerous
and inimicable to social structure, order, and system—precisely why
it has been enjoyed by Boswell, Della Valle, and generations of shape
changers. The ideal of social order first suggested by Plato is that
of a coherence—enforced if necessary—between how one is seen by
a multitude of familiar others and how one sees oneself, the gulf in
which reside the social liberties of travel. When such an equation
fails and accord appears impossible, there arise the conditions for
revolution or for that substitute for revolution, emigration and
travel, that recreation and play with identity Boswell so thoroughly
enjoyed.

Recognition of the social subversiveness of travel, the fluidity of
identity achieved through territorial mobility, has long been a justification for laws against itinerancy, and was the source of many of
the objections to humanistic claims of the moral improvement
brought by travel. Since a traveler must adapt to a variety of circumstances, Renaissance praisers of travel often confront the difficult
question: How does travel make travelers morally better if, by its
nature, it promotes lying and deceit? In many circumstances, travelers must, for their own security, keep secret their true status, wealth,
destination, point of origin, religion, and nationality. It is no surprise, then, that travelers have long enjoyed reputations as liars, fictionalizers, and simulators. Fynes Moryson, an English traveler who
buried his younger brother outside Aleppo on the road from Jerusalem, admitted being stumped by this question:

> Being to write of simulation, I am at a stay, and grope for direction
> as in a darke labyrinth: for the voyce of the vulgar esteems the vice
> of dissimulation proper to a traveler, and highly doth reproach
> him therewith. Shall we then say that he who knows so as to live

with the Italians, Spaniards and very barbarous pagans as he can gaine their well-wishing will be at home among friends subject to the odious vice of dissimulation, the very plague of true friendship?[27]

In Rome, the traveler must do as the Romans do, but must at home stop doing it, even if the Roman custom seems better than the local one. Thus, according to Moryson, the traveler should, on "returning home, lay aside the spoone and forke of Italy, the affected gestures of France, and all strange apparell, yea, even those manners with which with good judgment he allowes, if they be disagreeable to his countrymen: For we are not all borne reformers of the World."[28] But is this not, still, dissimulation? Moryson approved the Italian custom that considered it rude for one who had entered into conversation with another to turn to a third person, with whom one had some business, without some "solemn excuse" to the first; and contrasted this with the English custom of abruptly, and without any excuse, turning from a first interlocutor to a second. The return home required that one resume what on the journey had come to seem a barbarism.

On the journey itself, dissimulation is often a question of survival. Indeed, Moryson advised the traveler not to let on that he is on a long journey lest potential robbers realize that he carries much money; and, if a strong swimmer, he should conceal that fact on sea voyages lest, in the event of shipwreck, "others trusting therein take hold of him, and make him perish with them."[29] Moryson also introduced a number of fine distinctions in those aspects of self a traveler may and may not adapt to circumstances. One may lie about one's name, "since the name is for others," and change costume, but should not alter the diet: "We dress for others, eat for ourselves." But his defense against the accusation that such dissimulation, even if necessary, did not morally improve the traveler lay along familiar lines. He argued legitimately that social life is, in essence, acting; and that the best actor is the one who least appears to be doing so. But Moryson's main bastion of defense is a Machiavellian argument—that which is done by necessity is no vice:

[I]t is a point of art for a Traveller to know how to avoid deceit, and how to dissemble honesty (I mean to save himself, not to deceive others). Let him have a cleare Countenance to all men, and

an open breast to his friend, but when there is a question of his
countries good, of his enemies lying in waite for him, of his own
credit or life, let him shut his bosome close from his inward
friends.... That counsell thou woulds't have another keepe, first
keepe it thyself. A Traveller must dissemble his long journeys, yet
only in dangerous places, and among suspected persons.... In like
sort a Traveller must sometimes hide his money, change his habit,
dissemble his country, and fairly conceale his religion, but this hee
must doe only when necessity forceth.[30]

And yet the accusation is proved. Traveling does not make those
who lie of necessity morally better, and often it makes them a good
deal worse. But here Moryson, and many others who would defend
the moral salubrity of travel, rams his head against a wall: social
systems and orders are fixed entities that deify the concept of a continuous and unchanging self, equating it with honesty and character.
Even Machiavelli, who recognized the necessity of adapting to time
and place, refused to grant honor or respect to those who do so and
reserved the title of "greatness" to those of consistent character, who
did not change with the change of circumstances. Travelers, as Han-
nah Arendt said of rulers, enjoy the "right to lie," to manipulate
appearances, to seem what they are not and not to seem what they
are. If, under the weight of necessity, this is not a vice, neither is it
a virtue. The dissimulations of travel are the source of those things
considered pathological by those charged with the maintenance of
social health and virtue: multiple selves, role confusion, status anx-
ieties, superficiality.

The literature of travel associates profound discomforts as well
as elevated energies with this phenomenon—the necessity of travelers to adapt, change, pretend, and dissimulate. Such adaptations
are often the occasion of moral suffering, or guilt, as one finds one's
most fundamental identities to be those that are hardest to give up
while traveling. In traditional circumstances, where the fundamental
identity of an individual was often thought to lie in the most encompassing frame of common belief, in religion and common gods, the
necessity to conceal one's faith on journeys was often an occasion of
lasting guilt. Athanasius Nikitin, a seventeenth-century Russian merchant who traveled to India and was required for his own good to
renounce his Greek Orthodox identity, was deeply troubled by his
momentary apostasy:

> I have nothing with me; no books whatever; those that I had taken from Russia were lost when I was robbed, and I forgot the Christian faith and the Christian festivals, and know not Easter nor Christmas, nor can tell Wednesday from Friday, and I am between the two faiths. But I pray to the only God that he may preserve me from destruction. God is one, King of glory and creator of heaven and earth [31]

The oneness of God is a securing fiction here, freezing the fluidity of human identities by establishing one source of everlasting recognitions.

The guilt often attending the traveler who changes shape is significant evidence of the contradiction at the heart of social structure, which seeks to channel recognitions toward uniform and unchanging identities, creating a pressure to be one thing which creates a counterpressure to be many and to escape the confinements of a fixed and unitary self. T. E. Lawrence—Lawrence of Arabia—a master of disguises who sloughed off feelings of self-hatred in assuming the anonymity of the stranger or the garb of an Arab, contrarily admired travelers who refused to change or adapt to foreign circumstances. Charles Doughty, the first Englishman to live and travel in Arabia as an undisguised Englishman, was a particular hero to Lawrence. In the introduction to Doughty's classic *Travels in Arabia Deserta* (1923), Lawrence described two types of English traveler:

> We export two chief kinds of Englishmen, who in foreign parts divide themselves into two opposed classes. Some feel deeply the influence of the native people, and try to adjust themselves to its atmosphere and spirit: To fit themselves modestly into the picture and suppress all in them that would be discordant with local habits and colours. They imitate the native as far as possible, and so avoid friction in their daily life. However, they cannot avoid the consequences of imitation, a hollow, worthless thing. They are like the people but not of the people, and their half-perceptible differences give them a sham influence often greater than their merit. They urge people among whom they live into strange unnatural courses by imitating them so well that they are imitated back again. The other class of Englishmen is the larger class. In the same circumstances of exile they reinforce their character by memories of the life they have left. In reaction against their foreign surroundings they take refuge in the England that was theirs. They assert their

aloofness, their impassivity, the more vividly for their loneliness and weakness. They impress the people among whom they live by reaction, by giving them an example of the complete Englishman, the foreigner intact.[32]

The assimilator only confuses the natives, who think, regardless of his efforts at conforming to local circumstances, that he is still a particular but unfocused species of stranger, an Englishman. In the shape-changing traveler they see only a distorted image of a type, not a true performance of an identity. But the "authentic" Englishman is clearly a construct of travel—assuming departure, a land left behind, which the uprooted Englishman realizes in his performances before an audience of ethnic others. The authentic and uncompromising Englishman is a stereotype and, like all cultural stereotypes, is generated in the process of intercultural communication, observation, and identification. His defining traits are assembled, too, not just in order to give visibility to just any cultural type but to represent a *superior* cultural type, one deserving of honor and recognition everywhere. It was the successful performance of this persona to which Lord MacCartney—the first English ambassador to China, in 1793–94—attributed the Chinese anxiety to get rid of him and his party. Somehow he had inadvertently given expression to "that superiority which, wherever Englishmen go, they cannot conceal from the most indifferent observer."[33]

THE PUBLIC OF PASSING STRANGERS

Then one day some future traveler, sailing by in his good ship across the wine-dark sea, will say: "This is the monument of some warrior of an earlier day who was killed in single combat by illustrious Hector." Thus my fame will be kept alive forever.

—Homer, the *Iliad*

The necessity of a third person, a witness, distinguishes trade in social status from other kinds of trade. This auditor or witness in exchanges involving prestige is a significant indication of the source of the values being negotiated. Social values, because they are generated in recognitions, assume an audience, an all, an external eye.

The anthropologist Frederick Damon stresses that, in kula trade, it is the circulation of a shell to a third party that creates fame and the extension of a name beyond the limits of face-to-face relations. The ethnographical traveler John D. Leroy observes, in his study of the South Kiwa pig-kill, that exchanges of pigs that affect the standing of the transactors within the community are always triadic, requiring the presence of the two partners immediately involved in the exchange, and a third, observing person:

> To announce that trade is triadic is simply another way of saying that it occurs in the presence of others, and that these can condense into a single anonymous third person, who is anyone and everyone in the culture. He does not even have to be physically present for his influence to be felt; imagination and memory represent him. Indeed his importance is in representation not in action. Through his signifying glance, donor and recipient understand their act to be part of a wider public reality.[34]

This is the origin of the "public" and, I imagine, a source of the necessity of gods, who—in establishing a reflective reality over and against human actions—create a moral and social dimension and give human actions a moral significance. In most codes of honor, it is not necessary to avenge an unwitnessed insult, for no honor is lost, just as no honor can be gained from an unwitnessed act. This is another possible source of the equation of the stranger and the god common in traditional societies: both provide an external, observing, and judgmental eye in the gaze of which social value is focused and fixed; both supply a reflexive medium, a public opinion against which collective and individual honor is ratified.

Travelers have long played the role of anonymous witness necessary for recognizing social or heroic actions that bring fame and honor to the actors: "The claimant to honour must get himself accepted at his own evaluation, must be granted reputation, or else the claim becomes mere vanity, an object of ridicule or contempt—but granted by whom?"[35] The answer has often been the passing stranger who bears a name and a reputation across space and time. This, at least, was the assumption of Hector, as he thoughtfully arranged in advance for the interment of the bodies of the Achacan warriors who were bold enough to accept his challenge to a duel: "I shall send back his corpse to your well-found ships, so that the long-haired Achaeans may give him burial rites and make a mound above him by the broad Hellespont."[36] It was "some future traveler" passing by who was to be the trustee of Hector's fame and the guarantor of his immortality. Hector was, of course, correct: after three thousand years, touring hordes still gape at the site given significance by his deeds. His prescience was based on a clear understanding of the mechanism of fame and the necessity of a witness in the transactions of prestige. A plea for the prayers of passing strangers is the occasion of our knowledge of the first known traveler in Western history, one Harkuf, a caravan conductor of the ancient Egyptian king Pepi I, who stated his worthiness in terms likely to appeal to wayfarers: "I gave bread to the hungry, clothing to the naked, I ferried him who had no boat."[37]

The audience of travelers has traditionally been called on by claimants to eternal dignity and honor, suggesting that one of the most fundamental functions of the society of travelers is to be a court of public opinion: "Public opinion forms therefore a tribunal before which claims to honour are brought, 'the court of reputation' as it has been called, and against its judgment there is no redress."[38] The nature of the power wielded by the public of travelers makes it profitable, for example, for Gawan kula traders to save their largest and most perfect yams exclusively for the entertainment of foreign guests and their smallest, most damaged yams for domestic consumption, thereby conveying an image of plenty, potency, and hidden potential to an outside world of judgmental others who will establish the value of this community in relation to others.

The power wielded by the stranger derives from the relations engendered in mutual observation. Generated purely and simply through perception, this power is not independent of acts of recognition. In the recognitions exchanged between strangers lie the roots of social bonds, the fiber of society itself. It was a stranger and traveler who perceived this relationship in a way characteristic of curious, intelligent travelers who work from the surfaces into the human realities beneath. Goethe, in visiting the Roman amphitheater in Verona, naïvely but logically asked what its purpose and function might be and why the ancients preferred the circular seating arrangement to that of the modern theater, which strictly divorces the functions of seeing and being seen. Answering his own question, Goethe explained: "Such an amphitheatre, in fact, is properly designed to impress the people with itself," and to make the people "astonished at themselves."[39] From here, it is a small step to the thesis I have been arguing: society originates in acts of mutual recognition. In organizing such recognitions the amphitheater is a source of social power, and so is travel, for both structure those recognitions in which societies originate and by which they are changed.

As a historical experience, travel engenders an always new, always recurring species of social being: the stranger. Moderns have become increasingly conscious of this species of social being and, indeed, have in some sense canonized it by giving ultimate authority to the alienated, objective, scientific eye. The figure of the stranger must be defended, however, against both idealization and the age-old charges that travel is demoralizing—reducing the sanctity of values and patriotisms—and superficializing. "Only light minds travel," Emerson is reputed to have said, though he, too, traveled and wrote about it. The experience of social shape changing may be inevitable in travel through dangerous territory. Beloved by such travelers as Boswell, effective mourning for such as Della Valle, the experience of continually changing social masks may first awaken the idea of no-mask, or of a mask so general as to be transparent to all. It is out of some such transformation that humanity becomes something more than a concept. It becomes a performance, a script, a central part to play in an ongoing social drama, which may ultimately produce a new concept of self as something subsisting under or within the flux of appearances. In describing the end of learning in the "traveller's school of mere humanity," Charles Doughty wrote: "The traveller must be himself, in men's eyes, a worthy man to live under the tent of God's heaven, and were it without a religion: he is such who has a clean human heart and long-suffering under his hair-shirt; it is enough, and though the way be full of harms, he may travel to the ends of the world."[40]

Fellow citizens in the society of travelers: Visiting the Pyramids, 1963

(Photo copyright © Thomas Hoepker, Magnum Photos)

EPILOGUE

෨෨෨෨෨෨

THE MIND OF THE MODERN
TRAVELER

Journeys, those magic caskets full of dreamlike promises, will never again yield up their treasures untarnished. A proliferating and overexcited civilization has broken the silence of the seas once and for all. The perfumes of the tropics and the pristine freshness of human beings have been corrupted by a busyness with dubious implications, which mortifies our desires and dooms us to acquire only contaminated memories. . . . I can understand the mad passion for travel books and their deceptiveness. They create the illusion of something which no longer exists but still should exist.

—Claude Lévi-Strauss, 1975

To live in one land, is captivitie.

—John Donne, "Change," 1635

What conclusions, then, should author and readers draw? The contemporary mood would dictate a nostalgia for the time when travel was truly travel, when there were boundaries between known and unknown, civilized and uncivilized, when escape was still possible. As early as 1837, Alexander Kinglake felt the inevitability of a mechanized, wheel-going, industrialized world, the immanence of one world, one land. We cannot escape the global civility that generations of travelers, explorers, gentlemen and ladies of elegant curiosity, merchants, migrants have created. It is travel, generations of journeys, that has created a global culture now knit by international systems of transportation, production, distribution, communication, destruction. This world we cannot, as yet, leave. Travel as tourism has become like the activity of a prisoner pacing a cell much crossed and grooved by other equally mobile and "free" captives. What was once the agent of our liberty has become a means for the revelation of our containment.

This irony pervades contemporary journeys and travel literature, suffusing the works of Paul Theroux, V. S. Naipaul, Claude Lévi-Strauss. The bitterness and disillusionment of contemporary philosophical travelers weaned on the literature of the heroic age of European discovery—with its conception of uncorrupted beginnings beyond the periphery, its acceptance of the unknown as a source of the novel, a domain of possibility—reach epic proportions in Lévi-Strauss's *Tristes Tropiques*, which the travel writer John Krich has called the "guide-book" of modern travelers.[1]

The reality of one world may be sensed in the depth of the deprivation caused by the pervasive feeling that *real* travel—outward-bound, hard, dangerous, and individualizing—is no longer possible. John Krich suggests something of the depth of this wound: "Trying to escape—at least in the ways that travel brochures promise—is like trying to escape death. We know that we can't really do it, but that all the meaning we'll ever find will be in the effort."[2] In foreclosing the possibility of escape from civility, the modern structure of global tourism annihilates a time-honored escape from the limits that have always defined human existence; a means of liberty from a fixed and predictable death; a method of extending the male persona in time and space, as conqueror, crusader, explorer, merchant-adventurer, naturalist, anthropologist. The age of global tourism seems to have foreclosed those forms of immortality and sources of meaning found in travel from the time of Gilgamesh, by generations who have thought to escape death by crossing space and recorded this feat in bricks, books, and stories. Travel has been the medium of traditional male immortalities. That this is no longer so is disillusioning to many.

No wonder Paul Fussell finds "annoyance, boredom, disillusion, even anger" to be the characteristic emotions and voice of the era of "post-tourism," in which "standardization, multiplication and general . . . contempt for the customers have evaporated much of the pleasure that used to attend even tourism."[3] Self-contempt and a sense of fraudulence distinguish the attitude of contemporary, self-conscious travelers. There is a touching desperation in the attempts of professional tourists, well-funded anthropologists, and recording travelers, to distinguish themselves from the traveling masses and run-of-the-mill adventurers. The most characteristic mark of the tourist is the wish to avoid tourists and the places they congregate. But this is merely evidence of the fact that travel is no longer a means of achieving distinction. It is a way of achieving and realizing a norm, the common identity we all share—the identity of the stranger.

This identity is a product of centuries of journeys—of departures, passages, and arrivals. The modern mind of the traveler is relativistic, eschewing those absolutes and ultimate, timeless values that derive their reality, after all, from a stationary perspective. It is a mentality that is essentially comparative, formed by and subsisting upon comparisons. It finds its sources of orientation, its fixed points, in those forms and relations that persist through the variety of experienced objects and situations, and is acutely aware that these persistent forms and relations are provisional and might alter with a change of circumstances. It is a mentality that reflects upon surfaces and is adaptive rather than creative: wide rather than deep, mirroring rather than penetrating. It is a mind structured in the disciplines of alienation, removal, idealizing itself in the canonization of the objective, outside, disacculturated, and universal point of view. Restless, wide-ranging, alert to difference and to persistencies in the climate of change, it is content only when the possibility of happiness, of coherence within a home, a *patria* has been relinquished.

This mind is native to a global society of travelers. We live *within* this society; it is real, not metaphorical, pervading our identities and relations. Travel, once an exceptional experience, a "rare and plastic season" of life, is now a routine event, as unexceptional as getting into one's car and driving down the road beyond one's usual stopping places. Tourism with all its collateral services—automobiles, aviation, hotels, merchandising—will be the world's number-one industry by the year 2000. Travel has become common, the tourist a norm, the world a poster on a wall which may be consumed for the price of a ticket. Travel is not only common; it is the source of our commonality, our community—and that is the problem. Travel is no longer heroic and individualizing. The forests that once surrounded the zones of settlement, and in which generations of knights and would-be lords lost and found themselves, have now been encompassed and engulfed by those zones, becoming parks, wilderness areas, rain forests, fragile ecosystems given to our care.

Perhaps this is only to say that our time is the bitter end of the dialectic, and a time of sorrow for those who have defined their identities in terms of outer and opposing worlds of others. Those oppositions that once operated between civility and a surrounding antithesis of the wilderness are now boundaries within. The dialectic has been internalized and is a structural element within the society of travelers. Hegel is dead, buried, and incorporated into the contemporary consciousness, the modern mind of the traveler.

In a testimonial letter from a pleased client of Thomas Cook—who, in 1845, began to use the new railroads to organize tours, holidays, and outings and is thus a pioneer of the age of mass tourism—a Matilda reported that many of her friends regarded her and her three sisters as intemperate, "too independent and adventurous to leave the shores of Old England and thus to plunge into foreign countries not beneath Victoria's sway, with no protecting relatives of any kind. . . . [But] we could venture anywhere with such a guide and guardian as Mr. Cook."[4] Matilda and her sisters were among the many single, unattached women who now felt free to travel in an age of industrialized mobility, under the watchful eye of the tour guide, thus signaling the end of the genderization of mobility and of journeying as a purely masculine or masculinizing activity. This, too, is disillusioning to many males who would become men through the agency of travel. Our most representative travel writer is Jan Morris—for a long time a man, now a woman; and Paul Fussell finds "something feminine (in the old-fashioned sense) in the 'niceness' of her vision,"[5] which exempts her from the modern mood of tragic disillusionment characteristic of the post-touristic age.

Within the society of travelers, like earlier and persisting nomadic societies, mobility cuts across gender, age, and class differences and establishes fundamental, though transient, solidarities. In our society as in nomadic societies, men, women, and children (of flying age and of divorced parents) normally travel—with the difference that in those societies men, women, and children travel together, in collectivities, whereas in ours they often travel alone and separately, as individuals under the care of strangers. Karl Bücher, with his usual keen insight, noted that this was the feature of modern journeys and industrial migrations that most distinguished them from ancient migrations of peoples and expeditions, and from medieval migrations of trades and classes—soldiers, merchants, craftsmen, jugglers, and scholars—all of which were in some sense collective travels and migrations:

> Modern migrations, on the contrary, are generally a matter of private concern, the individuals being led by the most varied motives. They are almost invariably without organization. The process repeating itself daily a thousand times is united only through the one characteristic, that it is everywhere a question of change of locality by persons seeking more favorable conditions of life.[6]

The solitude of the traveler was once a feature of medieval heroic travel and, before that, an expression of the pathos of the wanderer and exile. But now the possibilities for solitude offered by journeys are a part of the purgative and therapy of travel, a means by which the mind is made clean and its involvement with a world of external objects focused and clarified. This was recognized and prized by the modern adventurer Freya Stark: "People who know nothing about these things will tell you that there is no additional pleasure in having a landscape to yourself. But this is not true. It is a pleasure exclusive, unreasoning and real."[7] Travel is a method of achieving a measure of solitude in the midst of inevitable solidarities, as well as a means of achieving a sense of coherence with others, a certain level of humanity.

The journey is a method of both detachment and attachment; it creates individuals as it creates communities. The communities formed in passage are known by all travelers, beginning in that sinking feeling of sharing a common fate that may overcome one as the plane's wheels leave the ground and one is shot across space in a silver tube crammed with strangers. The attachments constantly being formed and broken within the society of travelers are made at the moment of slipping into the wind-shadow of a sixteen-wheeler and becoming a follower for the long miles across Texas. The societies of passage may be found everywhere and anywhere. One was discovered by Sinclair Lewis's Dodsworth, aboard the transatlantic steamer that became the Dodsworths' "permanent home, for a week, to become more familiar, thanks to the accelerated sensitiveness which is one of the blessings of travel, than rooms paced for years. Every stippling of soot on the lifeboats, every chair in the smoking-room, every table along one's own aisle in the dining salon, to be noted and recalled, in an exhilarated and heightened observation."[8]

The society of travelers is made up of such segments, fissioning into smaller units or fusing in larger clusters in a ceaseless process of aggregation and disaggregation channeled through airports, streets, bus stations, rest areas, and systems of roads bounded but infinite. It is a society characterized by an extreme fluidity of identity and social attachments but one that nevertheless has its laws and rules, its "tendencies" and structure.

As in prior traveling societies, identity is achieved in the society of travelers not through work and labor but through consumption, leisure, and prestige trade organized on a global scale. We, even more than our ancestors, *are* what we eat, drink, use, drive, and wear. We are also where we came from, where we are, and where we are going. The politics of consumption and the ethics of use have yet to be worked out in the society of consuming travelers; this remains its intrinsic problematic, worked out individually in private lives or collectively in supermarkets, hospitals, prisons, drug clinics, or exported as drug wars and busts on an international scale.

It is a society organized, like former traveling societies, through oppositional strategies. Cohesion among the units of the society of travelers depends upon the level of opposition faced, contracting and expanding with the degree of threat posed by an enemy. Thus cold wars, racism, peculiarly international "nationalisms," the persistence of tribal identities in conditions of dispersal and homogenization (Norwegian-American, African-American, Italian-American), the obvious heating up of the battle between the sexes, are all structural features endemic to a society of segments cohering through their opposition to other federations, genders, power blocs, races, religious groups. The last cold war, which lasted forty-five years, from 1945 to 1990, ended for all of six months before a new confrontation in the Middle East was manufactured, new oppositions were created, a new sense of cohesion and common identity was engendered. This intransigent persistence of wars that are not fought, the need for ever-renewed oppositions, may be explained by the fact that in conditions of mobility, where all bear the anonymity of strangers, opposition is a primary source of cohesion and identity. We may not know who we are but we know who we are against—the enemy of the week. The need for enmity and opposition is a sign of the need for identity within the encompassing reality of anonymity and strangership.

This persistence of antagonism in a world in constant contact— through communication, transportation, consumption, destruction—suggests that the society of travelers needs difference. This traditional need of travelers has been recognized by the writer Paul Bowles, lifelong traveler, intellectual jet-setter, and American expatriot: "Each time I go to a place I have not seen before I hope it will be as different as possible from the places I already know.... I assume it is natural for a traveler to seek diversity, and that it is the human element which makes him most aware of difference. If people and their manner of living were alike everywhere, there would not be much point in moving from one place to another."[9] The love of difference creates a rationale for travel, for intercultural and interethnic contacts as a means by which differences are connected and oppositions overcome. The association through mobility of what is dissociated and distinct in mind and representation—races, sexes, classes, ethnicities—is a primary source of power and elevated energies in the society of travelers. In order for these sources of power to be maintained, dissociations and distinctions must be maintained, if only so that they may be overcome. This tension is clearly evident in the disillusionment of the post-touristic traveler who, expecting to find difference, finds sameness and experiences impotence rather than power.

The need for boundaries, for markers between East and West, for difference, is a need for power, the power evidenced in alterations of self, in the change of identity often experienced by travelers. It came upon Jack Kerouac in a hotel room in Des Moines, when he was on his first hitchhiking journey across the country in 1947:

> I woke up as the sun was reddening; and that was one distinct time in my life, the strangest moment of all, when I didn't know who I was—I was far away from home, haunted and tired with travel, in a cheap room I had never seen, ... and I looked at the cracked, high ceiling and really didn't know who I was for about fifteen strange seconds. I wasn't scared; I was just somebody else, some stranger, and my whole life was a haunted life, the life of a ghost. I was halfway across America, at the dividing line between the East of my youth and the West of my future, and maybe that's why it happened right there and then, that strange red afternoon.[10]

The need for change, for alterations of self, is both served and engendered in the situations of travel, and a primary motive of the tourist, who is defined by the sociologist Valene Smith as a "temporarily leisured person who voluntarily visits a place away from home for the purpose of experiencing a change."[11] Tourism assumes a return to the home, and a change of attitude toward it, in which the home becomes chosen rather than a fate and is seen from the outside rather than from the inside: "We are a new person who has gone through recreation and, if we do not feel renewed, the whole point of tourism has been missed."[12] The return home, for Kerouac, was an experience of seeing with innocent, alienated eyes what once had been assumed:

> I was back on Times Square; and right of the middle of a rush hour too, seeing with my innocent road-eyes the absolute madness and fantastic hoorair of New York with its millions and millions hustling forever for a buck among themselves. . . . I had my home to go to, my place to lay my head down and figure the losses and figure the gain that I knew was in there somewhere too.[13]

The loss that is a gain of innocence, simplicity, youth, is as I see it the chief transformation of passage and a chief feature of the society and mentality produced by generations of journeys. The force of travel is corrosive, stripping and wasting, an experience of continuous loss. The world travel has created is marked as much by what is missing as by what is present. The sense of absence almost palpable in Southern California, that something is missing here in the land created by people who went as far west as they could without getting their feet wet, is an objective fact, a product of all the unnecessary accoutrements of culture—books, pictures, pianos, elaborate furniture—discarded beside the trails on the way west.

The sense of emptiness characteristic of the society of travelers—the absence of content, richness, complexity in the land that journeys have produced—itself becomes a stimulus to travel, a motive for return to the land of beginnings. The historical journeys outward—no longer possible now without expensive space technology—create a necessity for the journey back, inward, to origins and what has been left behind. Modern migrations outward seem to create a new need for Florence, Prague, Paris, Rome, and Jerusalem, for that old world where may be found much that has been lost and forgotten on the journeys that generated the new.

Thus originates a new species of the old tradition of philosophical travel, a search for cultural origins, stimulated by a hunger for meaning and content which is itself the product of generations of wasting, simplifying, and reductive journeys. On these return journeys the old motives may operate in a new way, and a modern death may be avoided, postponed. Those do not die who connect their endings to their beginnings. Therefore wander.

NOTES

PREFACE

1. Bashō, *The Narrow Road to the Deep North and Other Travel Sketches*, ed. and trans. Nobuyuki Yuasa (Baltimore, Md.: Penguin Books, 1966), p. 85.

INTRODUCTION: FOR A HISTORY OF TRAVEL

1. John B. Lansing et al., *The Travel Market, 1958, 1959–60, 1961–62* (Lansing, Mich.: University of Michigan, Survey Research Center Reprint, 1963).

2. Donald E. Lundberg, *The Tourist Business* (New York: van Nostrand Reinhold, 1990).

3. Freya Stark, *The Journey's Echo* (New York: Ecco Press, 1963), p. 19.

4. See Arnold van Gennep, *The Rites of Passage* (Chicago: University of Chicago Press, 1972); Victor Turner, "Betwixt and Between: The Liminal Period in Rites of Passage," in *Betwixt and Between*, ed. Louise Mahdi, Stephen Foster, and Meredith Little (La Salle, Ill.: Open Court, 1987); and Mircea Eliade, *The Rites and Symbols of Initiation* (New York: Harper Torchbooks, 1965).

5. This is Frederik Barth's definition of metaphor in *Ritual and Knowledge Among the Baktaman of New Guinea* (New Haven: Yale University Press, 1975), p. 204.

6. Eliade, *Rites and Symbols*, p. 134.

7. See Carl D. Buck, *A Dictionary of Selected Synonyms in the Principal Indo-*

European Languages (Chicago: University of Chicago Press, 1949); and Alois Walde, *Vergleichendes Worterbuch der Indogermanischen Sprachen*, vol. 2 (Berlin and Leipzig: Walter De Gruyter, 1927).

8. N. K. Sandars, trans., *The Epic of Gilgamesh* (New York: Penguin Books, 1975), p. 103.

9. Ibid., p. 61.

10. Homer, the *Odyssey*, trans. Walter Schewring (Oxford: Oxford University Press, 1980), p. 183.

11. Ibid., p. 89.

12. Captain James Cook, *Journals*, vol. 1, ed. J. C. Beaglehole (London: Hakluyt Society, 1955), p. 461.

13. Claude Lévi-Strauss, *Tristes Tropiques* (New York: Atheneum Press, 1975), p. 17.

14. *Chicago Tribune*, 18 June 1989, sec. 12, p. 6, col. 1.

15. Albert Camus, *Notebooks, 1935–1942* (New York: Alfred A. Knopf, 1963); see pp. 13–14 for epigraph quote on p. 1.

16. Ibid., p. 57.

17. Gen. 4.12, 4.15.

18. Quoted from "Pilgrimage," in *Encyclopedia of Religion and Ethics*, vol. 10, ed. James Hastings (New York: Charles Scribners Sons, 1951), p. 23.

19. Jack Kerouac, *On the Road* (New York: New American Library, 1957); see p. 111 for epigraph quote on p. 7.

20. Seneca, *De Tranquilitas*, chap. 2, trans. Aubrey Stewart, quoted in Caroline Skeel, *Travel in the First Century after Christ* (Cambridge: Cambridge University Press, 1901), pp. 12–13.

21. William Wordsworth, "The Preludes," in *Poetical Works*, vol. 3 (Oxford: Clarendon Press, 1968), pp. 27–30.

22. Quoted in F. W. Maitland and Sir Frederick Pollock, *The History of the English Laws, Before the Time of Edward I*, vol. 1 (Cambridge: Cambridge University Press, 1968), p. 428.

23. Quoted in George Roppen and Richard Sommer, *Strangers and Pilgrims. An Essay on the Metaphor of the Journey* (Oslo: Norwegian Universities Press, Norwegian Studies in English, no. 11, 1964), p. 116. See also Charles Norton Coe, *Wordsworth and the Literature of Travel* (New York: Bookman Associates, 1953).

24. Michael Crichton, *Travels* (New York: Alfred A. Knopf, 1988), pp. ix, x.

25. Zora Neale Hurston, *Dust Tracks on a Road* (New York: Arno Press and the New York Times, 1969), p. 189.

26. Thomas Gibson, "The Sharing of Substances versus the Sharing of Activity Among the Buid," *Man* 20 (1985): 392.

27. Walter Schlesinger, "Lord and Follower in German Institutional History," in *Lordship and Community in Medieval Europe: Selected Readings*, ed. Frederic L. Cheyette (New York: Holt, Rinehart and Winston, 1968), p. 74.

28. Sinclair Lewis, *Dodsworth* (New York: New American Library, 1967), p. 41.

29. Joan Didion, *The White Album* (New York: Pocket Books, 1979), p. 83.

30. Sandars, *Gilgamesh*, p. 72.

31. Leiris quote from James Clifford, *The Predicament of Culture* (Cambridge: Harvard University Press, 1988), p. 165.

32. Karl Bücher, *Industrial Evolution* (New York: Henry Holt, 1901), p. 346.

33. Susanne Langer, *Feeling and Form: A Theory of Art* (New York: Charles Scribner's Sons, 1953), p. 102.

34. Van Gennep, *Rites of Passage*, p. 26.

35. Barth, *Ritual and Knowledge*, p. 255.

36. Thucydides, *History of the Peloponnesian War*, trans. Rex Warner (New York: Penguin Books, 1986), p. 37.

CHAPTER 1. REACHING FOR ABROAD: DEPARTURES

1. Pliny, *Natural History*, vol. 2, trans. H. Ruckhum (Cambridge: Harvard University Press, 1947), p. 257.

2. N. K. Sandars, trans., *The Epic of Gilgamesh* (New York: Penguin Books, 1975), p. 70; see pp. 70–71 for epigraph quote.

3. See Nancy Munn, *The Fame of Gawa* (New York: Cambridge University Press, 1986).

4. Sandars, *Gilgamesh*, p. 71.

5. Ibid., p. 72.

6. John Bowlby, *Attachment and Loss*, vol. 2 (New York: Basic Books, 1976), p. 26.

7. Ibid., p. 16.

8. *The Travels of Olearius in Seventeenth Century Russia*, ed. and trans. Samuel Baron (Stanford, Calif.: Stanford University Press, 1967), p. 82.

9. NEB, Gen. 2.16–18.

10. NEB, Gen. 3.21–24.

11. Wiesel quoted in Robert Thurman, "We Are All Witnesses: An Interview with Elie Wiesel," *Parabola: Exile* 10 (1985):27.

12. Pascal, *Pensées*, trans. A. J. Krailsheimer (Baltimore, Md.: Penguin Books, 1968), p. 92.

13. "The Wanderer," in *The Norton Anthology of English Literature*, 4th ed., vol. 1 (New York: W. W. Norton, 1962), p. 84.

14. Anders, quoted in Helene Maimann, "Exil als Lebensform," *Jahrbuch für Zeitgeschichte* 2 (1979):17.

15. Paul Fussell, ed., *The Norton Book of Travel* (New York: W. W. Norton, 1987), p. 13.

16. John MacDonald, *Travels, 1745–1779: Memoirs of an Eighteenth Century Footman* (New York: Harper and Bros., 1927).

17. Chrétien de Troyes, *Ywain: The Knight of the Lion* (New Haven: Yale University Press, 1987), p. 24.

18. Ibid., p. 14.

19. Erich Auerbach, *Mimesis* (Garden City, N.Y.: Doubleday Anchor, 1957), chap. 6.

20. Jean Bethke Elshtain, "Nuclear Discourse and Its Discontents, or Apocalypse Now or Never," *Vietnam Generation* 1 (Summer–Fall 1989):263.

21. Gutierre Diaz de Gomez, *The Unconquered Knight: A Chronicle of the Deeds of Don Pero Nino, Count of Buelna*, ed. and trans. Mrs. Wilfrid Jackson (London: Chapman and Hall, 1928), p. 11.

22. De Troyes, *Ywain*, p. 76.

23. Ibid., pp. 80–81.

24. Ibid., p. 84.

25. Ibid., pp. 184, 12.

26. Michael Nerlich, *Ideology of Adventure: Studies in Modern Consciousness, 1100–1750*, vol. 1 (Minneapolis: University of Minnesota Press, 1987), p. xxi.

27. Alexander W. Kinglake, *Eothen* (London: John Ollivier, 1845), pp. 2, 4.

28. Ibid., p. 27.

29. Ibid., p. 5.

30. Ibid., p. 176.

31. George L. Mosse, *Nationalism and Sexuality* (New York: Howard Fertig, 1985), pp. 121, 122.

32. Kinglake, *Eothen*, pp. 200, 259.

33. Moritz, in *A General Collection of Pinkerton's Voyages and Travels*, vol. 2 (London: Longman, 1808), p. 553.

34. James Gibson, *The Ecological Approach to Visual Perception* (Boston: Houghton Mifflin, 1979), pp. 20ff.

35. Freya Stark, *Letters*, vol. 1 (Salisbury, Wiltshire: Compton Russel, 1974), p. 139.

36. Johann Wolfgang von Goethe, *Italian Journey, 1786–1788*, trans. W. H. Suden and Elizabeth Mayer (New York: Schocken Books, 1968), pp. 28, 30; see p. 483 for epigraph quote on p. 25.

37. R. H. Majors, ed., *India in the Fifteenth Century: A Collection of Narratives of Voyages to India in the Century Preceding the Portuguese Discovery of the Cape of Good Hope* (London: Hakluyt Society, 1857), p. 9.

38. Maurice L. Farber, "Some Hypotheses on the Psychology of Travel," *Psychoanalytic Review* 3 (41[1954]):269.

39. Richard Lassels, *The Voyage of Italy or a Compleat Journey Through Italy in Two Parts*, vol. 1 (Paris: N.p., 1670), p. Eiii.

40. Ibid., p. Eiv.

41. Carl Erdmann, *The Origin of the Idea of the Crusade*, trans. Marshall W. Balwin and Walter Goffart (Princeton, N.J.: Princeton University Press, 1977), pp. 336–37.

42. Fulcher of Chartres, *A History of the Expedition to Jerusalem, 1095–1127*, trans. Frances Ryan (Knoxville: University of Tennessee Press, 1969), p. 71.

43. Erdmann, *Idea of the Crusade*, p. 340.

44. George P. Hammond, ed. and trans., *Narratives of the Coronado Expedition, 1540–1542* (Albuquerque: University of New Mexico Press, 1940), p. 113.

45. Mary Douglas, *Purity and Danger: An Analysis of Concepts of Pollution and Taboo* (New York: Penguin Books, 1970), pp. 50–51.

46. Margaret Mahler et al., *The Psychological Birth of the Human Infant* (New York: Basic Books, 1975), p. 158.

47. Ibid., p. 151.

48. John Knowles, *Double Vision: American Thoughts Abroad* (New York: Macmillan, 1964), p. 36.

49. In James Clifford, *The Predicament of Culture* (Cambridge: Harvard University Press, 1988), p. 166.

50. Claude Levi-Strauss, *Tristes Tropiques* (New York: Atheneum Press, 1975), p. 38.

CHAPTER 2. "SUCH SWEET WAYFARING": THE SEDUCTIONS OF PASSAGE

1. William Dampier, *Voyages*, 2 vols. (London: Hakluyt Society, 1906); see vol. 1, p. 34, for epigraph quote.

2. Patrick Brydone, *A Tour Through Sicily and Malta*, vol. 2 (London: A. Straton and L. Cahell, 1790), p. 50.

3. In Sir Francis Drake, *The World Encompassed* (London: Hakluyt Society, 1854 [1628]), p. 13.

4. W. D. Howells, *Italian Journeys* (Boston: James R. Osgood, 1872), p. 58.

5. *The Life of Thomas Gent, Written by Himself* (London: Thomas Thorpe, 1832), p. 54.

6. Mark Twain, *Travels with Mr. Brown* (New York: Russel and Russel, 1971), p. 21.

7. Paul Theroux, *The Kingdom by the Sea: A Journey Around Great Britain* (New York: Washington Square Press, 1983), p. 321.

8. Alexander W. Kinglake, *Eothen* (London: John Ollivier, 1845), p. 29.

9. Mihaly Csikszentmihalyi, *Beyond Boredom and Anxiety* (San Francisco: Jossey-Bass, 1975), p. 48.

10. N. K. Sandars, trans., *The Epic of Gilgamesh* (New York: Penguin Books, 1975), p. 61.

11. In Sir Percy Sykes, *A History of Exploration from the Earliest Times to the Present Day* (New York: Harper and Bros., 1961), p. 16.

12. Strabo, *Geography*, vol. 1, trans. H. L. Jones (London: William Heinemann, 1931), p. 25.

13. Kirchner, in Thomas Coryate, *Coryate's Crudities*, vol. 1 (Glasgow: James MacLehose and Sons, 1905), p. 129.

14. Richard Lassels, *The Voyage of Italy or a Compleat Journey Through Italy in Two Parts*, vol. 1 (Paris: N.p., 1670), p. Aviii.

15. Cecil Jane, ed. and trans., *Select Documents Illustrating the Four Voyages of Columbus*, vol. 2 (London: Hakluyt Society, 1930), p. 42.

16. In Antonio de Beatis, *Travel Journal: Germany, Switzerland, the Low Coun-

tries, France and Italy, 1517–1518, ed. and trans. J. R. Hale (London: Hakluyt Society, 1979), p. 19.

17. Jean Cocteau, *My Journey Round the World* (London: Peter Owen, 1958), p. 20.

18. Claude Lévi-Strauss, *Tristes Tropiques* (New York: Atheneum Press, 1975), p. 62.

19. Bronislaw Malinowski, *Argonauts of the Western Pacific: An Account of Native Enterprise and Adventure in the Archipelagoes of Melanesian New Guinea* (London: Routledge & Kegan Paul, 1964), p. 83.

20. Georg Simmel, *Soziologie* (Leipzig: Verlag von Dunker und Humblot, 1908), p. 688; see also Dennison Nash, "The Ethnologist as Stranger," *Southwestern Journal of Anthropology* 19 (1963): 152, for epigraph quote on p. 62.

21. Everett Verner Stonequist, "The Marginal Man: A Study in the Subjective Aspects of Cultural Conflict," Ph.D. diss., University of Chicago, 1930, pp. 94, 2.

22. James Gibson, *The Ecological Approach to Visual Perception* (Boston: Houghton Mifflin, 1979), p. 223.

23. William Wordsworth, "In a Carriage Along the Banks of the Rhine" (1790), in *Poetical Works*, vol. 3 (Oxford: Clarendon Press, 1968), p. 169; see vol. 4, p. 247, for epigraph quote on p. 58.

24. Colin Thubron, *Where Nights Are Longest: Travels by Car Through Western Russia* (New York: Random House, 1984), p. 6.

25. William James, *The Principles of Psychology*, vol. 1 (Cambridge: Harvard University Press, 1981), p. 478.

26. Johann Wolfgang von Goethe, *Italian Journey, 1786–1788*, trans. W. H. Suden and Elizabeth Mayer (New York: Schocken Books, 1968).

27. Henry James, *The Art of Travel: Scenes and Journeys in America, England, France and Italy* (Freeport, N.Y.: Books for Libraries Press, 1970), pp. 214, 213.

28. Antonello Gerbi, *Nature in the New World: From Christopher Columbus to Gonzalo Fernandez de Oviedo*, trans. J. Mole (Pittsburgh, Pa.: University of Pittsburgh Press, 1985), p. 6.

29. Joseph-Marie Degerando, *The Observation of Savage Peoples*, trans. F. C. T. Moore (London: Routledge & Kegan Paul, 1969), p. 62.

30. John Bowlby, *Attachment and Loss*, vol. 1 (New York: Basic Books, 1976), pp. 238–39.

31. James, *Art of Travel*, pp. 213, 215.

32. Blount, in *A General Collection of Pinkerton's Voyages and Travels*, vol. 10 (London: Longman, 1811), p. 223.

33. Charles M. Doughty, *Travels in Arabia Deserta*, vol. 1 (London: Jonathan Cape, 1923), p. 262.

34. *The Autobiography of Charles Darwin* (New York: W. W. Norton, 1958), pp. 120–21; see p. 79 for epigraph quote on p. 60.

35. Goethe, *Italian Journey*, p. 40.

36. Kinglake, *Eothen*, pp. viii–ix.

37. Darwin, *Autobiography*, p. 79.

38. Gregory Bateson, "Information and Codification: A Philosophical Ap-

proach," in Jurgen Ruesch and Gregory Bateson, *Communication: The Social Matrix of Psychiatry* (New York: W. W. Norton, 1951), p. 185.

39. James Clifford, *The Predicament of Culture* (Cambridge: Harvard University Press, 1988), p. 156; ibid., for Sengalen quote.

40. See Gibson, *Visual Perception*, esp. p. 122; see also p. 183 for epigraph quote on p. 71.

41. Theroux, *Kingdom by the Sea*, p. 121.

42. Leiris, quoted in Clifford, *Predicament of Culture*, p. 165.

43. Graham Greene, *Travels with My Aunt* (New York: Bantam Books, 1971), p. 02.

44. Albert Einstein, *Ideas and Opinions* (New York: Crown, 1954), p. 247.

45. John H. Flavell, *The Developmental Psychology of Jean Piaget* (Princeton, N.J.: D. Van Nostrand, 1963), p. 317.

46. Victor Turner, "Liminality, Play, Flow and Ritual: An Essay in Comparative Symbiology," in *Anthropological Study of Human Play*, ed. Edward Norbeck, *Rice University Studies* 60(3[1987]):70.

47. Csikszentmihalyi, *Beyond Boredom*, p. 48.

48. Ibid., p. 36.

49. Ibid.

50. See N. R. W. Pande, "Time, Space and Motion," Ph.D. diss., Nagpur University, 1969.

51. Yi-Fu Tuan, *Space and Place: The Perspective of Experience* (Minneapolis: University of Minnesota Press, 1977), p. 6.

52. In Studs Terkel, *Working* (New York: Pantheon Books, 1974), p. 383.

53. John Locke, *An Essay Concerning Human Understanding* (New York: New American Library, 1974), p. 171; see p. 166 for epigraph quote.

54. Theroux, *Kingdom by the Sea*, p. 230.

55. Strabo, *Geography*, vol. 1, p. 421.

56. Homer, the *Odyssey*, trans. Walter Schewring (Oxford: Oxford University Press, 1980), p. 61.

57. Richard Hakluyt, *The Principal Navigations, Voyages, Traffiques and Discoveries of the English Nation*, vol. 1 (London: J. M. Dent, 1927), p. 313.

CHAPTER 3. THE STRANGER AT THE GATES: ARRIVALS

1. Robert E. Park and Herbert A. Miller, *Old World Traits Transplanted* (Chicago: University of Chicago Society for Social Research, 1925), p. 55.

2. Chrétien de Troyes, *Ywain: The Knight of the Lion* (New Haven: Yale University Press, 1987), pp. 30–31.

3. Mary Douglas, *Purity and Danger: An Analysis of Concepts of Pollution and Taboo* (New York: Penguin Books, 1970), p. 15.

4. Exod. 19.12–14.

5. Douglas, *Purity and Danger*, p. 48.

6. NEB, 10 John: 1–2.

7. Russian Primary Chronicle, in Serge Zenkovsky, ed. *Medieval Russia's Epics, Chronicles, and Tales* (New York: E. P. Dutton, 1974), p. 49.

8. Dumezil, quoted in Marshall Sahlins, *Islands of History* (Chicago: University of Chicago Press, 1985), p. 73.

9. Ibid., p. 82.

10. N. K. Sandars, trans., *The Epic of Gilgamesh* (New York: Penguin Books, 1975), pp. 63, 67; see p. 65 for epigraph quote.

11. Quoted in H. Clay Trumbull, *The Threshold Covenant* (New York: Charles Scribner's Sons, 1896), p. 179.

12. Pedro Fernandez de Quiros, *Voyages, 1595–1606*, vol. 2, trans. Clements Markham (Nendeln, Liechtenstein: Hakluyt Society, 1967), p. 242.

13. *The Book of Ser Marco Polo the Venetian Concerning the Kingdoms and Marvels of the East*, ed. and trans. Col. Sir Henry Yule (London: John Murray, 1929), p. 383.

14. Chandra Mukerji, "Bullshitting: Road Lore Among Hitchhikers," *Social Problems* 25(1977–78):244.

15. Boas quoted in Julian Pitt-Rivers, "The Stranger, the Guest and the Hostile Host: Introduction to the Study of the Laws of Hospitality," in *Contribution to Mediterranean Sociology*, ed. J. G. Peristiany (The Hague: Mouton, 1968), pp. 13–14.

16. Ibid., p. 17.

17. Quoted in Everett Verner Stonequist, "The Marginal Man: A Study in the Subjective Aspects of Cultural Conflict," Ph.D. diss., University of Chicago, 1930, p. 218.

18. Ch'oe Pu, *Diary: A Record of Drifting Across the Sea*, trans. John Meskill (Tucson: University of Arizona Press, 1965), p. 70; see p. 65 for epigraph quote.

19. Ibid., p. 80.

20. Ibid., p. 82.

21. James G. Frazer, *The Golden Bough* (New York: Macmillan, 1948), p. 194.

22. P. J. Hamilton-Grierson, *The Silent Trade: A Contribution to the Early History of Human Intercourse* (Edinburgh: William Green and Sons, 1903).

23. Homer, the *Odyssey*, trans. Walter Schewring (Oxford: Oxford University Press, 1980), pp. 104–5; see p. 213 for epigraph quote.

24. Grubb, quoted in Lucien Levy-Bruhl, *Primitive Mentality* (New York: Macmillan, 1923), p. 362.

25. Alfred Russel Wallace, *The Maylay Archipelago* (London and New York: Macmillan, 1869), p. 359.

26. J. L. Cranmer-Byng, ed., *An Embassy to China Being the Journal Kept by Lord MacCartney During His Embassy to the Emperor Ch'un-Tung, 1793–1794* (London: Longmans, 1972), p. 114.

27. Quoted in Levy-Bruhl, *Primitive Mentality*, p. 364.

28. Quoted in M. M. Wood, *The Stranger: A Study in Social Relations* (New York: Columbia University Press, 1934), p. 80.

29. Bernal Diaz, *The Conquest of New Spain* (New York: Penguin Books, 1963), p. 151.

30. George P. Hammond, ed. and trans., *Narratives of the Coronado Expedition, 1540–1542* (Albuquerque: University of New Mexico Press, 1940), pp. 130, 44, 46.

31. Quoted in Sahlins, *Islands of History*, p. 124.

32. Gregory Bateson, "Information and Codification: A Philosophical Approach," in Jurgen Ruesch and Gregory Bateson, *Communication: The Social Matrix of Psychiatry* (New York: W. W. Norton, 1951), pp. 204–5.

33. Arnold van Gennep, *The Rites of Passage* (Chicago: University of Chicago Press, 1972), pp. 27–28.

34. Quoted in Wood, *The Stranger*, p. 67.

35. Moritz, in *A General Collection of Pinkerton's Voyages and Travels*, vol. 2 (London: Longman, 1808), p. 564.

36. Homer, *Odyssey*, p. 37; see p. 169 for epigraph quotes on p. 103.

37. Charles Darwin, *The Voyage of the Beagle* (Garden City, N.Y.: Doubleday, 1962), p. 43.

38. Magnus Magnusson, ed. and trans., *Laxdaela Saga* (New York: Penguin Books, 1983), p. 93.

39. Nels Anderson, *The Hobo: The Sociology of the Homeless Man* (Chicago: University of Chicago Press, 1923), p. 20.

40. Pitt-Rivers, "The Stranger," p. 16.

41. François Hartog, *The Mirror of Herodotus: The Representation of the Other in the Writing of History*, trans. Janet Lloyd (Berkeley: University of California Press, 1988), p. 230.

42. *The Voyages and Adventures of Fernand Mendez Pinto*, trans. H. Cogon (London: Dawsons of Pall Mall, 1963), p. 17.

43. *Letters of Lady Mary Wortley Montagu Written During Her Travels in Europe, Asia and Africa*, vol. 3 (London: T. Becket and P. A. de Handt, 1763), p. 2.

44. Ibid., vol. 2, p. 312.

45. *The Voyage of François Pyrard to the East Indies, the Maldives, the Moluccas and Brazil*, vol. 1, ed. and trans. Albert Gray (London: Hakluyt Society, 1887), p. 92.

CHAPTER 4. SPACE AND GENDER: WOMEN'S MEDIATIONS

1. *The Voyage of François Pyrard to the East Indies, the Maldives, the Moluccas and Brazil*, vol. 1, ed. and trans. Albert Gray (London: Hakluyt Society, 1887), p. 83.

2. Diodorus Siculus, *Library of History*, vol. 2, trans. C. H. Oldfather (New York: B. P. Putnam and Sons, 1933), p. 179.

3. Alexander von Humboldt and Aimé Bonpland, *Personal Narrative of Travels to the Equinoctial Regions of the New Continent During the Years 1799–1804*, vol. 2 (London: Longman, Hurst, Kees, Arme, and Brown, 1818), p. 2.

4. P. J. Hamilton-Grierson, "Strangers," *Encyclopedia of Religion and Ethics*, ed. J. Hastings (Edinburgh: T. & T. Clark, 1921), vol. XI, p. 886.

5. Claude Lévi-Strauss, *The Elementary Structures of Kinship* (Boston: Beacon Press, 1969), p. 116.

6. Pyrard, *Voyage*, vol. 2, p. 124.

7. Bernal Diaz, *The Conquest of New Spain* (New York: Penguin Books, 1963), p. 60.

8. Bronislaw Malinowski, *Argonauts of the Western Pacific: An Account of Native Enterprise and Adventure in the Archipelagoes of Melanesian New Guinea* (London: Routledge & Kegan Paul, 1964), p. 205.

9. Fynes Moryson, *An Itinerary*, vol. 3 (Glasgow: James MacLehose and Sons, 1907), p. 349.

10. Homer, the *Odyssey*, trans. Walter Schewring (Oxford: Oxford University Press, 1980), p. 99.

11. Nancy Munn, *The Fame of Gawa* (New York: Cambridge University Press, 1986); see p. 77 for epigraph quote on p. 111.

12. Paul Theroux, *The Kingdom by the Sea: A Journey Around Great Britain* (New York: Washington Square Press, 1983), p. 116; see pp. 157–58 for epigraph quote on p. 113.

13. Chrétien de Troyes, *Ywain: The Knight of the Lion* (New Haven: Yale University Press, 1987), pp. 59–60.

14. Homer, the *Iliad*, trans. E. V. Rieu (New York: Penguin, 1987), p. 129; see also E. Sidney Hartland, "Concerning the Rite at the Temple of Mylitta," in *Anthropological Essays Presented to Edward Burnett Tyler* (Oxford: Clarendon Press, 1907), p. 195, for epigraph quote on p. 117.

15. Gen. 20.13.

16. Gen. 20.14–16.

17. Bruce Chatwin, *The Songlines* (New York: Viking-Penguin Books, 1987), p. 178.

18. Arnold van Gennep, *The Rites of Passage* (Chicago: University of Chicago Press, 1960), pp. 33–34.

19. Munn, *Fame of Gawa*, p. 46.

20. Quoted in Malinowski, *Argonauts of the Western Pacific*, p. 337.

21. P. J. Hamilton-Grierson, *The Silent Trade: A Contribution to the Early History of Human Intercourse* (Edinburgh: William Green and Sons, 1903), p. 76.

22. Quoted in Fernando Henriques, *Prostitution and Society*, vol. 1 (London: MacGibbon and Kee, 1962), p. 24.

23. *The Travels of Marco Polo*, trans. Ronald Latham (New York: Penguin Books, 1982), pp. 88, 175.

24. Ibid., p. 172.

25. Ibid., pp. 175–76.

26. Strabo, *Geography*, vol. 5, trans. H. L. Jones (London: William Heinemann, 1931), p. 439.

27. Lodovico di Varthema, *Travels in Egypt, Syria, Arabia Deserta and Arabia Felix, 1503–1508* (New York: Burt Franklin, 1963), p. 203.

28. Claude Lévi-Strauss, *The Elementary Structures of Kinship* (Boston: Beacon Press, 1969), p. 512.

29. Henriques, *Prostitution and Society*, vol. 1, p. 38.

30. Jean S. La Fontaine, "The Free Women of Kinshasa: Prostitution in a City in Zaire," in *Choice and Change*, ed. J. Davis (London: Athlone Press, 1974), p. 111.

31. Erik Cohen, "Thai Girls and Farang Men: The Edge of Ambiguity," *Annals of Tourism Research* 9(1982):412.

CHAPTER 5. TRAVELING IN TIME: ANCIENT AND MEDIEVAL TRADITIONS

1 Joseph-Marie Degerando, *The Observation of Savage Peoples*, trans. F. C. T. Moore (London: Routledge & Kegan Paul, 1969), pp. 62–63.

2. Strabo, *Geography*, vol. 1, trans. H. L. Jones (London: William Heinemann, 1931), p. 469.

3. Pliny, *Natural History*, vol. 2, trans. H. Ruckhum (Cambridge: Harvard University Press, 1947), pp. 187, 31–32.

4. Diodorus Siculus, *Library of History*, vol. 2, trans. C. H. Oldfather (New York: B. P. Putnam and Sons, 1933), p. 105.

5. Strabo, *Geography*, vol. 2, p. 77.

6. Siculus, *Library of History*, vol. 2, p. 44.

7. Ibid., vol. 1, p. 53.

8. Ibid., p. 245.

9. Ibid., p. 239.

10 Alexander W. Kinglake, *Eothen* (London. John Ollivier, 1845), p. 320.

11. Quoted in James M. Osborn, "Travel Literature and the Rise of Neo-Hellenism in England," in *Literature as a Mode of Travel*, ed. Warner G. Rice (New York: New York Public Library, 1963), p. 44.

12. Kinglake, *Eothen*, p. 214.

13. Johann Wolfgang von Goethe, *Italian Journey, 1786–1788*, trans. W. H. Suden and Elizabeth Mayer (New York: Schocken Books, 1968), pp. 90, 212.

14. Siculus, *Library of History*, vol. 1, pp. 401–2.

15. Strabo, *Geography*, vol. 7, p. 112.

16. Seneca quote in Charles Lyell, *Principles of Geology*, vol. 1 (London: John Murray, 1834), p. 22.

17. Strabo, *Geography*, vol. 7, p. 113.

18. Ronald B. Levinson, ed., *A Plato Reader* (New York: Houghton Mifflin, 1967), p. 158.

19. Palestine Pilgrims' Text Society, *The Churches of Constantine at Jerusalem* (New York: Arno Press, 1971), p. 11.

20. Ibid., pp. 1, 3, 15.

21. Quoted in John Wilkinson, *Egeria's Travels* (London: S. P. C. K., 1971), p. 14.

22. Steven Runciman, "The Pilgrimage to Palestine Before 1095," in *A History of the Crusades*, ed. Kenneth M. Selton (Philadelphia: University of Pennsylvania Press, 1955), p. 70.

23. Carl Erdmann, *The Origin of the Idea of the Crusade*, trans. Marshall W. Balwin and Walter Goffart (Princeton, N.J.: Princeton University Press, 1977).

24. George B. Parks, *The English Traveler to Italy in the Middle Ages*, vol. 1 (Stanford, Calif.: Stanford University Press, 1954), pp. 67–68, 70; see p. 140 for epigraph quote on p. 148.

25. Quoted in Jeanette Mirsky, *The Great Chinese Travelers: An Anthology* (New York: Pantheon Books, 1964), pp. 33, 77, 79, 95.

26. Quoted in Helen Waddell, *The Wandering Scholars* (London: Constable, 1958), p. 32.

27. Quoted in Alan Cobban, *The Medieval Universities: Their Background and Organization* (London: Methuen, 1975), p. 52.

28. Quoted in Pearl Rebri, "Scholarly Privileges: Their Roman Origin and Medieval Expression," *American Historical Review* 51(1954):549–50.

29. Ibid., p. 557.

30. Cobban, *Medieval Universities*, p. 117.

31. Quoted in Waddell, *Wandering Scholars*, pp. 206, 189, 177.

32. Quoted in J. J. Jusserand, *English Wayfaring Life in the Middle Ages* (Boston: Milford House, 1973), p. 233.

33. Quoted in Waddell, *Wandering Scholars*, p. 53.

34. Elizabeth Eisenstein, *The Printing Press as an Agent of Change*, 2 vols. (New York: Cambridge University Press, 1979).

CHAPTER 6. THE ENCOUNTER WITH THE NEW WORLD: EUROPE'S DISCOVERY OF ITSELF

1. J. H. Elliott, *The Old World and the New, 1492–1650* (New York: Cambridge University Press, 1970), p. 47.

2. Michael T. Ryan, "Assimilating New Worlds in the Sixteenth and Seventeenth Centuries," *Comparative Studies in Society and History* 23(1981):525.

3. Quoted in Antonello Gerbi, *Nature in the New World: From Christopher Columbus to Gonzalo Fernandez de Oviedo*, trans. J. Mole (Pittsburgh: University of Pittsburgh Press, 1985), p. 261.

4. *De Orbe Novo: The Eight Decades of Pietro Martire d'Anghiera (Peter Martyr)*, vol. 1, trans. F. A. Macnutt (New York: B. P. Putnam and Sons, 1912), p. 79.

5. Cecil Jane, ed. and trans., *Select Documents Illustrating the Four Voyages of Columbus*, vol. 1 (London: Hakluyt Society, 1930), pp. 8, 92.

6. Ibid., vol 2, p. 66.

7. Michel de Montaigne, *Essays*, vol. 1, trans. George Ives (Cambridge: Harvard University Press, 1925), p. 285.

8. Ynca Garcilasso de la Vega, *Royal Commentary of the Yncas*, vol. 1 (London: Hakluyt Society, 1869), p. 61.

9. Father Joseph de Acosta, *The Natural and Moral History of the Indies*, vol. 2 (London: Hakluyt Society, 1970), pp. 449–50.

10. Homer, the *Odyssey*, trans. Walter Schewring (Oxford: Oxford University Press, 1980), p. 101.

11. Acosta, *History of the Indies*, vol. 2, p. 410.

12. Ibid., vol. 1, p. 189.

13. Anghiera, *De Orbe Novo*, vol. 1, pp. 103–4.

14. Acosta, *History of the Indies*, vol. 1, p. 72.

15. Elliott, *Old World and New*, p. 50.

16. See William G. Batz, "The Historical Anthropology of John Locke," *Journal of the History of Ideas* 35(1974):663–70.

17. John Locke, *Second Treatise of Civil Government* (New York: D. Appleton-Century, 1937), pp. 5, 24–25.

18. Acosta, *History of the Indies*, vol. 1, p. 105.

19. Francis Bacon, *The Great Instauration*, vol. 3 of *The Complete Works* (Philadelphia: A. Hart, 1851), p. 358.

20. Ibid.

21. Joseph-Marie Degerando, *The Observation of Savage Peoples*, trans. F. C. T. Moore (London: Routledge & Kegan Paul, 1969), p. 62.

22. Quoted in W. B. Greenlee, ed., *The Voyage of Pedro Alvares Cabral to Brazil and India* (London: Hakluyt Society, 1938), p. 23.

23. Degerando, *Savage Peoples*, p. 64.

24. Ibid., p. 24.

25. Montaigne, *Essays*, vol. 1, p. 274.

26. Jean F. de la Perouse, *A Voyage Round the World Performed in the Years 1785, 1786, 1787, and 1788*, vol. 1 (New York: Da Capo Press, 1968), pp. 329, 327.

27. Johannes Fabian, *Time and the Other: How Anthropology Makes Its Object* (New York: Columbia University Press, 1983), p. 35; see p. 25 for epigraph quote on p. 168.

CHAPTER 7. THE ALIENATED EYE: SCIENTIFIC TRAVEL

1. In Christian Zacher, *Curiosity and Pilgrimage: The Literature of Discovery in Fourteenth Century England* (Baltimore, Md.: Johns Hopkins University Press, 1976), p. 22.

2. Ibid., p. 37, for Petrarch quote.

3. Lodovico di Varthema, *Travels in Egypt, Syria, Arabia Deserta and Arabia Felix, 1503–1508* (New York: Burt Franklin, 1963), p. 9.

4. Elizabeth Eisenstein, *The Printing Press as an Agent of Change*, 2 vols. (New York: Cambridge University Press, 1979).

5. See Richard Hakluyt, *The Principal Navigations, Voyages . . . of the English Nation*, 3 vols. (Rpt. London: Dent, 1910); G. B. Ramusio, *Raccolta de Navigazioni et Viaggi*, 3 vols. (Vincenzi, 1550–59); Samuel Purchas, *Hakluytus Posthumus or Purchas His Pilgrimes*, 20 vols. (1625) (Glasgow: MacLehose and Sons, 1905).

6. Varthema, *Travels*, p. 55.

7. Erich Heller, *The Artist's Journey into the Interior and Other Essays* (New York: Vintage Books, 1968), p. 12.

8. Francis Bacon, *The Great Instauration*, vol. 3 of *The Complete Works* (Philadelphia: A. Hart, 1851), p. 337.

9. Ibid., pp. 435, 339.

10. Varthema, *Travels*, p. 52.

11. Henry Blount, *A Voyage into the Levant* (1634), in *A General Collection of Pinkerton's Voyages and Travels*, vol. 10 (London: Longman, 1811), p. 223.

12. E. S. Bates, *Touring in 1600: A Study in the Development of Travel as a Means of Education* (Boston: Houghton-Mifflin, 1911), p. 26.

13. Conrads, quoted in Antoni Maczak and Hans Jurgen Teuteberg, *Reiseberichte als Quellen europäischer Kulturgeschichte* (Wolfbüttel: Herzog August Bibliothek, 1981), p. 117.

14. Justin Stagl, "Der Wohl Unterbiesene Passagier: Reisekunst u. Gesellschaftsbeschreibung vom 16 bis zum 18 Jahrhundert," in *Reisen und Reisebeschreibungen im 18 u. 19 Jahrhundert als Quellen er Kulturbegiehungsborschungen*, eds. B. J. Krasnobow and H. Zeman Gert Kebel (Berlin: Verlag Ulrich Camen, 1980), pp. 353–84; see p. 354 for epigraph quote on p. 184.

15. See Walter J. Ong, *Ramus, Method, and the Decay of Dialogue* (Cambridge: Harvard University Press, 1958).

16. Antonio De Beatis, *Travel Journal 1517–1518*, ed., trans., and Intro. J. R. Hale (London: Hakluyt Society, 1979), pp. 30, 29.

17. M. Margaret Newett, *Canon Pietro Casola's Pilgrimage to Jerusalem* (Manchester: University Press, 1907), pp. 129 ff.

18. See Stagl above, note 14.

19. John Churchill and Awnsham Churchill, *A Collection of Voyages and Travels*, vol. 1 (London: N.p., 1704), p. lxxv.

20. Johann Wolfgang von Goethe, *Italian Journey, 1786–1788*, trans. W. H. Suden and Elizabeth Mayer (New York: Schocken Books, 1968), p. 31.

21. Charles L. Batten, *Pleasurable Instruction: Form and Convention in Eighteenth Century Travel Literature* (Berkeley: University of California Press, 1978), p. 13.

22. Louis Antoine de Bougainville, *A Voyage Round the World* (Ridgewood, N.J.: Gregg Press, 1967), pp. xxv–xxvi.

23. William Dampier, *Voyages*, vol. 2 (London: Hakluyt Society, 1906), pp. xviii–xix.

24. See R. W. Frantz, *The English Traveller and the Movement of Ideas, 1660–1732* (Lincoln: University of Nebraska Press, 1967), p. 34.

25. Captain James Cook, *Journals*, vol. 1, ed. J. C. Beaglehole (London: Hakluyt Society, 1955), p. vi.

26. Michel de Montaigne, *Essays*, vol. 1, trans. George Ives (Cambridge: Harvard University Press, 1925), p. 274.

27. Royal Society, "Directions for Seamen Bound on Far Voyages," *Philosophical Transactions* 1 (1665–66):140–41.

28. Bacon, *Works*, vol. 3, p. 430.

29. Churchill and Churchill, *Voyages and Travels*, p. lxxvi.

30. Alexander von Humboldt and Aimé Bonpland, *Personal Narrative of Travels to the Equinoctial Regions of the New Continent During the Years 1799–1804*, vol. 1 (London: Longman, Hurst, Kees, Arme, and Brown, 1818), p. 190.

31. Heller, *Artist's Journey*, p.14.

32. Royal Society, "Directions for Seamen," p. 73.

33. Quoted in Cook, *Journals*, vol. 1, p. cxxxvi.

34. Cecil Jane, ed. and trans., *Select Documents Illustrating the Four Voyages of Columbus*, vol. 1 (London: Hakluyt Society, 1930), p. 6.

35. Quoted in Bernard Smith, *European Vision and the South Pacific, 1768–1850* (Oxford: Clarendon Press, 1960), p. 6.

36. Royal Society, *Philosophical Transactions* 22(1700–1701):539.

37. Quoted in Archibald Geikie, *The Founders of Geology* (London: Macmillan, 1905), p. 341.

38. Ibid., pp. 384 and 34, for Smith quotes.

39. Quoted in Roy Porter, *The Making of Geology: Earth Science in Britain, 1666–1815* (New York: Cambridge University Press, 1977), p. 142.

40. Quoted in Frantz, *English Traveller*, p. 8.

41. Humboldt, *Personal Narrative*, vol. 1, p. 4.

42. Ibid., pp. iii–iv.

43. Ibid., pp. xxxviii, xiv.

44. Saussure, quoted in Geikie, *Founders of Geology*, p. 184.

45. For Hutton see Charles Lyell, *Principles of Geology*, vol. 1 (London: John Murray, 1804); and Geikie, *Founders of Geology*, pp. 285 ff.

46. Humboldt, *Personal Narrative*, vol. 1, p. 136.

47. Quoted in Lyell, *Principles of Geology*, vol. 1, p. 91; see frontmatter for Playfair quote in epigraph.

48. Ibid., p. 91.

49. Quoted in Geikie, *Founders of Geology*, pp. 292–93.

50. *The Autobiography of Charles Darwin* (New York: W. W. Norton, 1969), pp. 78, 77.

51. Charles Darwin, *The Voyage of the Beagle* (Garden City, N. Y.: Doubleday, 1962), pp. 169, 69.

52. Ibid., p. 217.

53. Ibid., p. 121.

54. Charles Darwin and Alfred Russel Wallace, "On the Tendency of Species to Form Varieties; And on the Perpetuation of Varieties and Species by Natural Means of Selection," *Journal of the Linnean Society*, Zoology (1858), III, 45–62.

55. Alfred Russel Wallace, *The Maylay Archipelago* (London and New York: Macmillan, 1869), p. 14.

56. Ibid., p. 9.

57. Ibid., p. 217.

58. Ibid., p. 332.

59. Darwin, *Voyage of the Beagle*, p. 205.

60. Wallace, *Maylay Archipelago*, pp. 282, 475.

61. Clifford Geertz, *Local Knowledge* (New York: Basic Books, 1983).

62. Wallace, *Maylay Archipelago*, p. 375.

63. Ibid., pp. 257–58.

64. Ibid., pp. 339–40.

CHAPTER 8. THE SPERMATIC JOURNEY

1. Frederik Barth, "Models of Social Organization," *Occasional Paper No. 23, Royal Anthropological Institute of Great Britain and Ireland* (1966), p. 1.

2. Bashō, *The Narrow Road to the Deep North and Other Travel Sketches,* ed. and trans. Nobuyuki Yuasa (Baltimore, Md.: Penguin Books, 1966), p. 33.

3. Quoted in Elkan Nathan Adler, *Jewish Travelers* (London: Routledge and Sons, 1930), p. 329.

4. Homer, the *Odyssey*, ed. and trans. Walter Schewring (Oxford: Oxford University Press, 1980), p. 6.

5. Magnus Magnusson, ed. and trans., *Laxdaela Saga* (New York: Penguin Books, 1983), p. 96.

6. Mary O'Brien, *The Politics of Reproduction* (London: Routledge & Kegan Paul, 1981), p. 49.

7. Ibid., pp. 34, 60.

8. Albert Camus, *Notebooks, 1935–1942* (New York: Alfred A. Knopf, 1963), p. 59.

9. O'Brien, *Politics of Reproduction*, p. 55.

10. Mircea Eliade, *Rites and Symbols of Initiation* (New York: Harper Torchbooks, 1965), pp. 128, 101–2.

11. Captain James Cook, *Journals*, vol. 1, ed. J. C. Beaglehole (London: Hakluyt Society, 1955), p. 237.

12. Chandra Mukerji, "Bullshitting: Road Lore Among Hitchhikers," *Social Problems* 25(1977–78):244.

13. Snorri Sturluson, *The Heimskringla*, vol. 2, trans. Samuel Laing (London and Stockholm: Norraena Society, 1907), pp. 591, 608.

14. Frederic William Maitland and Sir Frederick Pollack, *The History of the English Law Before the Time of Edward I,* vol. 1 (Cambridge, England: Cambridge University Press, 1968), p. 407.

15. Leopold Genicot, "Recent Research on the European Nobility," in *The Medieval Nobility: Studies on the Ruling Classes of France and Germany from the Sixth to the Twelfth Century,* ed. Timothy Reuter (Amsterdam: North-Holland, 1979), p. 21.

16. Karl Marx, "On the Jewish Question," in *The Marx–Engels Reader*, ed. Robert C. Tucker (New York: W. W. Norton, 1972), p. 40.

17. Isaiah Berlin, *Four Essays on Liberty* (London: Oxford University Press, 1969), p. 158.

18. Quoted in Stephen Lukes, "Durkheim's 'Individualism and the Intellectuals,' " *Political Studies* 17 (March 1979):112.

19. Jean-Jacques Rousseau, *Émile* (New York: Dutton, 1977), p. 147.

20. Georges Duby, *The Early Growth of the European Economy: Warriors and Peasants from the Seventh to the Twelfth Century* (Ithaca, N. Y.: Cornell University Press, 1974), p. 33.

21. Alan MacFarlane, *The Origins of English Individualism* (New York: Cambridge University Press, 1979), p. 163.

22. Thomas Hobbes, *Man and Citizen*, ed. Bernard Gert (Garden City, N. Y.: Anchor Books, 1972), p. 216.

CHAPTER 9. TRAVELING SOCIETIES: AGENTS OF HISTORY

1. Ibn Battuta, *Travels in Asia and Africa, 1325–1354*, trans. H. A. R. Gibb (New York: Robert M. McBride, 1929), p. 45; see also Ch'oe Pu, *Diary: A Record of Drifting Across the Sea*, trans. John Meskill (Tucson: University of Arizona Press, 1965), p. 49, for epigraph quote.

2. Lodovico di Varthema, *Travels in Egypt, Syria, Arabia Deserta and Arabia Felix, 1503–1508* (New York: Burt Franklin, 1963), p. 103.

3. Jay W. Vogt, "Wandering: Youth and Travel Behavior," *Annals of Tourism Research* 4 (1[1976]):35.

4. Thucydides, *History of the Peloponnesian War*, trans. Rex Warner (New York: Penguin Books, 1986), pp. 35–36.

5. François Hartog, *The Mirror of Herodotus: The Representation of the Other in the Writing of History*, trans. Janet Lloyd (Berkeley: University of California Press, 1988), p. 205; see also Freya Stark, *The Journey's Echo* (New York: Ecco Press, 1963), p. 28, for epigraph quote.

6. Diodorus Siculus, *Library of History*, vol. 2, trans. C. H. Oldfather (New York: B. P. Putnam and Sons, 1933), p. 123.

7. Thucydides, *Peloponnesian War*, pp. 341–42.

8. Charles M. Doughty, *Travels in Arabia Deserta*, vol. 2 (London: Jonathan Cape, 1923), pp. 21–22.

9. Siculus, *Library of History*, vol. 1, pp. 160–61.

10. Lawrence, in Doughty, *Travels*, vol. 1, p. xix.

11. Ibn Khaldun, quoted in Bruce Chatwin, *The Songlines* (New York: Viking-Penguin Books, 1987), p. 196.

12. See Barth, in Cynthia Nelson, ed., *The Desert and the Sown: Nomads in the Wider Society* (Berkeley, Calif.: Institute of International Studies, 1973).

13. Pierre Bonté, "Conditions et éffets de l'implantation d'industries minieres in milieu Pastoral: l'exemple de la Mauritanie," in *Pastoralism in Tropical Africa*, ed. Theodore Monod (Namez: International African Seminar, 1972), p. 260.

14. Elman Service, *The Hunters* (Englewood Cliffs, N. J.: Prentice-Hall, 1979), p. 4.

15. Captain James Cook, *Journals*, vol. 1, ed. J. C. Beaglehole (London: Hakluyt Society, 1955), p. 399.

16. Elisha Kent Kane, *Arctic Explorations in Search of Sir John Franklin, 1853, '54, '55*, vol. 1 (New York: Arno Press, 1971), p. 114.

17. Frederik Barth, *Nomads of South Persia: The Basseri Tribe of the Ramasch Confederacy* (New York: Humanities Press, 1961), p. 153.

18. T. G. H. Strehlow, "Geography and the Totemic Landscape in Central Australia: A Functional Approach," in *Australian Aboriginal Anthropology*, ed. Ronald M. Berndt (Nedlands, Western Australia: University of Western Australia Press, 1970), p. 94.

19. Lawrence, in Doughty, *Travels*, vol. 1, p. xxii.

20. Richard B. Lee and Irven De Vore, eds., *Man the Hunter* (Chicago: Aldine, 1968).

21. See Service, *Hunters*.

22. Doughty, *Travels*, vol. 1, p. 91.

23. Strabo, *Geography*, vol. 2, trans. H. L. Jones (London: William Heinemann, 1931), p. 87.

24. Barth, *Nomads of South Persia*, p. 21.

25. Walter Goldschmidt, "Independence as an Element of Pastoral Social Systems," *Anthropological Quarterly* 44 (1971):141.

26. P. H. Gulliver, *The Family Herds: A Study of Two Pastoral Tribes in East Africa, The Ju and Turkana* (London: Routledge & Kegan Paul, 1966), p. 12.

27. Strehlow, "Geography and the Totemic Landscape," p. 100.

28. Joseph Birdsell, "Some Predictions for the Pleistocene Based on Equilibrium Systems Among Recent Hunter-Gatherers," in *Man the Hunter*, ed. R. B. Lee and I. De Vore, pp. 229–40.

29. Quoted in James Hastings, ed., "Pilgrimage," in *Encyclopedia of Religion and Ethics*, vol. 10 (New York: Charles Scribner's Sons, 1951), p. 24.

30. Quoted in Sidney Heath, *Pilgrim Life in the Middle Ages* (New York: Kennikat Press, 1971), p. 34.

31. Ibid., p. 44, for More quote.

32. Ibid., for Chaucer quote.

33. Marshall Sahlins, "The Segmentary Lineage: An Organization of Predatory Expansion," *American Anthropologist* 63 (1961): p. 333.

34. Quoted in Chatwin, *Songlines*, p. 220.

35. Sahlins, "Segmentary Lineage," p. 326.

36. Karl Polanyi, *The Livelihood of Man*, ed. Harry W. Pearson (New York: Academic Press, 1977), p. 92.

37. Gulliver, *Family Herds*, p. 110.

38. Johannes Pederson, *Israel: Its Life and Culture*, vol. 1 (London: Geoffrey Cumberlege, 1964), p. 14.

39. Fulcher of Chartres, *A History of the Expedition to Jerusalem, 1095–1127*, trans. Frances Ryan (Knoxville: University of Tennessee Press, 1969), pp. 271–72, 88.

40. Alfred Russel Wallace, *The Malay Archipelago* (London and New York: Macmillan, 1869), p. 336.

41. Barth, *Nomads of South Persia*, p. 21.

42. Thucydides, *Peloponnesian War*, pp. 582–83.

43. Elkan Nathan Adler, *Jewish Travelers* (London: Routledge and Sons, 1930), p. 65.

44. Charles Wendell David, ed. and trans., *De Expurgatione Lisbonensi* (New York: Columbia University Press, 1936), p. 13.

45. Fynes Moryson, *An Itinerary*, vol. 2 (Glasgow: James MacLehose and Sons, 1907), p. 38.

46. Doughty, *Travels*, vol. 1, p. xxxii.

47. Claude Lévi-Strauss, *Tristes Tropiques* (New York: Atheneum Press, 1975), p. 310.

48. Xenophon, *Anabasis*, trans. W. D. Rouse (Ann Arbor: University of Michigan Press, 1982), p. 9.

49. Sahlins, "Segmentary Lineage," p. 327.

50. *Voyages of Sir James Lancaster to the East Indies* (London: Hakluyt Society, 1877), p. 16.

51. Fredcrik Barth, "Models of Social Organization," *Occasional Paper No. 23, Royal Anthropological Institute of Great Britain and Ireland* (1966), p. 10.

52. Magnus Magnusson and Hermann Palson, trans., *Njal's Saga* (New York: Penguin Books, 1980), p. 86.

53. Snorri Sturluson, *The Heimskringla*, vol. 7, trans. Samuel Laing (London and Stockholm: Norraena Society, 1907), p. 23.

54. Xenophon, *Anabasis*, trans. W. D. Rouse (Ann Arbor: University of Michigan Press, 1974), p. 63.

55. Plutarch, *The Rise and Fall of Athens*, trans. Ian Scott-Kilvert (New York: Penguin Books, 1981), pp. 88, 89.

56. Thucydides, *Peloponnesian War*, pp. 424, 51.

57. Xenophon, *Anabasis*, p. 130.

58. Yvon Garlan, *War in the Ancient World*, trans. Janet Lloyd (New York: W. W. Norton, 1975), p. 91.

59. Franz Oppenheimer, *The State: Its History and Development Viewed Sociologically* (Indianapolis: Bobbs-Merrill, 1914), p. 55.

60. Walter Schlesinger, "Lord and Follower in German Institutional History," in *Lordship and Community in Medieval Europe: Selected Readings*, ed. Fredric Cheyette (New York: Holt, Rinehart and Winston, 1968), p. 77.

61. Ibid., pp. 70, 74.

62. Sturluson, *Heimskringla*, vol. 7, p. 253.

63. See Bernal Diaz, *The Conquest of New Spain*, trans. J. M. Cohen (New York: Penguin Books, 1963), p. 47.

64. In Cecil Jane, trans. and ed., *Select Documents Illustrating the Four Voyages of Columbus* (London: Hakluyt Society, 1930), vol. 2, p. 54.

65. In Schlesinger, *Lordship and Community*, p. 75.

66. Fr. Pedro Simon, *The Expedition of Pedro de Ursua and Lope de Aguirre in Search of El Dorado and Amazu in 1560–1561*, trans. William Bollaert (New York: Burt Franklin, 1971), p. 70.

67. Ibid., pp. 213, 94, 184.

68. Ibid., p. 3.

CHAPTER 10. TRAVEL AND THE TRANSFORMATIONS OF SOCIAL BEING

1. Marcel Mauss, *Sociology and Psychology: Essays* (London: Routledge & Kegan Paul, 1979), p. 88; see also Pierre Bourdieu, "The Sentiment of Honor in Kabyle Society," in *Honor and Shame: The Values of Mediterranean Society*, ed. J. G. Peristiany (Chicago: University of Chicago, 1966), p. 211, for epigraph quote.

2. James Boswell, *On the Grand Tour, Germany and Switzerland, 1764*, ed. Frank Brady and Frederick Pottle (New York: McGraw-Hill, 1953), p. 75.

3. James Boswell, *On the Grand Tour, Italy, Corsica, and France, 1765–1766*, ed. Frank Brady and Frederick Pottle (New York: McGraw-Hill, 1955), p. 164; see p. 54 for epigraph quote on p. 263.

4. Boswell, *Germany and Switzerland*, p. 52.

5. Ibid., pp. 101, 61.

6. Ibid., pp. 126, 68, 44, 54.

7. Ibid., pp. 170, 110.

8. *The Travels Of Pietro Della Valle in India*, ed. and trans. Edward Grey, vol. 2 (New York: Hakluyt Society, 1892), p. 334.

9. Ibid., vol. 1, p. 126.

10. Ibid., vol. 2, p. 335.

11. Ibid., vol. 1, p. 173.

12. Ibid., vol. 2, p. 331.

13. Ibid., vol. 1, p. 259.

14. Ibid., vol. 2, pp. 276, 333.

15. Quoted in Robert E. Park and Herbert A. Miller, *Old World Traits Transplanted* (Chicago: University of Chicago Society for Social Research, 1925), p. 92.

16. Villa, quoted in Everett Verner Stonequist, *The Marginal Man: A Study in the Subjective Aspects of Cultural Conflict*, Ph.D. diss., University of Chicago, 1930, p. 223.

17. *The Voyage of François Pyrard to the East Indies, the Maldives, the Moluccas and Brazil*, vol. 2, ed. and trans. Albert Gray (London: Hakluyt Society, 1887), p. 200.

18. Ibid., vol. 2, p. 120.

19. Ibid., p. 121.

20. Alexander von Humboldt and Aimé Bonpland, *Personal Narrative of Travels to the Equinoctial Regions of the New Continent During the Years 1799–1804*, vol. 2, trans. H. M. Williams (London: Longman, Hurst, Kees, Arme, and Brown, 1818), p. 271.

21. Della Valle, *Travels in India*, vol. 2, p. 158.

22. Bronislaw Malinowski, *Argonauts of the Western Pacific: An Account of Native Enterprise and Adventure in the Archipelagoes of Melanesian New Guinea* (London: Routledge & Kegan Paul, 1964), p. 86.

23. Frederick H. Damon, "The Kula and Generalized Exchange: Considering Some Unconsidered Aspects of *The Elementary Structures of Kinship*," *Man* 15 (1980): 288.

24. Quoted in Malinowski, *Argonauts of the Western Pacific*, p. 339.

25. Quoted in Andrew J. Strathern, "The Kula in Comparative Perspective," in *The Kula: New Perspectives on Massim Exchange*, ed. Jerry Leach (New York: Cambridge University Press, 1983), p. 85.

26. Quoted in Malinowski, *Argonauts of the Western Pacific*, p. 336.

27. Fynes Moryson, *An Itinerary*, vol. 3 (Glasgow: James MacLehose and Sons, 1907), pp. 409–10.

28. Ibid., p. 422.

29. Ibid., p. 389.

30. Ibid., p. 410.

31. R. H. Majors, ed., *India in the Fifteenth Century: A Collection of Narratives of Voyages to India in the Century Preceding the Portuguese Discovery of the Cape of Good Hope* (London: Hakluyt Society, 1857), p. 18.

32. Lawrence, Introduction to Charles M. Doughty, *Travels in Arabia Deserta*, vol. 1 (London: Jonathan Cape, 1923), p. xviii.

33. J. L. Cranmer-Byng, ed., *An Embassy to China Being the Journal Kept By Lord MacCartney During His Embassy to the Emperor Ch'un-Tung, 1793–1794* (London: Longmans, 1972), p. 128.

34. John D. Leroy, "The Ceremonial Pig-Kill of the South Kiwa," *Oceania* 49 (1979): 185.

35. Julian Pitt-Rivers, "Honor and Social Status," in *Peristiany* (1966), p. 22.

36. Homer, the *Iliad*, trans. E. V. Rieu (New York: Penguin Books, 1987), p. 134.

37. Charles Horne, ed., *The Sacred Books and Early Literature of the East*, vol. 2 (London: Parke, Austin, and Lipscomb, 1917), p. 43.

38. Pitt-Rivers, "Honor and Social Status," p. 27.

39. Johann Wolfgang von Goethe, *Italian Journey, 1786–1788*, trans. W. H. Suden and Elizabeth Mayer (New York: Schocken Books, 1968), p. 33.

40. Doughty, *Travels*, vol. 1, p. 56.

EPILOGUE: THE MIND OF THE MODERN TRAVELER

1. Claude Lévi-Strauss, *Tristes Tropiques* (New York: Atheneum Press, 1975), p. 285; John Donne, Third Elegy.

2. Krich, quoted in Paul Fussell, *The Norton Book of Travel* (New York: W. W. Norton, 1987), p. 755.

3. Ibid., p. 757.

4. Quoted in Edmund Swinglehurst, *The Romantic Journey: The Story of Thomas Cook and Victorian Travel* (London: Piece Editions, 1974), p. 38.

5. Fussell, *Book of Travel*, p. 715.

6. Karl Bücher, *Industrial Evolution* (New York: Henry Holt, 1901), p. 349.

7. Freya Stark, *The Journey's Echo* (New York: Ecco Press, 1963), p. 36.

8. Sinclair Lewis, *Dodsworth*, quoted in Fussell, *Book of Travel*, p. 688.

9. Paul Bowles, *Their Heads Are Green and Their Hands Are Blue* (New York: Random House, 1963), p. vii.

10. Jack Kerouac, *On the Road* (New York: New American Library, 1957), p. 16.

11. Valene Smith, ed., *Hosts and Guests: The Anthropology of Tourism* (Philadelphia: University of Pennsylvania Press, 1977), p. 2.

12. Ibid., p. 23.

13. Kerouac, *On the Road*, pp. 89–90.

INDEX

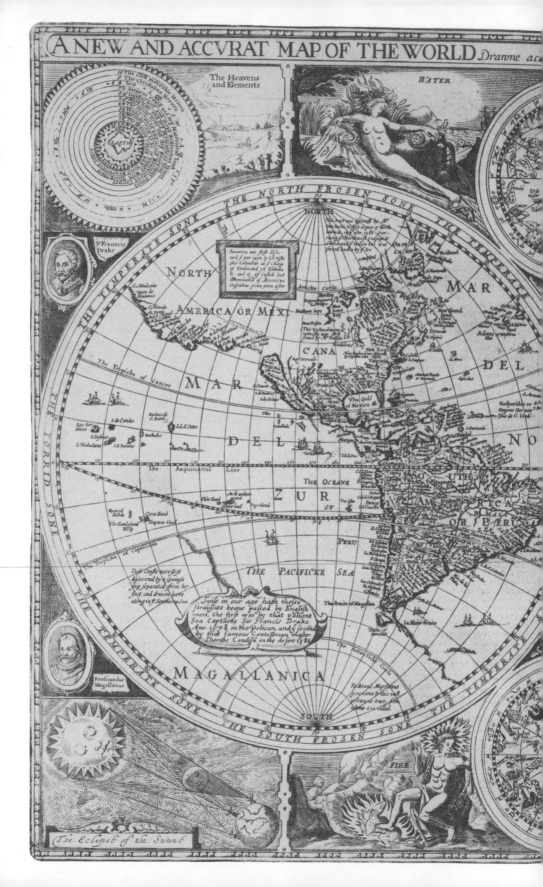